MW00643274

THE ARK OF TASTE

DELICIOUS AND DISTINCTIVE FOODS
THAT DEFINE THE UNITED STATES

THE ARK OF TASTE

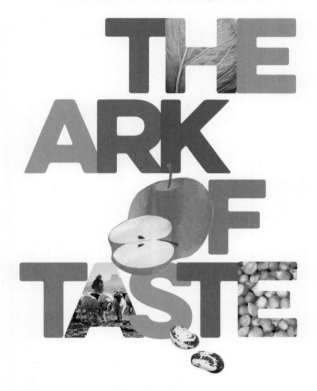

SLOW FOOD USA

GISELLE KENNEDY LORD AND DAVID S. SHIELDS

ILLUSTRATIONS BY CLAUDIA PEARSON

VORACIOUS
LITTLE, BROWN AND COMPANY
NEW YORK BOSTON LONDON

Slow Food USA®

Voracious / Little, Brown and Company
Hachette Book Group
1290 Avenue of the Americas, New York, NY 10104
voraciousbooks.com

First Edition: August 2023

Voracious is an imprint of Little, Brown and Company, a division of Hachette Book Group, Inc. The Voracious name and logo are trademarks of Hachette Book Group, Inc.

The publisher is not responsible for websites (or their content) that are not owned by the publisher.

The Hachette Speakers Bureau provides a wide range of authors for speaking events. To find out more, go to hachettespeakersbureau.com or email hachettespeakers@hbgusa.com.

Little, Brown and Company books may be purchased in bulk for business, educational, or promotional use. For information, please contact your local bookseller or the Hachette Book Group Special Markets Department at special.markets@hbgusa.com.

Image credits: Aaron Yoshino/*Honolulu* Magazine, 252-253; Aliaksei Design/Shutterstock, 113; Gabe Sachter-Smith, 251; Gabriella Marks, 229-231; Jamie Thrower, 283-285; Jennifer Jones, 242-243; Julia Byshrova/Shutterstock, 70, 122; MM Memo/Shutterstock, 61; Margaret Houston Dominick, 108-110; Maxim Cherednichenko/Shutterstock, 125; Micah Green, 92-94; Michael Benanav, 217-219; Pink.mousy/Shutterstock, 193; Rob Barreca/Farm Link Hawaii, 251; We Are The Rhoads, 277-279

INDELIBLE
EDITIONS

Book design and production by Indelible Editions

ISBN 9780316477321
LCCN 2022952094

10 9 8 7 6 5 4 3 2 1
IM
Printed in China

3122314 7947478

CONTENTS

SOUTHEAST

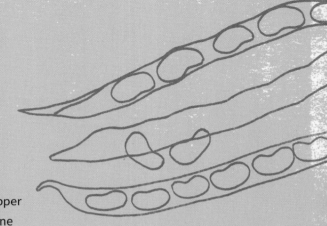

MIDWEST

ROCKY MOUNTAIN
AND SOUTHWEST

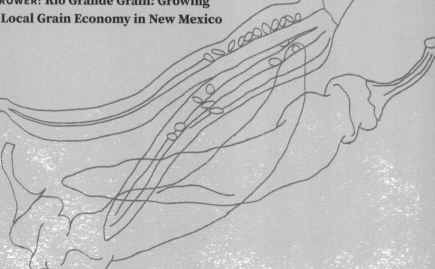

PACIFIC AND NORTHWEST

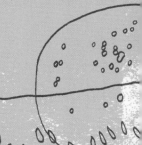

INTRODUCTION

The next time you are in a grocery store, take a walk over to the produce section and look at the tomatoes. If you're lucky, there will be a few varieties, such as beefsteak and cherry, as well as maybe the country of origin and a bar code on a plastic sticker. And . . . that's it. That minimal data is all that's typically given about the food that nourishes our families, takes center stage during holidays, and satisfies cravings every day.

But did you know that there are more than 10,000 different varieties of tomatoes in the world? Some are purple and sweet, some are green and more acidic, and others are red and yellow. They can be both misshapenly large and comically tiny. These varieties have been cultivated by humans over generations to maximize nutrients, to delight taste buds, and to thrive in a specific climate. This amazing biodiversity is a testament to a beautiful reciprocal relationship between humans and plants. Each variety tells a story of culture and history, of movement and climate.

As our food system becomes more industrialized and colonized, produce like tomatoes has become a commodity with a barcode to ship across borders and ultimately land on your grocery shelf. As a result, we are losing biodiversity at an alarming rate. The Food and Agriculture Organization of the United Nations estimates that 75 percent of our global crop diversity was lost in the 20th century, and today, only nine plant species account for 66 percent of total crop production. A similar story is happening with fish species and breeds of livestock. The sharp decline of food biodiversity has a huge impact on the ability of people to feed themselves, has wide-ranging and negative impacts on soil and animals, and reduces the resiliency of farms facing extreme weather from climate change. When it comes to our plate, the loss of biodiversity also means nutrient-poor options and boring flavors.

Slow Food's Ark of Taste is all about the joy and justice of biodiversity. It's a global and grassroots effort to catalog the amazing range of foods around us before they disappear and to raise awareness about how we can act together to preserve and promote these fantastic finds. The pages ahead of you are packed with delightful profiles of farmers, recipes for you to explore, and stories of delicious and distinctive foods facing extinction in the United States. Arranged by region where the food is currently produced, this book includes a whole host of tomatoes not found in your grocery store produce aisle, including the Amish Paste, Cherokee Purple, and Livingston Globe. We hope you will take this book to your local farmers market, talk to farmers about what varieties they grow, and perhaps try growing new varieties in your own backyard or windowsill!

For joy and justice,

Anna Mulè and Mara Welton
Executive Director and Programs Director
Slow Food USA

Slow Food USA®

CK CLAPP'S FAVORITE PEAR DIANA HAMB
RG APPLE FAIRFAX STRAWBERRY FIDDLE
DER HANK'S X-TRA SPECIAL BAKING BEA
HINKELHATZ PEPPER JACOB'S CATTLE BEA
IN MARSHALL STRAWBERRY MARY WASH
ANOVER GROUND CHERRY PINK CHAMPA
CHICKEN RHODE ISLAND GREENING APPL
LE SASSAFRAS SHEEPSHEAD FISH STO
CE TUSCARORA WHITE CORN WELLFLEET
NUT ATLANTIC WOLFFISH BAR-SECKEL P
S FAVORITE PEAR DIANA HAMBURG GRA
IRFAX STRAWBERRY FIDDLEHEADS FISH
S X-TRA SPECIAL BAKING BEAN HANSON
EPPER JACOB'S CATTLE BEAN JENNY LIN
STRAWBERRY MARY WASHINGTON ASPAR
D CHERRY PINK CHAMPAGNE CURRANT
ISLAND GREENING APPLE RHODE ISLAN
S SHEEPSHEAD FISH STOWELL'S EVERGR
WHITE CORN WELLFLEET OYSTER WHITE
ISH BAR-SECKEL PEAR BOSTON MARROW
HAMBURG GRAPE EARLY ROSE POTATO E
DLEHEADS FISH PEPPER GULF OF MAINE
BEAN HANSON LETTUCE HENDERSON
BEAN JENNY LIND MELON LONG ISLAND
NGTON ASPARAGUS MEECH'S PROLIFIC Q
PAGNE CURRANT PINK PLUME CELERY PLY
RHODE ISLAND WHITE CHICKEN ROXBU
LL'S EVERGREEN SWEET CORN TENNIS BA
OYSTER WHITE CAP FLINT CORN AMERICA
R BOSTON MARROW SQUASH CAYUGA DU
EARLY ROSE POTATO ESOPUS SPITZENBU
PPER GULF OF MAINE YELLOW TAIL FLO

G GRAPE **EARLY ROSE POTATO**
EADS **FISH PEPPER** GULF OF MAR
HANSON LETTUCE HENDERSO
JENNY LIND MELON **LONG ISLAND CHEE**
GTON ASPARAGUS **MEECH'S PROLIFIC QU**
NE CURRANT PINK PLUME C
RHODE ISLAND WHITE CH
ELL'S EVERGREEN SWEET CO
YSTER **WHITE CAP FLINT CORN**
R **BOSTON MARROW SQUASH** CA
E **EARLY ROSE POTATO ESOPUS SP**
PPER GULF OF MAINE YELLOW T
TTUCE HENDERSON'S BUSH LIM
MELON **LONG ISLAND CHEESE PU**
GUS **MEECH'S PROLIFIC QUINCE** N
K PLUME CELERY **PLYMOUTH ROC**
WHITE CHICKEN ROXBURY RUS
EN SWEET CORN **TENNIS BALL LE**
AP FLINT CORN **AMERICAN CHESTNUT**
SQUASH **CAYUGA DUCK** CLAPP'S
OPUS SPITZENBURG APPLE FAIRF
ELLOW TAIL FLOUNDER HANK'S
BUSH LIMA BEAN **HINKELHATZ PEPPER**
CHEESE PUMPKIN **MARSHALL STR**
NCE NEW HANOVER GROUND C
OUTH ROCK CHICKEN RHODE IS
Y RUSSET APPLE SASSAFRAS SH
L LETTUCE **TUSCARORA WHITE CORN**
CHESTNUT ATLANTIC WOLFFISH
K CLAPP'S FAVORITE PEAR DIAN
G APPLE **FAIRFAX STRAWBERRY**
DER HANK'S X-TRA SPECIAL BA

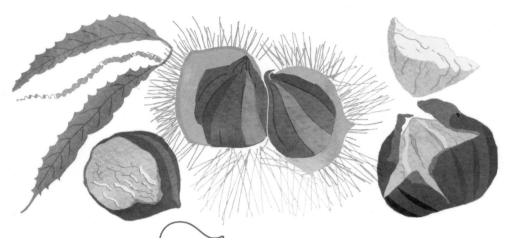

American CHESTNUT

US ORIGIN OR MOST PREVALENT IN
Appalachia

CHARACTERISTICS
Piquant, sweet, toothy in texture, small nut, large tree

USDA PLANT HARDINESS ZONES
4-9

CLOSE RELATIVES
Asian chestnut, Sicilian chestnut

NOTABLE PRODUCER
American Chestnut Foundation

In late September 1874, the Appalachian ridge newspapers from Maine to Georgia published a notice that read simply: "The chestnut trees will soon be ready to be clubbed." This announcement was common before the chestnut blight of the early 20th century. Until then, one of the great autumn recreations of the region was "nutting." Drumming the trunk with a hammer or beam would shake ripe nuts to the ground for collection, provided the trunk was not too broad and the tree not too tall. If one chanced upon a giant (not unusual for the robust American chestnut), a nutting party would resort to other methods of harvest, like shimmying up a trunk using a leather cinch belt. "These excursions of old hold a delightful place in all reminiscences of youth," reported the *Greensboro Record* in 1909. "Even those who do not roam the countryside to gather the fallen nuts amid the leaves welcome the less romantic appearance of the roaster and the vendor in the city streets, while the roasting of the

The edible portion of the American chestnut is piquant, sweet, small, and rather toothy in texture. When dried, the nut makes a versatile meal and flour. Because of its culinary quality, the American chestnut inspired an expansive set of dishes and regional foodways.

delectable nut in the coals of the fireplace is a delight known in those homes where the fireplace survives."

Sometime shortly after 1900, a fungus arrived with chestnut trees imported from Asia and spread to the American chestnut trees in the northeastern hardwood forests of the US. Arborists identified the blight in 1904 and, to their great dismay, discovered that no remedy could counter its lethal effect on the cambium layer beneath the tree's bark that serves as a tree's hydraulic system. Blight spread steadily, first in the northern chestnut forest from Maine to Maryland, then down into the Appalachian ridge, until the whole eastern range of the tree sickened and died. Thus, this dominant tree of the eastern uplands essentially expired in an ecological disaster that still haunts the minds of those who enforce biological security in the United States. Animal populations that had depended upon the autumnal nut fall for sustenance came under great stress. Deer and raccoons turned to the upcountry cornfields to survive.

Human foodways disappeared with the tree, among them the masting of hogs in October beneath chestnut groves, the making of Native chestnut breads from nut meal, the boiling and mashing of chestnuts into spoon meat, and the making of chestnut gruels and grits. To these common dishes, one could add the refined preparations of chestnut soufflés and chestnut puddings that graced the side tables of Eastern households during the holidays. These dishes were all but lost with the trees, and all that remained after the blight was the Christmastide appearance of imported "roasting chestnuts" and perhaps a few additional nuts for the traditional stuffing or dressing. The most reputable of European strains is the Sicilian chestnut, larger and more meaty in texture, pleasantly sweet but not so distinctive in taste as the American chestnut. Both Chinese and Japanese chestnuts are significantly less sweet, and sometimes tend to be chalky in texture.

All hope is not lost, though, as forest ecologists, geneticists, and scientific arborists have labored to restore the American chestnut tree to its traditional range since the mid-20th century. In the 1970s, a hypovirulent but nonlethal strain of the blight was imported from Italy, and diseased chestnut trees were inoculated in their cankers to counteract their destruction. This proved to be an effective local remedy for infestations in the northeast. However, the most promising path forward has been the breeding of resistant hybrids of the American chestnut. Using a breeding scheme devised by Charles Burnham, blight-resistant Asian trees are crossed with American trees, and their offspring crossed again with just an American chestnut tree. The resultant trees from these back crossings are predominantly, though not absolutely, American chestnut. The American Chestnut Foundation selected these hybrids as the instrument for the reforestation of the old eastern range.

The edible portion of the American chestnut is piquant, sweet, small, and rather toothy in texture. When dried, the nut makes a versatile meal and flour. Because of its culinary quality, the American chestnut inspired an expansive set of dishes and regional foodways. Chestnut-fed pork and chestnut-fed venison stood high in the judgment of connoisseurs. Holiday turkeys were stuffed with chestnut dressing. An array of chestnut-centered delights—chestnut pudding, deviled chestnuts, chestnut soup, chestnut soufflé, chestnut bread, chestnut caramels, and chestnut porridge—were common and cherished dishes of the eastern United States in the 19th century.

Today, a population of resistant American chestnuts are being consolidated for seed in forests in Virginia, Georgia, and other places in the United States. While the great commercial impetus behind the revival is for timber—American chestnut is the fastest growing straight-trunked large American hardwood tree—the culinary revival of the distinctive chestnut will be the silver lining of the revival's success. When it returns in force in the coming years, the regional food of Appalachia will have its center restored.

Boston MARROW Squash

This squash spurred unforeseen drama in the 19th-century horticultural world. The Massachusetts Historical Society awarded an inscribed silver cup to John M. Ives of Salem to honor his introduction of the Autumnal Marrow squash into general cultivation in 1853. Contemporary reporters were stunned at the $50 value of the award. The value of the cup reflected the horticultural community's esteem of the squash as a garden vegetable but also brought out some subsequent claims to the squash's discovery. To quash the whisper campaign against him, Ives laid out the history in the pages of the *New England Farmer* magazine in 1858: "A specimen of this vegetable was brought to my place in North Salem by a friend from Northampton in this State, in 1831. In the spring of 1833, I distributed seeds to many members of our Mass. Horticultural Society, they never having seen it previously. At the Annual Exhibition of this Society at Faneuil Hall, Sept., 1834, I exhibited a specimen, merely marked

'New Squash.' This was previous to the description or cut being made. One month from this (in Oct. 1834), I forwarded the name, autumnal marrow, together with a wood cut, to the *N. E. Farmer*."

In other words, Ives brought the variety to the Massachusetts market but did not "discover" the squash. Ives himself recorded that the squash had been brought to Massachusetts from Buffalo, New York, by Indigenous visitors. These Natives were probably the Seneca, keepers of the "western door" of the Iroquois Confederacy, whose homeland included the place where Buffalo was located. Terrylynn Brandt, a Mohawk seedswoman, recognizes the Boston Marrow as a Haudenosaunee variety known as the Buffalo Creek squash, the first in the evolution of names the squash would come to bear. Ives's original name pointed to the great advantage of this squash variety in that it came to maturity at a point in the season before all other winter squashes were ready to harvest. It was the perfect succession crop, arriving at the produce stand when no rival squashes were available. But by 1858, growers had begun calling it Boston Marrow squash in regions outside Massachusetts.

Weighing upwards of 8 pounds, this thin-skinned, orange-fleshed, white-seeded squash has a custardy consistency and rich flavor when cooked. It has a famously delicate grain. Ives described the skin color as "reddish cream, with

Weighing upwards of 8 pounds, this thin-skinned, orange-fleshed, white-seeded squash has a custardy consistency and rich flavor when cooked.

LANDRACE VS. CULTIVAR

A **landrace** is a plant or animal improved by seed selection or breeding to take on distinctive characteristics by farmers; its forms and behaviors are shaped by the environments in which it was developed. A landrace has genetic diversity and so can adapt in changes to the environment. In contrast, a **cultivar**, created by geneticists, commercial breeders, or academic biologists, is purposely genetically inbred and incorporates traits that are economically or agronomically desirable, regardless of the environment in which they may be raised. Cultivars tend to have little flexibility in responding to environmental change.

dashes of bright ochre when mature," and the skin texture is moderately warty. It has a pronounced neck on one end and is rotund in the middle. The stem is thick, turning up at almost a right angle from the body of the vegetable. For a landrace variety, it has a remarkable consistency of texture and shape. Breeders have expanded the size and weight of the Boston Marrow squash so that it has the potential to produce mammoth fruits, and the base weight is now up to 11 pounds.

The Boston Marrow squash ranked among the most frequently planted squash varieties in the United States for a century. Its long reign in the hearts of farmers and consumers began to be challenged in the 1940s with the introduction of the Butternut squash into mass cultivation. While the flavor is not superior, the Butternut's one great advantage over the Boston Marrow was that a larger percentage of the body of the vegetable was edible flesh, as the fat neck of the Butternut was more substantial that the spindly neck of the Boston Marrow. Perhaps the greatest irony of this overtaking was that Boston was the city that first and most vehemently embraced the Butternut squash, in 1942 and 1943. Dishes made with Butternut squash exploded onto hotel and restaurant menus in the city in the midst of World War II. The decline in acreage devoted to the Boston Marrow squash began gradually in 1945, then more drastically as the 20th century wore on. Boston Marrow is effectively no longer included in listings or inventory of popular winter squashes, where you'll see Butternut, Acorn, Delicata, and even the Boston Marrow's near contemporary, the Blue Hubbard. Yet the Boston Marrow has not been wiped from the countryside. Heirloom seed companies still carry seeds, and a number of home gardeners do well to keep the Boston Marrow growing.

In its early days, Boston Marrow squash was substituted for pumpkin in pies. By the 1870s, processors in Connecticut were producing ten-pound supersized cans of Boston Marrow squash meat for the use of boardinghouses and hotels. Squash pies came into vogue after the Civil War, and many slices of pumpkin pie served in New England were in actuality made with Boston Marrow squash. For those familiar with the tasty variety, it retains its famed flavor and texture. The most popular usage for the creamy, earthy squash is as a basis for soup. It's hard not to argue that they are dual purpose, as they also look fabulous among the squashes that grace your porch or kitchen counter in the autumn season.

CAYUGA

Duck

The Cayuga duck may be the most flavorsome domesticated strain of duck bred in America, though the precise origins of the Cayuga have never been ascertained. Gourmands in the 1800s judged the wild canvasback that fed on water celery as the paragon of duck flavor. Mr. J. R. Page of Cayuga County, New York, the foremost breeder of the Cayuga during the Civil War era, first encountered a flock on the Seneca River in New York State in 1838. Page presumed that the wild Black duck must have been an ancestor, but later confessed that he held no reliable information about its origins.

The Cayuga duck was bred extensively in New York and Massachusetts by 1857, and nationally known through the 1850s. In 1874, the American Poultry Association registered the Cayuga and defined for it a "Standard of Excellence" to guide breeding. One poultry breeder explained why he chose to raise the Cayuga over the more famous domestic Rouen and Aylesbury ducks: "The Cayuga duck is hardy, good size, and for the table is superior to all

The 1890s were a decade obsessed with white food and ill-conceived notions of purity, making it difficult to compete with the remarkably pale carcass of the white Pekin duck. The dark-plumed Cayuga was reckoned rather sooty looking in comparison.

other ducks or poultry of any sort: flesh quite dark and high flavored. If well fed they become very fat." Modern poultry raisers liken the taste of the grilled red-fleshed breast to roast beef. In terms of flavor, the Redheaded duck ranked second; the Black duck, third. These game birds were deeply savory and fatty, infused with the richness of their wild diet. In addition, the Cayuga was a prolific egg layer, dropping about 90 eggs each spring and up to 60 or 70 in the fall. Their eggs vary in color, presenting as black and gray early in the laying season and white late in the season.

In the 1870s and 1880s, the Cayuga became a commodity duck. Its quality as a roasting bird inspired a following among farmers, but its docility and relative immobility clinched its place as one of the great duck breeds produced in America. The Cayuga duck put on weight quickly and in a very short time was incapable of flying more than 3 or 4 inches off the ground in short bursts. In terms of farmyard management, the Cayuga proved a much easier fowl to keep than the Muscovy or Pekin ducks. It is also a capable forager, and if one were to choose a variety for a pet, the Cayuga would be an excellent choice.

The appearance of the Cayuga duck has changed over time. It seems to have begun as a dull black and brown bird of medium size with a white collar or white flecks on the neck and breast. Its head, neck, and wing feathers had a green tinge, and the legs were short. Breeders in the 19th century selected for deeper black coloring and fewer white mottles, and the West India Black duck was interbred with it to give a greater gloss to the green sheen of its head and wing feathers. When the Pekin duck was introduced in the 1890s and began taking a significant market share of the roasting duck category, breeders fought back by interbreeding the Cayuga with the Rouen duck to create a bigger, meatier bird. Unfortunately, these attempts at remaining competitive on the commodity market were an insufficient countermeasure.

The 1890s were a decade obsessed with white food and ill-conceived notions of purity, making it difficult to compete with the remarkably pale carcass of the white Pekin duck. The dark-plumed Cayuga was reckoned rather sooty looking in comparison. With startling rapidity, the light-colored Pekin duck became the domestic duck of commerce. The number of breeding pairs of the Cayuga dwindled with every passing decade. Today, the Cayuga duck is listed as "threatened" on the Livestock Conservancy's Conservation Priority List. This means that there are fewer than 1,000 breeding birds in the US, with 10 or fewer primary breeding flocks. The Cayuga duck is also globally endangered.

While it's nearly impossible to source Cayuga duck meat, it is possible to buy live Cayuga ducklings. Some suppliers also offer fertile Cayuga duck eggs. Only those lucky enough to know a heritage poultry operation stocking the Cayuga duck can put this rare variety on the table.

EARLY ROSE
Potato

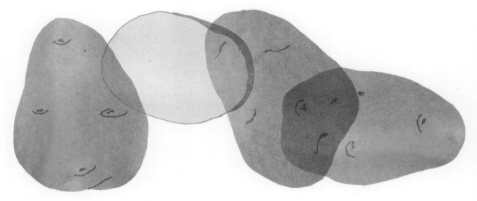

US ORIGIN OR
MOST PREVALENT IN
Vermont

CHARACTERISTICS
*Rose color,
quick maturation,
productivity*

USDA PLANT
HARDINESS ZONES
5b–8b

CLOSE RELATIVE
Burbank potato

NOTABLE PRODUCERS
*The Kenosha Potato
Project, The Seed
Savers Exchange*

The Early Rose potato combined four great virtues—ample size, quick maturation, excellent flavor, and productivity—to become the most important potato created in the US in the latter half of the 19th century. The potato was discovered by Albert Bresee of Hubbardtown, Vermont, in 1861 and captured his attention because it was ready for harvest almost two weeks earlier than the most popular early potato then on the market. It would prove to be the horticultural sensation of the late 1860s and remain popular for a great deal longer than most of its potato peers.

The story of the Early Rose potato gives us a good look at the exciting world of seed sales and plant swapping at the time. Bresee experimented with the potato for three years before selling his entire seed stock to potato broker D. S. Heffron of Utica, New York. Heffron built up the numbers of plants by sending some to John P. Gray in the hopes of winning his enthusiastic endorsement of the variety. He

In 1873, five years after first being offered for sale, the potato "attained a popularity unrivaled in the history of the potato."

gave the variety an attractive name—Early Rose—and then cashed out when he sold his supply to the Conovers in New Jersey and, more significantly, to B. K. Bliss and Sons, who would make the Early Rose a pillar of their potato catalog. Bliss would become the greatest broker of potatoes in the United States, and the Conovers sold seed potatoes of Early Rose potatoes to seedsmen and the general public in spring of 1868, when potato lovers across the country fell in love with the variety.

The first professional response to the performance of this variety can be found in the 1869 Ferre, Batchelder & Co. seed catalog: "This new and fine variety has proved all that was claimed for it when offered for the first time the past Spring. It is very productive, and reports of a yield of one hundred fold is an everyday occurrence. Two to three weeks earlier than the Early Goodrich. The tubers are quite smooth, nearly cylindrical, varying to flattish, largest at the center, tapering gradually towards each end; skin a dull rose color; flesh, white, and one of the best flavored varieties in cultivation. Highly recommended for early marketing on account of its large and uniform size and productiveness." Early trials documented Early Rose generating 558 bushels per acre of potatoes— about five times the recorded average yield of potatoes in the late 1800s.

The success of the Early Rose was explosive. In 1873, five years after first being offered for sale, the potato "attained a popularity unrivaled in the history of the potato. It has now become the standard variety for earliness, quality and productiveness." During this early period of cultivation, rumors floated in newspapers that good Early Rose potatoes retailed for $100 per bushel, with a 12-bushel limit per purchaser.

One curiosity of the Early Rose was that many plant breeders immediately began improvement programs despite its great performance. B. K. Bliss even employed a scheme of sensory testing to determine a better tasting, more starchy potato. He branded his better-tasting red potato the Extra Early Vermont. The Red Bliss potato, which now enjoys popularity, took the genetics in another direction, making the white flesh of the potato more waxy than starchy; it would prevail in the contest for public favor.

The reign of potato varieties as premier cultivars tends to be relatively brief—20 years is reckoned a good run. Disease vulnerability often dethroned the top potato. An important component of the success of the Early Rose was its resistance to the fungal disease anthracnose, though it was unfortunately vulnerable to potato blight and prone to viral potato diseases—the same maladies that doomed the Mercer potato, the most popular American variety of the first half of the 19th century. Yet the virtues of the Early Rose potato were so pronounced that the varieties that ruled in its wake were often genetically derived from the Early Rose. Luther Burbank's famous Burbank potato was a seedling—even more productive than its parent, and more field hardy.

The cooking qualities of the Early Rose potato inspired such respect that the variety remained a commodity potato into the early 1930s. After World War II, when commercial production of slips and seed for the Early Rose ceased due to its vulnerabilities, individual gardeners maintained the variety. It survives in most of the world's major potato breeding collections maintained by governments and universities, and in the research plots of seed companies.

The Early Rose has become exceedingly scarce in American heirloom seed collections as viral infections tainted some lines in the US, forcing growers to look to Canada for disease-free plant material. The primary issue with reviving the Early Rose at any scale is its relative lack of resistance to plant-damaging pathogens. But we should hope for a more robust restoration of this variety because it is the well-loved and reigning potato of the time when major haute cuisine chefs made potato recipes central to their vegetable cookery. The Early Rose potato provided a flavorful foundation for countless significant recipes of the 1880s and 1890s, the apogee of early American fine dining. The potato remains central to vegetable dishes across the United States, and bringing this iconic and historic potato variety back to the table may serve to bolster the concept of American cuisine.

ESOPUS SPITZENBURG
Apple

US ORIGIN OR MOST PREVALENT IN
New York

CHARACTERISTICS
Crisp, juicy, luscious fragrance

USDA PLANT HARDINESS ZONES
6a–8b

CLOSE RELATIVE
Jonathan apple

NOTABLE PRODUCERS
FRUIT:
Albemarle CiderWorks, Salt Spring Apple Company, Out on a Limb Apples, Three Springs Fruit Farm
CIDER:
Stormalong Cider, Eve's Cidery, and Hudson Valley Farmhouse Cider
TREES:
Trees of Antiquity, Orange Pippin Trees, Fedco Seeds, Century Farm Orchards

An early American apple, the Esopus Spitzenburg was a seedling found by a New York Dutch farmer on Esopus Creek in the Hudson Valley. The Spitzenburg won fame as a dessert apple, one that was eaten uncooked from the hand. Its complex aromatics added dimension to ciders, and its body allowed it to be a useful canning apple throughout the 19th century. For an heirloom variety, it displays a noteworthy versatility, and contemporary sources classify it as a "culinary apple"—that is, one adaptable to a range of uses other than eating out of hand.

The Esopus Spitzenburg was first named in a 1769 advertisement for apple varieties in the October issue of the *New York Gazette*. Interestingly, the ad also notes a "Newtown Spitzenburg" (Newtown was a settlement in Queens), suggesting that the apple had been grown long enough in New York and was well-esteemed enough by the late 1760s for orchardists to have developed a variant. After the American Revolution, pomologist and nurseryman

Its fame was established before the formation of the United States, and it has remained—along with the Jonathan, the Winesap and the Newton Pippin—as one of the founding apples of American orchards.

William Prince listed the Esopus Spitzenburg with the Newton Pippin as the only two named apples in his advertisements of fruit trees. By the end of the 18th century, Prince had spread the apple's fame well beyond New York State. Its fame was established before the formation of the United States, and it has remained—along with the Jonathan, the Winesap, and the Newton Pippin—as one of the founding apples of American orchards.

In Spencer Ambrose Beach's 1905 classic *Apples of New York,* the fruit is carefully described and illustrated as "medium to large; pretty uniform in size and shape. Form rather broad and flat at the base, varying from oblong rounding towards the cavity to roundish ovate or to roundish inclined to conic; somewhat irregular and obscurely ribbed. . . . Skin touch, sometimes waxy, slightly roughened by the russet dots, deep rich yellow often almost completely covered with bright red inconspicuously striped with darker red, in the sun deepening to a very dark, almost purplish blush, marked with pale yellow and russet dots which are small and numerous. . . . Flesh tinged with yellow, firm, moderately fine, crisp, rather tender, juicy, aromatic, sprightly subacid, very good to best."

ORGANIC VS. HEIRLOOM

Because of Esopus Spitzenburg's many vulnerabilities to disease and fungus, you will almost never encounter organically grown Spitzenburg apples. They will all have been subjected to some kind of chemical regimen. If you choose to grow the trees yourself, you will likely resort to a nonorganic intervention in order to attain a crop. This is an unfortunate circumstance found in growing heirloom apples and peaches.

Indeed, the Esopus Spitzenburg apple boasts a complex flavor, a sugary apple with a spice edge and a good balance of acid that plays on the tongue in the somewhat grainy texture. The sugar intensifies when the apple is stored over winter.

With the variety maturing late in the fall season, the prudent grower began feasting on the apples at Thanksgiving and tried to keep some in supply in cold storage until spring. But the Esopus Spitzenburg has never been a commodity apple. The annual production per tree tends to be modest, and the size of the apples depends heavily on weather and sunlight hours. The trees themselves are slow growers and have slender twigs. But it was the trees' vulnerability to fungal scab and apple canker that turned many orchards sickly over the 19th century and inhibited new plantings. It attracts every pest and pathogen that visits American orchards, and finding one untouched by beasts, birds, insects, scale, and canker can pose a challenge.

While the variety did not find success on the commercial market, the flavor was so exceptional that a substantial number of growers keep yard trees. Indeed, some devotees—Thomas Jefferson included—consider it the finest-tasting apple in North America, so there have always been plantings despite being shunned by commercial operations since the end of the 19th century. Those who keep the tree now graft it onto more disease-resistant stocks. The rise of the artisan cider movement at the end of the 20th century led to a renewed interest in old apple varieties traditionally used in the coppice, and a number of cideries embraced the apple. Because of Thomas Jefferson's particular attachment to the variety, historic Monticello has always supplied the public with saplings, so that people can understand the enthusiasm of the nation's third president for this unique fruit.

FAIRFAX
Strawberry

US ORIGIN OR MOST PREVALENT IN
Maryland

CHARACTERISTICS
Solid heart, beautiful flavor

USDA PLANT HARDINESS ZONES
7a–9b

CLOSE RELATIVE
Royal Sovereign strawberry

NOTABLE PRODUCER
Edible Landscaping

The Fairfax strawberry is the creation of George Darrow, one of the greatest small-fruit breeders in the US during the first half of the 20th century. A cross between the Royal Sovereign and Howard 17 strawberries, the Fairfax came into existence at the USDA experimental station at Glenn Dale, Maryland. Darrow fine-tuned the strawberry's genetics from 1923 until 1928, when he launched the variety and won a devoted following, despite its middling size. In 1933 it was widely adopted by commercial growers. In 1979, horticulturist Donald Hyde Scott in his *Strawberry Varieties of the United States* suggested that the greatest berry creation of the 20th century was the Fairfax strawberry, on account of its fresh eating and dessert quality.

The Fairfax strawberry combined all of the qualities esteemed by strawberry fanciers. It was juicy, mildly sour, and fragrant without being cloyingly perfumy. It did not degrade in texture when frozen, and it did not lose flavor or fragrance when cooked. Its taste was clear, resonant, and long-lasting on the tongue. A sense of the standing of this wonderful berry can be had from the Rayner Brothers Inc.'s 1942 *Berry Book*: "The flavor is exceptionally rich, full bodied and very sweet." W. F. Allen's 1950 *Book of Berries* elaborated

"You've never tasted the best if you've never tasted Fairfax!"

by quoting customer S. E. Hurdle: "If there is anything tastier than the Fairfax it must grow in celestial regions." Allen further observed, "Since its introduction in 1933, Fairfax has set a new standard in quality. . . . This superb quality explains why we receive more enthusiastic letters about Fairfax from those to whom we sell plants than about any other variety. . . . For the roadside markets, Fairfax is the most popular berry in the country. . . . You've never tasted the best if you've never tasted Fairfax!"

Rayner describes the berry's successful trajectory from home garden to commercial market: "Fairfax is the most popular home garden berry, which plus unusual firmness, large size, and productiveness give it high commercial value. Fairfax is now one of the major early varieties, is being successfully grown as far South as North Carolina, and in all Central and Northern States . . . [and] has an exceptionally long fruiting season." Rayner noted that the variety was also free from leaf spot and scorch and doesn't diminish foliage when fruiting, a strong note for general plant health.

In the mid-20th century there was a contest of strawberry aesthetics between those who favored the lighter, pinker sort—the Dorset was the paragon of this category—and those who favored darker, redder berries—for which the Fairfax was the model. The judgment in favor of lighter strawberries was, in part, founded on the fact that strawberries darkened once they had passed maturity. But the Fairfax scrambled this old criterion for rejection. Since the advent of the Fairfax, dark red has been the ideal of most crop strawberry breeders.

Unfortunately, the Fairfax was phased out of widespread cultivation in the 1970s and 1980s when monocropping required cultivars with extremely high disease resistance and a berry so firm it could bounce without bruising in long transportation. "Fairfax strawberry plants are not [as] fully disease resistant as some modern cultivars are . . . ." wrote Erik at StrawberryPlant.org. "[They] have a softer and delicious texture, but this makes them more prone to bruising and damage during the picking/packing/shipping steps. Berries that don't ship well don't sell well at grocery stores. So, with the changing demands of commerce, Fairfax strawberry plants fell out of favor with growers in favor of more robust, but often less flavorful, cultivars."

The organization of a national market for berries and the concentration of the business into the hands of very few companies hastened the near extinction of the Fairfax after the 1980s. A home gardener could no longer buy a plant from a nursery in 2000, but that changed when Mike Wellik, a grower from Middletown, Delaware, noticed his favorite strawberry had vanished. Wellik thought it bizarre that the best-tasting strawberry that American genetics produced was bordering on extinction. "The flavor [of] Fairfax is phenomenal. I have never tasted any hybrid like it. That's why I keep it around! . . . Fairfax flavor is very mild [and] sweet and should be the standard that everyone compares to when breeding new stock." Securing plant material from the USDA Clonal Germplasm Repository, Wellik brought the plant back, supplying pots of rooted Fairfax strawberries to growers. Arthritis forced Wellik to suspend sales in 2018, but before he did, he put plant material into enough growers' hands and gardens to keep the beloved variety alive today.

DARK RED is *Not* DECAY

W. F. Allen's 1942 *Book of Berries* addressed Fairfax's unusual color in a market of lighter berries:

"Fairfax started as a variety under a cloud because of the tendency of the berries to turn dark on holding. The Fairfax cloud was quickly found to have a silver lining as Fairfax went to work. And as consumers learned about varieties, the rich dark red of Fairfax became a symbol of quality—not of decay. On any market where consumers are close enough to the producer to come back to him, they not only demand those dark berries, Fairfax, but are willing to pay a premium to get them."

FIDDLEHEADS

Before the fiddlehead became celebrated in New England produce stands each spring, Indigenous people had long been harvesting and eating the furled fronds of young Ostrich ferns, or sometimes Cinnamon ferns. The name fiddlehead has applied to both. The Ostrich fern is native to the Northeastern US. Indigenous communities in every region of the country were deeply knowledgeable about and resourceful with wild and native foods. A few country people in Maine and New Hampshire who had observed the Abenaki forage for the fern brackens ate the wild greens in the 19th century. In 1897 the W. S. Wells and Son cannery in Wilton, Maine, became the first commercial supplier offering canned fiddleheads to a very local New England clientele. Until the 1970s, the vast majority of New Englanders had never even heard of the vegetable. Canadians had to teach them about it.

The citizens of New Brunswick, Canada, embraced this essential piece of the First Peoples' diet in the region and proclaimed that fiddleheads and salmon were as poetic an evocation of spring as lamb and minted garden peas. In 1972 a food distributor in King of Prussia, Pennsylvania, began importing fresh Canadian fiddleheads to supply US restaurants and high-end grocery stores. Newspapers began publishing recipes for fiddlehead quiche. By 1976 they had become fixed on the spring menus of high-end restaurants in Boston. The mid-1970s also saw the freezing and shipping of ferns as an alternative to canning. By 1980, they had become a fixture at high-end gourmet produce and specialty food markets in New York and New England.

Publication of recipes and appreciations in newspapers and magazines with national readerships made people outside of New England realize that the Cinnamon fern had an expansive range, growing as far south as the Alabama coastal plain. Foragers from the South and Midwest began adding brackens to their late winter and early spring haul. The Ostrich fern, which is plumper and less fibrous, is more restricted in the upper Midwest and north of West Virginia.

Harvested when just 4 inches or so spring from the ground, the sprouts of a fern are delicate, vegetal, and tender, imparting a flavor somewhere between asparagus and spinach, and a texture somewhat like asparagus or a green bean. They were traditionally steamed or boiled and served with butter and salt. Eventually, they became particularly prized as a raw ingredient in spring salads.

The consumption of fiddleheads, particularly raw, is not without controversy. A number of medical studies since the 1950s have documented that the fronds contain a carcinogenic chemical called ptaquiloside. Any linkage between instances of cancer and the consumption of fiddleheads was only documented in Japan, where they are ingested as a regular feature of diets for extended parts

Harvested when just 4 inches or so spring from the ground, the sprouts of a fern are delicate, vegetal, and tender, imparting a flavor somewhere between asparagus and spinach, and a texture somewhat like asparagus or a green bean.

of the year. The seasonal consumption of cooked fiddleheads has not been linked with any verifiable instance of cancer in the United States. Cooking—particularly boiling in water—breaks down ptaquiloside, eliminating its harmfulness. Broccoli actually contains more carcinogens than fiddleheads, though some would not advise making a regular habit of eating raw fiddleheads from Ostrich ferns.

New Englanders seized upon the fiddlehead as an emblem of local identity by the mid-1980s. In 1985, Vermont state representative Peter Youngbaer introduced a bill to name the fiddlehead Vermont's official state vegetable. This attempt at symbol making provoked the residents of New Brunswick, Canada, for fiddleheads appeared on the province's coat of arms. Protests in many forms, including poems, were dispatched to New England papers. CBC radio personality Paddy Gregg recited one such poem:

> How many times stood we idly and watched
> Events that made us see red.
> Our pines they took, our salmon gone . . .
> Now it's the fiddlehead.
> Stand up to the grasping Yankee I say;
> It's time for the worm to turn,
> You can have the trees, take the damn fish,
> But not our beloved fern.

Vermont did not put the fiddlehead on the state flag. And if they checked the sourcing information on the bin of fiddleheads at the local produce stand, they would find that the majority of the product sold hailed from Canada. That said, many New Englanders range the April woods foraging for young ferns, as they are not a cultivated crop. As *Modern Farmer* observed in a June 2015 article, "Born to Be Wild," fiddleheads "have never been successfully cultivated on a large scale." The Native Peoples of New England and New York continue to regard them as an enduring gift of spring, the most anticipated green to appear in the wake of maple sugar season.

FISH *Pepper*

The fish pepper is easy to pick out in a field. The fruits go through a sequence of color stages—first white, then pale green, then streaky green, then orange with brown stripes, and finally deep red. The plant is a compact shrub almost two feet tall, with variegated white and green leaves.

All members of the pepper family have their ultimate origin in the Americas. Within a century of the Spanish conquest of Central and South America, a great many varieties found their way around the globe to become inextricable ingredients and flavors of a whole host of colorful culinary traditions of the Eastern Hemisphere. Though the specific origin of the name and history of the Fish pepper are unclear, the variety is largely believed to have come from the Caribbean to the United States in the late 19th century.

Upon arrival, this unique variety of the species *Capsicum annuum* was adopted, nurtured, and adapted to the distinctive fish and shellfish cookery of the Chesapeake Bay by members of the African diaspora, persisting entirely in their gardens and on their farms.

The great revival effort on its behalf came about through the work of African American growers and cooks.

The Fish pepper never became a common variety in commercial markets at the time and was exclusively nurtured by African American growers who recognized its beauty and culinary virtue. It also amplified one important theme of African American cooking—the encounter with an entire range of new ingredients and their ability to recognize the nutritional, medicinal, and spiritual virtues of unfamiliar plants. According to culinary historian Michael Twitty, the power of capsicum to nullify certain kinds of bodily pain, its power as a dewormer, and its ability to uplift food led to the adoption of hot peppers—Bird pepper, Cayenne pepper, Cherry pepper, and the Fish pepper when it appeared in the 19th century.

William Woys Weaver is an ethnographer, author, and heritage seed connoisseur who discovered Fish pepper seeds among a seed collection his grandfather, H. Ralph Weaver, compiled in the 1920s. Ralph Weaver had received the seeds from artist and serendipitous seed saver Horace Pippin sometime after World War I. Weaver shared the seed with the Seed Savers Exchange in the 1990s, who publicly offered it in their 1995 seed catalog. It is from that stock that a number of seed companies and growers have added Fish pepper to their own catalogs and developed strains of the variety. Weaver's grandfather, a great gardener, speculated that the origin of the pepper was the West Indies.

Fish peppers thrive in full sun, grow readily from seed, and should be spaced 18 inches apart, and will grow about as tall. Most people germinate the seeds indoors and then transplant them into the garden. They also grow well in pots. After their slow and beautiful color palette progression, the fruits will be fully red ripe 80 days from transplant. The pepper pods will grow up to 3 inches in length and rate between 5,000 and 30,000 on the Scoville scale, ranging in heat from milder than a jalapeño to hotter than a serrano, depending on terroir and stage of ripeness when harvested. Because the plant is so attractive, many people buy the Fish pepper for ornamental reasons.

The great revival effort on its behalf came about through the work of African American growers and cooks. When chefs in the Chesapeake Bay region learned from Twitty and others of the existence of a local hot pepper significant in traditional African American cookery, they began sponsoring its cultivation around Baltimore and Washington, DC. Urban farmer and *Soilful City* founder Xavier Brown, in Washington, DC, has manufactured a hot sauce—Pippin Sauce—named in honor of the Black artist and seed saver Horace Pippin, who transmitted the seeds to our times. Spike Gjerde of the James Beard Award–winning Woodbury Kitchen concocted Snake Oil Hot Sauce and sells dried Fish pepper flakes.

Most 21st-century chefs and their processors used the fully ripe red forms of the pods. But the level of heat in the pepper varies at each stage of growth and color. The creamy-white young pepper pod is mild and flavorful in a vegetal way—perfect for sneaking its flavor into delicate and creamy sauces. The green form of the pepper takes on a mild heat and can be chopped up as a salad pepper without eaters suffering from Scoville scorch. Some pepper processors prefer to emulsify the pepper in its orange or brown stage—when the heat packs a subtle punch but the pepper still holds a substantial meatiness.

Pippin's PEPPER

Artist Horace Pippin's arm was injured in World War l. To combat the pain, Pippin received bee sting therapy from a nearby beekeeper, H. Ralph Weaver. In exchange, he gave Weaver seeds for his collection, including ones for the Fish pepper. After Weaver's death, his grandson William Woys Weaver found the seeds in baby food jars in his basement. He reintroduced these heirloom peppers, which, when light colored foods were prized, added heat and not color to white sauces often served with fish.

La POBLANITA

COCKTAIL

DANNY CHILDS, *mixologist*
THE FARM AND FISHERMAN TAVERN, NEW JERSEY

For thousands of years, four of the world's five domesticated pepper species didn't venture far from the areas adjacent to their homelands in Bolivia and Peru. These ajíes, as they're known locally, were domesticated in this region around 8,000 years ago and are still an incredibly important part of the cuisine today. All of the pepper varieties used in this cocktail are descendants of these C. annuum *ancestors. These are blended into a syrup with the herb pápalo, which is widely used in Mexican cuisine. There are a lot of strong flavors vying for your attention in this drink; the magnificent final product is greater than the sum of its parts.*

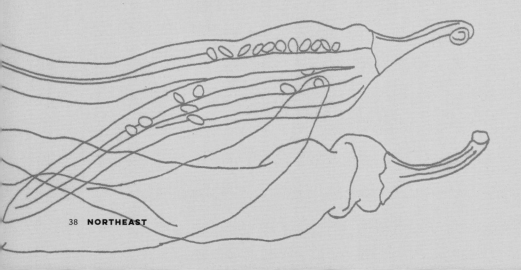

FOR THE SIMPLE SYRUP

1 cup (240 ml) boiling water

1 cup (200 g) sugar

FOR THE PEPPER SYRUP

5 Jimmy Nardello Frying peppers
or a similar sweet red varietal

1 Fish pepper or a similar mildly hot,
red pepper such as ripe jalapeño,
serrano, or Chile de Árbol

12 fluid ounces (355 ml) of simple syrup

FOR THE LA POBLANITA

1½ fluid ounces (45 ml) blanco tequila

½ fluid ounce (15 ml) mezcal

¾ fluid ounce (2 ml) lime juice

1 fluid ounce (30 ml) pepper syrup

Pinch of salt

1 pápalo or cilantro leaf,
for garnishing

SPECIAL EQUIPMENT

Cocktail shaker

Hawthorne strainer

Blender

Fine-mesh colander

Hand juicer

Large ice cube

Rocks glass

MAKE THE SIMPLE SYRUP

Heat the water in a saucepan over high
heat. When the water begins to boil,
add the sugar. Remove from the heat
and stir until the sugar is dissolved.
Let cool completely.

MAKE THE PEPPER SYRUP

Remove the stems from the peppers and
roughly chop the flesh. Place the peppers
in a blender. Add the simple syrup and
blend. Strain through a fine-mesh strainer
and store in an airtight container in the
refrigerator for up to one week.

MAKE THE POBLANITA

Add all ingredients to a cocktail shaker
and shake vigorously for 10 seconds.
Using a Hawthorne strainer and fine-
mesh colander, double strain over a
large ice cube in a rocks glass. Place a
pápalo or cilantro leaf in your hand and
firmly slap it, then garnish the cocktail
with the leaf.

*Danny Childs is a mixologist at the Farm and
Fisherman Tavern in New Jersey, a cocktail
columnist for* Edible Jersey, *and a member
of the Slow Food Northeast/New England Ark of
Taste Committee as well as the Cooks' Alliance.*

HINKELHATZ
Pepper

US ORIGIN OR MOST PREVALENT IN
Pennsylvania

CHARACTERISTICS
Small, conical, moderately hot

USDA PLANT HARDINESS ZONES
6a–8a

CLOSE RELATIVE
Cascabella Pepper

NOTABLE PRODUCERS
Hudson Valley Seed Company, Nature and Nurture Seeds

Shaped like a chicken heart, the Hinkelhatz is an heirloom hot pepper cultivated since the early 19th century in Pennsylvania Dutch country by the resident Mennonites. All hot peppers derive ultimately from Central American ancestors; Mexico is likely the original homeland of the Hinkelhatz. The spread of peppers via trade and conquest was so complex during the colonial era that the route from the fields of Indigenous residents of Mexico to the gardens of Swiss Mennonites in Pennsylvania cannot be traced with any certainty. Scholars have identified a form of the Hinkelhatz in an illustration from the 1611 *Curae Posteriores* by Charles de L'Ecluse. William Woys Weaver, the foremost historian of Pennsylvania Dutch horticultural and culinary traditions, wrote that it was first mentioned in the 1848 cookbook *Die Geschickte Hausfrau*, citing the pepper's usefulness in sauces and pickling mixtures.

Peppers vary greatly in regard to their heat, depending on the soil in which they grow, the seed strain, and sunlight exposure

The Hinkelhatz is a moderately hot pepper, though evaluators behind the Pepper Scale website observe that it has "a surprising heat here for the diminutive size of this chili."

during its initial growth. The Hinkelhatz is a moderately hot pepper, though evaluators behind the Pepper Scale website observe that it has "a surprising heat here for the diminutive size of this chili. At a minimum they match the medium heat of our reference point— the jalapeño pepper (5,000 Scoville heat units). But Hinkelhatz peppers can range up a good deal more. At their top, they can be a similar heat to a milder cayenne pepper (30,000 Scoville heat units). That makes the Hinkelhatz often sit outside of 'family-friendly' eating level, though this chili isn't typically eaten fresh."

The fruits are rather small—from 1 to 2 inches in length—and bluntly conical in shape, with some bumps and wrinkles along their edges. The plant reaches a height between 2 and 3 feet and bears lanceolate leaves. Its coloration is diverse when ripe, ranging from mostly red to sometimes yellow and infrequently orange. Many Hinkelhatz fruit set on the bush over the course of several months. The plant enjoys more cold tolerance than other hot pepper varieties, an important characteristic for growers in regions above the Mason-Dixon line. The fruits are easy to process. They are not commonly eaten raw, according to Weaver. Weaver notes that the peppers were most often roasted or panfried and then pureed with vinegar to make a spicy hot sauce, as roasting deepened the flavor, which tends to be rather vegetal without much fragrance.

The survival of the Hinkelhatz pepper depended on a scant handful of Mennonite families until Weaver made it a restoration project. Boarding on the Ark of Taste also increased public exposure. Today, the pepper is widely carried by American seed companies that have heirloom pepper lines and has been adapted to new uses, such as making salsa.

Long Island
CHEESE PUMPKIN

US ORIGIN OR MOST PREVALENT IN
Long Island, New York

CHARACTERISTICS
Flat, tan-skinned, with firm orange flesh

USDA PLANT HARDINESS ZONES
2–10

CLOSE RELATIVES
Seminole pumpkin, Dutch Fork pumpkin

NOTABLE PRODUCERS
Johnny's Selected Seeds, Baker Creek Heirloom Seeds, Seed Savers Exchange

In the early 1800s, Indigenous people along the eastern seaboard grew flattened varieties of sutured Moschata squash that settlers began calling Cheese pumpkins. Each Indigenous group in the region grew a version of the tan-skinned pumpkin. Originating in Guatemala, the Moschata squashes had spread into North America in the Woodland era and were cultivated for seeds and flesh. Today its most popular representative is the ubiquitous Butternut squash.

Three forms of these native landraces are boarded on the Ark of Taste—the Seminole pumpkin from the Gulf Coast, the Dutch Fork pumpkin from South Carolina, and the Long Island Cheese pumpkin from New York. Other forms of these native Moschata survive in smaller numbers—the Old Timey Cornfield pumpkin from North Carolina and the Maryland Cheese pumpkin to name two. These old varieties share certain virtues. They abound in oil-rich nutritious seeds and ample, sugary meat inside a shell that is sturdy enough to overwinter without rotting when stored in a cool place. Moschata squashes, however, manifest surprisingly varied shapes. They can have long necks like the Butternut, conical or round shapes like the Dutch Fork, or the flattened oblate shape of the Cheese pumpkin. All are splendid tasting and versatile, though some of the southern Moschatas tended to be used not just as human food but as livestock feed as well. The Cheese pumpkin, however, was cultivated primarily for human consumption.

The Long Island Cheese pumpkin tends to set two pumpkins per vine that take 105 to 110 days to mature. They are vulnerable to vine borers and other pernicious garden insects, but have good resistance to many diseases and are quite drought resistant. If heavily fertilized, they tend to generate vegetation rather than increasing pumpkin size. The firm flesh is orange.

Philadelphia seedsman Bernard M'Mahon listed a Cheese pumpkin in his 1806 seed catalog, although he miscategorized it as a Pepo squash. Pepo squashes were field pumpkins, whereas Cheese pumpkins resembled winter squashes and were "flat shaped and salmon colored." As a landrace, the Cheese pumpkin may vary greatly in size from region to region, even farm to farm, depending on the seed saving practices of the grower. Cheese pumpkins were valued as pie and roasting pumpkins, and they had a national following until the mid-20th century, when they stopped being offered in catalogs. But one enthusiast made sure that the Long Island Cheese pumpkin variety did not disappear altogether.

In the 1970s, Ken Ettlinger, a botany instructor at Suffolk Community College on Long Island, began growing pumpkins from seed collected from Long Island farm stands. He organized the Long Island Seed Project and began offering the locally adapted version of the Cheese pumpkin to the public for their gardens. Ettlinger did so to ensure that people might continue to enjoy the pleasure he experienced in the 1950s. "My family would always go to a farm and pick up a cheese pumpkin so mom could make the pie. If you talk to old timers, if you want to make a pumpkin pie, you use cheese pumpkin."

From the store of seeds collected by Ettlinger in the 1970s, seed companies like Johnny's Selected Seeds, Baker Creek Heirloom Seeds, and Seed Savers Exchange began offering a locally adapted strain of the Long Island Cheese pumpkin. The variety was distinctive in being smaller, at just 6 to 10 pounds, than the rather large New England Cheese pumpkins offered by a variety of companies from 1850 to 1940. But the smaller size was a selling point. Peter Henderson's own miniature Sugar pumpkin supplanted the Cheese pumpkin as the pie preference in its own catalog over the 1950s as families were getting smaller. Today, the Long Island Cheese pumpkin enjoys a substantial fandom in New England, with market farmers and home gardeners dedicated to growing and promoting the variety. It is still a popular and excellent choice for pie.

PARMIGIANO
REGGIANO
PARMIGIANO
REGGIANO

FABRIZIO FACCHINI, *chef and entrepreneur*
NEW YORK

The rich, smooth flesh of the beloved Long Island Cheese pumpkin serves as a great partner to risotto here. While the pumpkin gets its name from its resemblance to a wheel of cheese, some generous grates of Parmigiano Reggiano bring a bright, sharp cheesiness to this dish. Making your own vegetable stock is a must here.

SERVES 8

FOR THE VEGETABLE STOCK

1 medium yellow onion

2 large carrots

2 celery stalks

2 garlic cloves, peeled

2 sprigs rosemary

1 small bunch thyme

FOR THE PUMPKIN PURÉE

1 (4 pound/1.8 kg) Long Island Cheese pumpkin

Extra-virgin olive oil, for drizzling

1 recipe vegetable stock

Salt and freshly ground black pepper

FOR THE CRISPY PANCETTA

5 slices flat, cured pancetta

FOR THE RISOTTO

2 shallots

½ pound (2 sticks/225 g) salted butter, cubed

2¼ cups (400 g) carnaroli rice

1 cup (240 ml) Chardonnay

1 recipe vegetable stock (see left)

1 recipe pumpkin purée (see left)

½ cup (50 g) Parmigiano Reggiano, grated

Extra-virgin olive oil, for drizzling

Vincotto, for serving

Salt and freshly ground black pepper

CONTINUED >>

MAKE THE VEGETABLE STOCK

Wash the onion and cut it in half (do not peel it). Clean the carrots and celery and cut them in half. Smash the garlic using the flat side of a large knife blade. Add the onion, carrots, celery, and garlic to a large pot with enough water to cover them. Add the rosemary and thyme. Bring to a boil, then reduce the heat, cover, and simmer to infuse for about 2 hours.

MAKE THE PUMPKIN PURÉE

Preheat the oven to 375°F (190°C). Peel and dice the pumpkin. Lightly coat the pieces with a large drizzle of olive oil. Season with salt and pepper. Wrap the pumpkin pieces in foil and bake until tender but still slightly firm when pierced with a fork. Unwrap the pieces and broil them for 5 minutes. Strain the stock to remove the vegetables and herbs. Divide the stock between two pots. Set one pot over low heat to keep warm. Add the broiled pumpkin to the other pot, season with salt and pepper, bring to a boil, and simmer for 10 to 15 minutes. Turn off the heat and let cool for 5 to 10 minutes. Blend using an immersion blender until creamy and smooth. Set aside to keep warm.

PREPARE THE CRISPY PANCETTA

Place the pancetta slices on a baking sheet and bake in a 375°F (190°C) oven until crisp. Pour off any excess fat and pat the pancetta dry using a paper towel. Crumble the pancetta and set aside.

MAKE THE RISOTTO

Dice the shallots. In a rondo or risotto pan (or other large, straight-sided skillet) set over medium heat, melt ¼ pound (1 stick/113 g) of the butter and add the shallots. Cook until the shallots are slightly softened, 2 to 3 minutes. Add the rice and cook while continually stirring until slightly toasted, 2 to 3 minutes. Add the wine to deglaze the pan and cook until most of the liquid has evaporated. Add one ladle of stock and a half ladle of the pumpkin purée to the rice and stir. Continue adding stock and purée in this way until the rice is cooked al dente and the risotto achieves a creamy and wavy texture. Turn off the heat and add a little more of the purée (reserving a small amount to drizzle as a garnish), the Parmigiano Reggiano, and the remaining butter. Season with pepper and add a drizzle of olive oil. Stir, taste, and adjust the seasoning, if desired. Set aside for 5 minutes, covered.

Ladle the risotto onto a flat risotto plate and tap the underside of the plate with the palm of your hand to spread the risotto out into a thin, circular shape. Garnish with a drizzle of purée, a drizzle of Vincotto, and a drizzle of olive oil. Top with pieces of the crispy pancetta.

Fabrizio Facchini is a chef and entrepreneur with restaurants in both New York and Italy as well as the Cardinali Bakery and Italian Markets on Long Island. He is a member of the Slow Food Cooks' Alliance in both the United States and Italy.

MARSHALL
Strawberry

**US ORIGIN OR
MOST PREVALENT IN**
Massachusetts

CHARACTERISTICS
*Sweet dark red berry
with a hollow heart*

**USDA PLANT
HARDINESS ZONES**
5b–8a

CLOSE RELATIVE
Hovey strawberry

NOTABLE PRODUCER
Raintree Nursery

The Marshall strawberry, discovered by Marshall Ewell, was first exhibited at the Massachusetts Horticultural Society Exhibition in 1892. After winning two first prizes for the plants, he then offered Marshall strawberry plants to select nurserymen at the price of $10 per dozen. At the time, it was the highest price ever asked for strawberry plants. The Marshall first appeared for public sale in catalogs in 1893, after supplanting the Hovey strawberry as the model for berry "excellence."

The Hovey strawberry had reigned as the preferred crop fruit in the United States for much of the 19th century, but a shift in berry aesthetics occurred after the Civil War. Southerners opted for more acidic and sweet strawberries—first the Neunan's Prolific, then the Hoffman's Seedling, then the Klondike, then the Blakemore—while Northerners opted for very prolific, large, sweet fruits of balanced flavor. Within five years of its introduction, the Marshall strawberry had installed itself as the favorite crop berry among large commercial growers from Maryland northward. After the turn of the

"The Marshall originated in the town of Marshfield, MA, from a wild strawberry found in an old stone heap, where its enormous growth attracted the attention of its introducer. It retains that sweet and delicious flavor of the wild strawberry."

20th century, growers in California and the Pacific Northwest also adopted the Marshall strawberry with great enthusiasm.

Almost immediately a mystique grew up about the strawberry. Its history was described in the 1895 handbook *Rawson's Vegetable and Flower Seeds*: "The Marshall originated in the town of Marshfield, MA, from a wild strawberry found in an old stone heap, where its enormous growth attracted the attention of its introducer. It retains that sweet and delicious flavor of the wild strawberry. The color is dark crimson, glossy, and very handsome; flesh is dark, rich and highly flavored, very firm and solid." The belief that the Marshall was a sport—a spontaneous mutation—of the wild American strawberry was deeply attractive to New Englanders in the 1890s, but in actuality, it's a hybrid of the Hovey and another unknown parent variety.

Bridgeville Nurseries in Delaware, a pioneer supplier, described the variety as "Of the very largest size, far surpassing in that respect any other sorts, in color very dark rich crimson to the core, flesh fine grained and of a delicious flavor and with the peculiar aroma of the native wild strawberry, from which it is thought to have sprung, and is undoubtedly the finest sort ever grown in this country. The blossom is perfect. . . . The plants are the strongest and most vigorous I have ever seen. The foliage is heavy, and thick enough to protect the blossom from late frosts and the roots from winter cold. . . . 3000 quarts grown on ¼ acre."

Marshall strawberries set large fruit, send out few runners (15, contrasted with 35 for the Klondike and Dunlap varieties), and form large, compact plants. It was ideal for the mound method of cultivation used by commercial farmers at the time of its rise in popularity. Although advertised as being self-fertilizing, large-scale cultivation showed it performed best when fertilized by another variety. Because irrationally high prices were paid for out-of-season strawberries grown in glasshouses and harvested during the holiday season, having a variety that would produce ripe fruit in late autumn under artificial conditions was a no-brainer for many growers. It was quickly reckoned to be the best forcing strawberry (a plant that growers can make sprout and fruit out of season in greenhouses) available on the American market.

For all its virtues, the Marshall strawberry's liabilities would doom it as a commodity berry. It required very rich, heavily fertilized soil, and "fails completely on poor and sandy soils," according to S. W. Fletcher's *Strawberry Growing*. Not every grower had fine, fertile, loamy soil, and other varieties were more productive and more resistant to the fungal disease strawberry rust. Finally, some strains with particularly large berries tended to develop hollow hearts, called the "empty center," which became a point of criticism among breeders in the 1920s. Despite its sweetness, the Marshall strawberry was unfortunately among the hollow-hearted varieties, and growers began to look for fuller hearts.

George Darrow's Fairfax strawberry was smaller, more solid, and arguably more nuanced in flavor. It would eventually become the model for mid-20th-century strawberries. Yet, the Marshall's size and visual appeal sustained interest in the mid-20th century in the Pacific Northwest, where it remained in cultivation well into the 1960s. Many of the important West Coast culinary personalities of the 20th century grew up with the Marshall strawberry as their standard of strawberry taste.

The Marshall ceased to be a crop strawberry by 1970, but its reputation kept it in cultivation. Plants were preserved at the USDA Clonal Germplasm Repository, and the variety was frequently requested. The Marshall strawberry that is available nowadays through Raintree Nursery and other sources sets fruit a bit smaller than what was produced in the early decades of the variety's existence. This may be because conservators sought to exclude the fat, hollow-hearted strains when preserving the plant for future generations. The Marshall strawberry is an excellent example of plant variation in a product that has been largely homogenized in the commodity market. If you are lucky enough to come across a Marshall strawberry, or another that doesn't quite match the grocery store version, aim for the heart and thoughtfully assess the flavor—you may be surprised and delighted at what those rather unusual red gems have to offer.

Meech's
PROLIFIC
QUINCE

Meech's Prolific quince is the finest heirloom variety of quince bred in the United States. The seedling offspring of an apple-shaped Orange quince pollinated by a pear-shaped Portugal quince, it appeared in an anonymous fruit grower's orchard in Connecticut sometime in the decade before the Civil War. Once widely grown and consumed in the United States, the quince has become a rarity in yards and in produce bins because it is not a convenient fruit.

Quince is an ancient fruit symbolically connected with marriage and fertility. Some argue it was the apple in Eden. Quince spread from its Asian homeland into Europe in antiquity, and it has been cultivated throughout southern Europe to the present day. The Pilgrims transported it to New England alongside pears and apples. Britain has retained its traditional love of the quince, though Americans now regard it as a specialty product.

CLASSIC *Quince* PREPARATION

Meech's Prolific quince, because of its superlative fragrance (melding tangerine with green apple), was deemed suitable for all classic quince preparations:

Quince Wine—Made of equal parts quince juice (crushed from fruit with seeds removed), water, and 3¼ pounds of sugar per gallon, left to ferment.

Quince Syrup—Once a favorite flavoring in American soda fountains. Chop quinces and boil in water in which sugar is dissolved. Strain fruit matter out after the syrup has attained body.

Quince Preserves—First fruits are cooked soft, then an equal weight of sugar is added. Follow the usual procedures of canning to complete.

Quince Marmalade—Fruits are cooked soft, crushed to pulp, and cooked slowly with an equal weight of sugar. Sometimes apple is added to enhance the taste.

Quince Butter—Fruit is cooked soft at low temperature until its natural sugars concentrate to the point of caramelization. Once a favorite Philadelphia food.

Quince Compote—Pare, halve, and core quinces and put in a preserving vessel with enough simple syrup to cover them. Add lemon juice and boil until tender. Extract the fruit and put into a vessel, reduce the syrup, then pour over quinces.

Baked Quinces—Core whole quinces and fill the cavity with sugar. Place in a pan whose bottom is covered with water. Bake until fork-tender.

Quince Jelly—The skin of the quince contains ample pectin, contributing body to the most famous of quince preparations, quince jelly/paste (membrillo). Core the quinces to eliminate the seeds. Chop the quinces finely, including skin. Barely cover with water and bring the quinces to a boil. After they have boiled 3 minutes, put a lid on the vessel and simmer for 30 minutes. Drain the juice through a jelly bag. Because quinces contain little acid, add lemon juice or some fruit acid. For 4 cups of juice, add ¼ cup lemon juice, and depending on how sweet you wish your jelly, anywhere from 2 to 3 cups of sugar. Boil until the mixture sheets on the back of a spoon. Pour into a pan to form jellied sheets or put into a jar.

The fruit is . . . very large,
of a bright golden yellow,
exceedingly fragrant, and
of high flavor.

Because the Prolific quince bore fruit only in its second year of growth, it was passed around as a novelty in the 1850s, eventually coming into the possession of the foremost quince pomologist in America, William W. Meech. Unlike the unproductive Portugal quince, it set fruit amply on its branches. It had the pear shape, golden color, and culinary quality of the Portugal quince, but the hardiness, fruit weight (from 12 to 15 ounces each), and versatility of the Orange quince. Its unique virtues include being entirely free of the lumps or hard spots that often spontaneously appeared in the flesh of other varieties. Meech adopted and improved the plant and became so active a champion of the variety that growers named the quince after him.

Meech characterized his namesake fruit in his popular handbook on quinces, *An Illustrated Hand-book for the Propagation and Cultivation of the Quince*: "The trees of this variety are exceedingly vigorous. . . . The trunk is smooth, and entirely free from the excrescences of some other kinds. The bark of the young tree is darker than that of the Orange [quince], and is beautifully flecked with lenticels. . . . The fruit is . . . very large, of a bright golden yellow, exceedingly fragrant, and of high flavor. The skin is of a very fine texture." For an heirloom fruit tree it has good resistance to rust and moderate resistance to fabraea leaf spot, but a vulnerability to fire blight. Meech's Prolific quince entices with its sweet scent, yet the quince is hard textured and astringent to taste when plucked ripe off the tree. Its best characteristics are unlocked by cooking or fermentation.

Pink CHAMPAGNE Currant

US ORIGIN OR MOST PREVALENT IN
New England

CHARACTERISTICS
Splendid appearance, sprightly flavor

USDA PLANT HARDINESS ZONES
5b–7a

CLOSE RELATIVES
Red currant, White currant

NOTABLE PRODUCERS
Bushes available from Nourse Farms, Restoring Eden, and Stark Bros

The Pink Champagne currant looks like a gem-encrusted shrub from some enchanted realm with its clusters of pink spherical jewels, semi-translucent, luminous, and arrayed on sprigs of mini florets. Many varieties of heirloom currants survive in the United States—including Ark of Taste entries for the Cherry, Chautauqua Climbing, Diploma, Fay's Prolific, Giant Red, Moore's Ruby, Perfection, Red Cross, and White Imperial currants. But the Pink Champagne currant best conveys the splendor of appearance and flavor that made the currant seem the paragon of utility and sumptuousness in America, before fear of blister rust set the country to a panic about the tiny, delicious berry. In a time when strawberries, blueberries, raspberries, and blackberries stand foremost in consumer esteem for berries, we can scarcely grasp the immense regard that Americans once held for currants. At the outset of the 19th century, William Forsyth wrote, "The currant is the most useful of all the small fruit, either for the table and kitchen, or for preserving, making wine, etc. and continues longer in succession than any other."

The Pink Champagne currant appeared under the Red currant variety in John Abercrombie's 1779 *The British Fruit-Gardener,* though it's difficult to ascertain the true starting point in time of the variety. In their 1802 *A Treatise on the Management and Culture of Fruit Trees,* William Forsyth and William Cobbett identify it as a specialty fruit maintained by nurserymen, while the public more commonly grew the White Dutch currant and common American Black and Red currant varieties. Pomologists speculated whether the Pink Champagne might be a cross between Red and White varieties.

Native to northern Europe, currants require cool weather to flourish, so New England was their initial region of cultivation in the United States. While the Black currant was by far the culinary favorite of Europeans, and remains so, Americans have traditionally preferred the Red and Pink varieties. The Pink Champagne is sweeter than the Black or White and less tart than the Red currant. While few eat the fruit of Red or Black currants straight from the bush, the Pink Champagne is sweet and delicate enough to be a satisfying handful.

POMOLOGISTS

Pomologists are those who study and cultivate fruit trees. Over time the name expanded to include people concerned with trees that bore nuts and drupes. Traditionally they were the most literate kind of cultivator, always seeking saplings, cuttings, and fruits from other parts of the world to transplant.

The Pink Champagne variety has none of the funky "cat pee" scent that is known to emanate from the foliage of the Black variety (*Ribes nigrum*). The shrubs grow from 3 to 5 feet tall and produce densely clustered stems of pinkish fruit. The plants grow quickly, and the amount of fruit they set tends to exceed the expectation of gardeners, much to their delight. Only the Blanka White currant rivals the Pink Champagne for size, but the Pink Champagne entirely eclipses the Blanka in taste tests.

Despite its proven and beloved flavor, this luscious tiny fruit fell victim to the heavy hand of regulatory agencies and their century-long campaign to demean the currant as a fruit and restrict its interstate commerce. Early in the 20th century, inaccurate observation led to an assertion that currants, particularly Black currants, were vectors for white pine blister rust, a rust fungus that severely impacts and weakens cone-bearing trees. Pressured by the American timber industry, the Department of Agriculture imposed a federal ban on the cultivation of

*The Pink Champagne is
sweeter than the Black
or White and less tart
than the Red currant.*

Black currants in 1920. Northern states extended these restrictions to Pink, Red, and White varieties. Despite evidence in the 1960s that currants were not vectors, but victims, of white pine blister rust, the restrictions endure in several states, and interstate commerce of currants remains limited. Even though the beloved Pink Champagne currant has little of the rust vulnerability of the Black currant varieties, its cultivation was starkly affected by the restrictions.

When currant plants are managed well, harvests can continue from June to November, but the Pink Champagne currant does not lend itself well to machine harvesting on account of its delicacy. What's more, the Pink Champagne currant does not keep for more than nine days once harvested. Since hand harvesting limits the scale of cultivation and its shelf life is so short, it is not a lucrative crop. Furthermore, the Pink Champagne is one of the more difficult of the currants to pick because of the way the fruit adheres to the stems, despite the large size of the berries.

So it has been the home gardener that has kept the Pink Champagne currant continuously available as nursery stock since its introduction more than a century ago. The most frequent use of the fruit is as a preserve, since its distinctive quality and delicacy are lost when frozen. The fruit contains ample pectin, so it readily forms into a jam with body. A master preserver who processes the fruit into jam or syrups can conserve the fruit's quality and extend its shelf life almost indefinitely. (The culinary world has favored the syrup and preserves from Black currants for centuries.) Thus, the Pink Champagne is a true niche berry, remaining in hearts and soil by way of its enthusiasts, but its unique flavor and whimsical appearance make it worth the effort it will require to keep it growing.

PLYMOUTH ROCK
Chicken

US ORIGIN OR MOST PREVALENT IN
Massachusetts

CHARACTERISTICS
Docility, vitality, egg laying, flavorful flesh

CLOSE RELATIVES
Rhode Island Red chicken, White Jersey Giant chicken, Columbian Wyandotte chicken, Dominique chicken

NOTABLE PRODUCER
McMurray Hatchery

The Plymouth Rock is arguably *the* American chicken. The breed presently exists in seven configurations, but the earliest stable form of the bird, a barred white and dark gray fowl introduced in 1869, is the form referred to in the Ark of Taste. It became a dual-purpose commodity chicken in the 1870s, valuable for home egg production and supply-chain meat generation.

The tale of how the Plymouth Rock chicken came to be reveals how uncertain livestock breeding was before Gregor Mendel's 1865 explanations of the laws of genetic inheritance. In the United States, even the most scientific thinkers didn't

Bennett had bred a bird that was "one half Cochin China, one fourth Fawn-colored Dorking, one eighth Great Malay, and one eighth Wild Indian." He called it the Plymouth Rock and exhibited it at the 1849 fair, inspiring a lively popular demand.

have a clue how to fix traits from a certain strain of animal into a new hybrid. The Plymouth Rock chicken is the poster child for breeders learning how to make that happen—it had to be bred twice before breeders achieved that goal.

John C. Bennett of Plymouth, Massachusetts, was one of about 30 New England professionals smitten with Asian fowl. In the 1840s, having a yard full of unusual-looking birds signaled belonging to an elite agricultural brotherhood, and every collector sought multiple varieties. When Dorking, West Indian, Malay, and Brown Cochin birds occupied the same yard, the distinct varieties inevitably mixed and unintentional crossbreeding occurred. To counter this promiscuous mash-up of exotic birds, Bennett staged the great Fowl Fair of 1849. He insisted on tying traits to breeds, and instead of encouraging the promiscuous crossing of birds, he wished to combine specific traits into ideal hybrids. This first great exhibition of attractive Asian and European fowl meant to impress images of undiluted varieties of birds into the eyes and consciousness of onlookers. The fair proved to be a wildly popular public spectacle. Bennett reinforced the aesthetic point by publishing *The Poultry Book* in 1850, which described each breed's characteristics, behaviors, and food use. Bennett had bred a bird that was "one half Cochin China, one fourth Fawn-colored Dorking, one eighth Great Malay, and one eighth Wild Indian." He called it the Plymouth Rock and exhibited it at the 1849 fair, inspiring a lively popular demand. But when people tried to replicate the features of the Plymouth Rock by breeding pairs of birds at home, recessive traits popped up. Bennett later came to realize that six generations of interbreeding were needed to stabilize traits in plants and animals.

The first Plymouth Rock chickens were speckled or russet, not barred. Their size, egg laying, and docile demeanor were excellent. The breed reemerged in 1869 when Dyer A. Upham of Wilsonville, Connecticut, exhibited an "improved" barred version of the bird, with the barring derived from adding Dominique chicken, an old American breed, into the mix with Cochin and Dorking. Like Bennett's earlier Plymouth Rock, Upham's striking barred Plymouth Rock had unstable features, such as feathered legs, yet it was stable enough for the American Poultry Association to formulate for it a Standard of Excellence in 1874. H. B. May of Essex finally interbred the barred Plymouth Rock to fix their traits in 1877.

According to the Livestock Conservancy, "Plymouth Rock hens grow to 7½ pounds and cocks to 9½ pounds and their rate of lay is very good at around 200 per annum. Temperament is calm and the birds are cold-hardy with early feathering. This chicken has a bright red single comb, face, wattles, and earlobes. The comb of this breed has five evenly serrated points with those in the front and rear shorter than those in the middle. The plumage should have feathers that are crossed by sharply defined, regular, parallel bars of alternate light (short of positive white) and dark (short of positive black) color."

In mapping the genome of the White Plymouth Rock, a strain descended from an 1878 spontaneous mutation of the barred Plymouth Rock, geneticists at Virginia Tech University, Uppsala University, and the Livestock Conservancy discovered that the Dominique was in fact the major contributor to the Plymouth Rock breed. Dominique, Black Java, and Cochin breeds contributed to the maternal ancestors, while Black Java, Cochin, Langshan, Light Brahma, and Black Minorca contributed its paternity.

For the next century, the Plymouth Rock was the most widely raised bird in the United States. In the mid-20th century, a hybrid broiler bird bred from a cross between the White Plymouth Rock and the Cornish became the chief meat variety. This cross began to be genetically tweaked to increase speed of development and size with the introduction of Jersey Giant genetics. The modern day meat industry has little want of the barred Plymouth Rock and only retains breeder lines of the White Plymouth Rock developed in the 20th-century forms. The attractive heirloom barred Plymouth Rock endures on farms primarily as a laying chicken, producing up to 200 eggs per year, and is a popular choice for people raising heirloom chickens at home.

TENNIS BALL
Lettuce

**US ORIGIN OR
MOST PREVALENT IN**
Massachusetts

CHARACTERISTICS
*Compact head, buttery
leaf texture*

**USDA PLANT
HARDINESS ZONES**
5b–8a

CLOSE RELATIVE
Boston lettuce

NOTABLE PRODUCERS
*I & Me Farm,
Yonder Hill Farm*

The Tennis Ball lettuce was one of the most popular lettuces at the turn of the 20th century, first imported into North America from the United Kingdom by enterprising Boston seedswoman Bethiah Oliver in 1768. In 1809, Thomas Jefferson grew the variety at Monticello and quickly recognized its two virtues—splendid texture when eaten as salad and impressive hardiness in the garden. Of the 15 lettuce varieties in the Monticello kitchen garden, the Tennis Ball variety required the least maintenance.

Tennis Ball lettuce bears an unusually small head, buttery leaves, and resistance to pests and diseases, and so it quickly became a garden favorite. The black-seeded variety grows small, tight rosettes of light green leaves with a slippery, silky texture. The white-seeded variety matures two weeks earlier than the black and is sometimes called Early Tennis Ball lettuce. According to *Kalispell Montana Bee*, "young plants [of the black-seeded Tennis Ball variant] are of a lighter shade of green than the white-seeded Tennis Ball—leaves smooth

...Glasshouse gardeners around America's major cities [seized] upon the Tennis Ball lettuce as a forcing vegetable—a salad green that could be sold in the holiday season and in winter.

at first, becoming very much crumpled and plaited after the heads begin to form. The heads are larger and looser than those of the white seed variety, and they mature about two weeks later. The leaves of this variety are rarely if ever shaded with red."

Southern gardeners manifested a decided preference for the black-seeded form of the Tennis Ball lettuce during the 19th century, while the white-seeded variant became popular in the North, despite its being a degree more bitter than the black-seeded. The tenderness of the leaves in both forms made it a very desirable salad lettuce but posed challenges as a market product, since it bruised easily in transport. Well into the 1830s, both variants remained within the realm of home gardens. In 1835, the editor of the *Connecticut Herald* noted, "[I] would observe that it is grown in several private gardens here, but it is not offered in the market. We would observe that it is one of the finest salads, and its cultivation should be extended."

One undeniable factor transformed the Tennis Ball lettuce into a market variety. In the 1830s, growers began to notice the variety's cold hardiness and apparent indifference to day length. A squib appeared in a December 1830 newspaper reporting that the stewards of a Boston market garden were harvesting Tennis Ball lettuce, "which grew in the open air without protection or any extra care. This instance of winter vegetation . . . is the most remarkable within his recollection." This caused the glasshouse gardeners around America's major cities to seize upon the Tennis Ball lettuce as a forcing vegetable—a salad green that could be sold in the holiday season and in winter. In January 1869, Rhode Island agriculturist, sanitation engineer, and author George E. Waring spoke of "several hot houses, containing at this moment seven hundred dozen heads of Tennis Ball Lettuce, just ready for market."

From the time of the Civil War to World War I, market gardeners tried to make Tennis Ball lettuce available year-round. Its grand appeal to consumers only loosened when giantism conquered vegetable breeding aesthetics and the-bigger-the-better mentality took hold. Breeders developed the larger Boston lettuce from the Tennis Ball, and that variety supplanted the compact original in the hearts of salad lovers. Thus the heyday of the Tennis Ball as a market favorite faded in the 1920s. The rise of the larger and more compact iceberg lettuce, with its crisp leaves, moved consumer aesthetics ever further away from the Tennis Ball.

Nonetheless, spurred by Thomas Jefferson's enthusiasm for the variety, the Tennis Ball lettuce was one of the first localized heirloom crops to capture the fancy of heritage gardeners. The Tennis Ball was distinctive in shape, inviting in texture, and ancient in history. Since the early 1990s, the heirloom line of Tennis Ball lettuce seeds has remained on offer from a number of seed companies, particularly those specializing in heirloom varieties. Tennis Ball lettuce is worthy of praise as one of the essential vegetable varieties that shaped the public image of what an heirloom vegetable is. And it still makes for a divine homegrown salad.

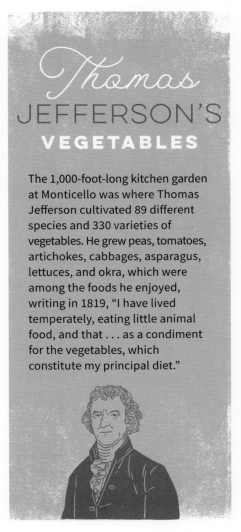

Thomas JEFFERSON'S VEGETABLES

The 1,000-foot-long kitchen garden at Monticello was where Thomas Jefferson cultivated 89 different species and 330 varieties of vegetables. He grew peas, tomatoes, artichokes, cabbages, asparagus, lettuces, and okra, which were among the foods he enjoyed, writing in 1819, "I have lived temperately, eating little animal food, and that . . . as a condiment for the vegetables, which constitute my principal diet."

TUSCARORA WHITE *Corn*

US ORIGIN OR MOST PREVALENT IN
Iroquois lands, North Carolina

CHARACTERISTICS
Red cob, long ears

USDA PLANT HARDINESS ZONES
6b–9a

CLOSE RELATIVE
Tennessee Red Cob corn

NOTABLE PRODUCERS
Seeds from Meadowview Farm, Grá Den Talún Farm, Seedkeeper.ca

Tuscarora White corn is the favorite source of tamal flour among the Iroquois nations. It is a native landrace white meal corn nurtured by the Tuscarora people in modern-day North Carolina, Pennsylvania, and New York. The Tuscarora (meaning "hemp gatherers") are an Iroquois-speaking people native to the territory that would later become North Carolina and with whom the corn traveled north when a major segment of the population migrated by force or necessity after the Tuscarora War of 1711–1713. In 1722, the Tuscarora were incorporated as one of the Six Nations of the Iroquois Confederacy, also known as the Haudenosaunee. The white corn the people had long stewarded was then incorporated into the foodways of the Confederacy as a whole. The Tuscarora people and the Iroquois Confederacy have prompted stewardship campaigns to sustain this important maize variety in recent years.

Tuscarora White corn makes a long red cob with ears that

*Chef Dave "Smoke" McCluskey,
an Indigenous foods educator
and member of the Mohawk Nation,
is one of the foremost advocates
of Tuscarora White corn as a
foodstuff and cultural expression.*

reach 12 inches on average and large, round-capped white kernels. Its starch is not flinty but soft. The Tuscarora dry their corn by pulling the husks back from the ear and plaiting them together to form strings of 40 to 50 ears to hang from the rafters, protected from moisture and mice. When the kernels are dry enough to process, they are soaked in water mixed with lye—made from the ashes of burnt hickory or oak—until the kernel cap begins to swell and slip off the grain. The whole kernels are then rinsed and used as hominy or roasted and incorporated into soup. Ground kernels are worked to meal for corn mush or to make tamal flour.

Chief Clinton Rickard, his son Norton Rickard, and his grandson George Rickard of the Bear Clan in New York waged a vocal and effective campaign against hybrid commercial corn varieties to protect Tuscarora White corn. Norton appeared as the central figure in *The Gift*, a 1997 film about preserving the Tuscarora's signature grain. The Tuscarora people in North Carolina labored to sustain the variety, and it is from this strain that farmers crossed it with flint corns to fashion the large-kerneled, thin-cobbed, white Southern dent corn that became a mainstay crop in the fields of the Southern US.

In 1993, John Mohawk, the internationally known Seneca cultural leader and pioneering voice of Indigenous food sovereignty, sought to preserve the past to provide a future. He organized the Iroquois White Corn Project to ensure the future of unmixed lines of landrace flour corn, in collaboration with Yvonne Dion-Buffalo of the Samson Cree Nation. Mohawk's death in 2006 occasioned a brief hiatus for the project, but the project was revived and sited at Ganondagan Historic Site in New York in 2012. Angel Jimmerson oversaw the revival of the project and now manages the annual harvest of a healthy crop and volunteer husking in October to process the corn for culinary use by the community. Mohawk promoted a generous attitude toward this important Native resource, encouraging the sale of processed corn to restaurants and people who respected the integrity and history of the corn, while maintaining the variety in the foodway and public health of the Iroquois Confederacy.

Chef Dave "Smoke" McCluskey, an Indigenous foods educator and member of the Mohawk Nation, is one of the foremost advocates of Tuscarora White corn as a foodstuff and cultural expression. Based in Augusta, Georgia, he uses traditional lye soaking methods to make his signature Longhouse Hominy Grits. McCluskey is connected to a group of Tuscarora farmers in North Carolina who grow the form of white meal corn that remained in the South, and McCluskey has developed a line of indigenous corn products that undergo nixtamalization. While culture and taste are the primary reasons for processing corn with lye, nixtamalization enables niacin (an essential B vitamin) to be taken into the body from corn. White settlers who simply ground dry dent corn for their corn-meal found that their corn-centered diet often led to a disease called pellagra, which results from severe niacin deficiency. Indigenous people had long ago discovered the treatments and processes necessary to leverage the nutritional benefits of corn as a staple of one's diet. Fortunately, there is a wealth of documentation about the corn foodways of the Iroquois Confederacy since the contact period, including detailed information about the tools used in planting and processing.

In the last decade, heirloom seed companies have made Tuscarora White corn seed available to the general public. In all cases, the seed sold by these companies derives from the Northern strains of the corn. As of 2021, seed for the Southern strains of the corn have not passed out of the community of Indigenous growers in North Carolina. The variety remains important to the Tuscarora people and the Iroquois Nations as a first food and marker of identity and culture.

WELLFLEET
Oyster

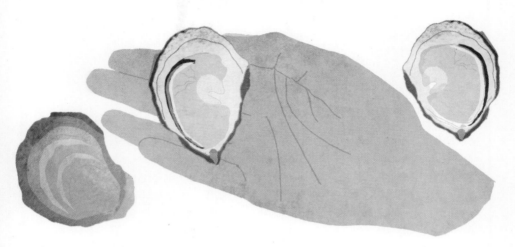

US ORIGIN OR MOST PREVALENT IN
Wellfleet, Massachusetts

CHARACTERISTICS
Three-inch bivalve, salty, buttery flavor

NOTABLE PRODUCERS
Holbrook Oyster, Wellfleet Shellfish Company, Big Rock Oyster Co., Billingsgate Shellfish, Red's Best, Island Creek Oysters, Mac's Seafood

Today the harbor town of Wellfleet, Massachusetts, reigns as the premier oyster town in New England. Its namesake oyster—an Eastern-bred, 3-inch, salty, buttery bivalve—has been a brand for two centuries. Grown in the saltwater shallows around the harbor, the small Wellfleets are nowadays sustainably grown, beginning in spat hatcheries and nurtured in bags or in Breton-style iron cages (protection against predatory fish and birds) and harvested at three years of age. With just over 100 small-scale farmers who maintain proprietary oyster grounds around the harbor, intense demand in New England makes the Wellfleet difficult to obtain in other regions. In a remarkable act of public service, the state maintains a common oyster ground off Indian Neck, where visitors possessing a permit can harvest modest quantities of Wellfleet oysters themselves.

Wellfleet Bay, which is 4 miles long and 2 miles wide, encompasses an extensive area of flats, for the rise and fall of the tide can range 11 feet. The vast majority of the oyster beds and plantings occur between the tide lines. The flats are predominately made of coarse dark sand, with occasional gravel banks and some mud basins, and they have been partitioned by farmers into proprietary plots marked by yellow floats.

...It was the Wellfleet's flavor that distinguished it from the other New England strains found in Narragansett Bay to the Damariscotta River in Maine.

In times past, the harvest of oysters was not so well governed. In the 19th century and well into the 20th, oysters fixed to masses of shell called oyster rocks and were exposed to predators, winter ice, and oyster pirates harvesting illegally on someone's proprietary bed. Piracy was a shooting offense, and the oyster shallows that extended along the waters of Massachusetts Bay near the tip of Cape Cod were a violent place. In the colonial era, the harbor earned the nickname Billingsgate, after the famous London fish market and the famously abusive fishmongers, because of the abundance of seafood and the roughness of manners. The exploitation of the shellfish beds was brutal throughout the 19th century—so much so that at times shiploads of Chesapeake Bay soft-lipped oysters were hauled up the coast and dumped into the waters for a brief baptism so they could be sold as Wellfleets at Boston. A side effect of this transshipment was that a portion of this Chesapeake material became incorporated into the depleting reefs.

On one level, using Chesapeake oysters as a substitute for locally grown Wellfleets is not an entire misdirection. Both populations of oysters are made up of the same Eastern oyster *(Crassostrea virginica)* species. Yet growing in different environments and ingesting the different sorts of plankton found in Massachusetts and Virginia does impart a different flavor in them. Two weeks in Wellfleet Bay would readjust a Chesapeake oyster's salinity to that of Wellfleet Bay, but not the base flavor of the oyster itself. And it was the Wellfleet's flavor that distinguished it from the other New England strains found in Narragansett Bay to the Damariscotta River in Maine.

Before the end of the 19th century, watermen in Wellfleet realized that the oyster grounds risked exhaustion. In the 1910s, efforts were made to collect oyster larvae known as spat with plankton nets to set up an oyster hatchery. A successful hatchery would not be created until around 1960, when the Aquacultural Research Corporation began selling spat to shell fishermen. Before that time, however, the watermen of Wellfleet did enter into occasional cooperative arrangements. In 1931 the sudden appearance of the predatory oyster drill snails in Wellfleet Bay threatened the destruction of the entire fishery.

Commercial rivals became allies in efforts to clear the bay of these pests. Yet it wasn't until 2008 that any concerted program of habitat restoration took place in Wellfleet Bay when Mass Audubon, the Nature Conservancy, the Town of Wellfleet, and the National Oceanic and Atmospheric Administration began rebuilding the reefs in an oyster restoration project. Their effort was completed in 2011. The various oyster harvesters in the region, witnessing the positive effect of this concerted effort, realized that formal organization might prove a boon in their effort to keep the fishery afloat. In 2018, for the first time, a producers group, the Wellfleet Shellfishermen's Association, came into existence. Immediately they organized a festival and location to sell their oysters.

Because oysters are transportable and can be shipped or mailed, the internet has made them available nationally. While shellfishing has been historically a male-dominated vocation, there are some women who work the water. Karen Johnson sells her oysters at the Wellfleet Shellfishermen's Farmers Market, held either at the Wellfleet Pier or at Holbrook Oyster.

THE DISAPPEARANCE OF Billingsgate Island

Rich beds of shellfish were found off Billingsgate Island, which in the 19th century sat at the mouth of Wellfleet Harbor. The 60-acre island, a center for fishing and whaling, was home to a lighthouse built in 1822, as well as 30 homes and a schoolhouse. Storms and erosion caused the island to be cut in two in 1855, with residents moving to the mainland by 1912. The lighthouse was abandoned in 1915 and was destroyed by a storm months later. Billingsgate was completely submerged by 1942. However, during low tide, the remnants of the island are still a popular place for shellfishing.

WELLFLEET OYSTERS

ON THE HALF SHELL WITH

BRADFORD *Watermelon* MIGNONETTE

KEVIN MITCHELL, *chef and culinary historian*
SOUTH CAROLINA

This floral mignonette pairs well with the salty, buttery Wellfleet but would work wonderfully with your favorite oyster. The Bradford watermelon rind is thick and holds up really well in the pickling process.

MAKES 2 CUPS (480 ML) SAUCE FOR 100 OYSTERS

FOR THE PICKLED WATERMELON RIND

½ cup (80 g) coarsely chopped Bradford watermelon rind (see page 88)

½ cup (120 ml) apple cider vinegar

½ cup (120 ml) water

1 tablespoon Diamond kosher salt

½ tablespoon granulated sugar

FOR THE MIGNONETTE

1½ cups (230 g) coarsely chopped Bradford watermelon

½ cup (80 g) pickled watermelon rind

1 tablespoon pickling juice from the watermelon pickles

¼ teaspoon smoked sea salt

¼ teaspoon freshly ground black pepper

Ice-cold oysters, shucked, up to 100

Micro arugula, to garnish (optional)

MAKE THE PICKLED WATERMELON RIND

Place the watermelon rinds in a jar big enough to allow the rinds to reach the rim. Put the vinegar, water, salt, and sugar in a small saucepan and bring to a boil over high heat, stirring until the sugar and salt have dissolved. Remove from heat and carefully pour the pickling juice to just below the rim of the jar. Seal the jar with a lid and let it cool to room temperature. Put in the refrigerator and let marinate for at least 24 hours.

MAKE THE MIGNONETTE

Combine all ingredients in a stainless steel bowl. Top each oyster with about 1 teaspoon of the mignonette. Top with micro arugula, if desired. Serve immediately.

Kevin Mitchell is a chef, culinary historian, author, and educator in Charleston, South Carolina, who serves on the board of Slow Food USA.

White Cap
FLINT CORN

Rhode Island's White Cap flint corn is a Narragansett landrace, eight-row flint corn (see page 122) that became central to settler foodways in the early 19th century, and later the invariable ingredient of the quintessential Rhode Island dish, the jonny cake (aka johnnycake or journey cake). Many parts of the West Indies and the eastern seaboard of North America are well known to prepare jonny cakes, but Rhode Island has a unique connection with turning the native white landrace flint corn variety into flour to make the timeless dish.

Originally created by the Indigenous Narragansett people, the preparation was appropriated by New England settlers. Jonny cakes were made from milled cornmeal, mixed dry with salt (and in late colonial times with sugar as well), wetted with boiling water, and thinned with a bit of milk to create a dough to be fried in a hot skillet or on a griddle for 15 to 30 minutes. The jonny cake must be served piping hot, and cooking them in bacon fat certainly adds wonderful, savory flavor. Consumed with butter and/or maple syrup, the distinctive texture of the Rhode Island jonny cake depended upon the milling of the flour. The tradition in Rhode Island has long been to mill the grains fine, using New England granite millstones.

There is a sketch by Thomas R. "Shepard Tom" Hazard titled "First Baking," in his *Jonny-Cake Papers* published in the 1879 *Providence Gazette*. It vividly describes the practice of milling White Cap flint corn. Phillis, the Hazard family cook, insisted on having White Narragansett corn—the same White Cap flint corn—ground by what is now called Hammond's Mill, just above Pettaquamscutt Lake in Rhode Island. Phillis would not touch meal ground at any other mill for the reason that they made harsh "round" meal, whereas Hammond's made soft-feeling "flat" meal, ideal for her jonny cakes. In fact, millstones made from the Narragansett granite rock are the only millstones on earth that will grind cornmeal fit for a genuine jonny cake. The distinction of round and flat meal arose from the variation in quality of the flour ground at these mills.

CORN ROWS

The rows on an ear of corn indicate how many kernels form on the circumference of the ear. Northern flint corns tended to have 8. Southern flint corns had 12. Gourdseed corns could have 16 to 24. The dent corns created by settlers in the early 19th century had 12 to 18 rows.

Sweet corns were mutations of flint corns, and originally had 8 rows; but 19th-century breeders wished to have more kernels on the cob and interbred the original sweet corn variety (papoon corn) taken from the Six Nations during the American Revolution with gourdseed corns to increase the number of rows. Now commercial sweet corn has 12 rows at a minimum.

White Cap flint corn takes 100 to 110 days to mature, more time than more northerly flint corns such as King Phillip corn (85 days) or the Abenaki Flint (90 to 95 days) grown in northern New England. The plants grow about 6 feet high and bear one or two ears per stalk. Like all flint corns, White Cap is hard and densely packed with starch, and has round kernels. The narrow ears vary from 6 to 9 inches in length, and the kernels cover the tip of the ear, giving it a rounded apex. Though the name suggests a snowy color, White Cap is an antique cream color. It is almost always dried and milled for use in mush and jonny cakes, instead of boiled or roasted like sweet corn.

White Cap flint corn is the only landrace flint corn from

White Cap flint corn is the only landrace flint corn from Rhode Island to survive into the 21st century. It endured because of the jonny cake's emblematic connection with Rhode Island identity . . .

Rhode Island to survive into the 21st century. It endured because of the jonny cake's emblematic connection with Rhode Island identity and White Cap flint's necessary role in making those jonny cakes. In 2020, the USDA retained seven different strains of White Cap flint corn in its germplasm collection. There were no other Rhode Island landrace or heirloom corn varieties. "In 1924, the Connecticut Agricultural Station published a report on corn in the state," wrote the Ayer's Creek Farm Newsletter. "For the most part, modern New Englanders have no idea about this legacy and have never tasted a good flint corn, with the possible exception of Rhode Islanders who have preserved their 'White Cap' flint in statute as the legally correct corn for making Jonny Cake." Whether you're a rule follower or interested in sustaining the culinary practice to which we owe the survival of this treasured corn variety, don't you dare make jonny cakes with anything but White Cap flint corn, and be sure to eat them piping hot.

BELLE OF GEORGIA PEACH BENNE OIL
BRADFORD WATERMELON CANDY ROAS
T CAROLINA GOLD RICE CHARLESTON WA
CKE'S PROLIFIC CORN COONTIE (FLORIDA
EENS (UPLAND CRESS) CREOLE CREAM
USE CHERRY GALLBERRY HONEY GEORG
SHAW GROUNDNUT CAKE GULF COAST
N SWEET POTATO HERBEMONT GRAPE HI
EEP HOOVER APPLE INDIAN BLOOD PEA
WATERMELON LANDRACE RED CREOLE
N LOUISIANA SATSUMA MAYHAW JELLY
LL SWEET POTATO NATIVE CHINQUAPIN
SABAW ISLAND HOG PANTIN MAMEY SAP
NTO PEPPER PINEYWOODS CATTLE PURPL
MAN TAFFY CANDY ROYAL PALM TURKEY
RN SEASHORE BLACK RYE SEVEN TOP T
NIS SHEEP TUPELO HONEY TURKEY CRA
UM WHITE VELVET OKRA WILD CATFISH
DO YATES APPLE YELLOW CABBAGE COL
ALACHICOLA OYSTER APIOS AMERICANA
NNE OIL BLACK LIMBERTWIG APPLE BOU
ROASTER SQUASH CAROLINA AFRICAN RU
KEFIELD CABBAGE CHEROKEE PURPLE TO
ARROWROOT) COTTON PATCH GOOSE
EESE DATIL PEPPER DUNCAN GRAPEFRU
RATTLESNAKE WATERMELON GREEN-ST
EEP HANDMADE FILE HATCHER MANGO
WES CRAB APPLE HOG ISLAND FIG HOG I
ACH KENTUCKY LIMESTONE BIBB LETTUC
E ONION LEMON CLING PEACH LOUISIAN
AND SYRUP MISSISSIPPI SILVER HULL PEA
ODELL'S WHITE WATERMELON OGEECH
OTE PARSON BROWN ORANGE PERFECT

ACK LIMBERTWIG APPLE BOURB
ER SQUASH CAROLINA AFRICAN RUNNER
EFIELD CABBAGE CHEROKEE PURPLE TON
ARROWROOT) COTTON PATCH G
HEESE DATIL PEPPER DUNCAN G
A RATTLESNAKE WATERMEL
HEEP HANDMADE FILE HA
VES CRAB APPLE HOG ISLAN
KENTUCKY LIMESTONE BIBB L
ONION LEMON CLING PEACH LO
ND SYRUP MISSISSIPPI SILVER HU
DELL'S WHITE WATERMELON OG
PARSON BROWN ORANGE PE
RIBBON SUGAR CANE PURPLE ST
SEA ISLAND RED PEAS SEA ISLAN
RNIP SOURWOOD HONEY TENNIS
BEAN WHIPPOORWILL PEA WHIT
WILD GULF COAST SHRIMP WILSON POPEN
RD YELLOW CREOLE CORN AMERICAN G
RKANSAS BLACK APPLE BELLE OF GEORGI
BON RED TURKEY BRADFORD WATERMEL
INER PEANUT CAROLINA GOLD RICE
ATO COCKE'S PROLIFIC CORN C
EASY GREENS (UPLAND CRESS)
DYEHOUSE CHERRY GALLBERR
PED CUSHAW GROUNDNUT CA GULF
AYMAN SWEET POTATO HERBEM
AND SHEEP HOOVER APPLE IN
KLECKLEY WATERMELON LAN
MIRLITON LOUISIANA SATSUMA
NANCY HALL SWEET POTATO NA
LIMES OSSABAW ISLAND HOG
PIMENTO PEPPER PINEYWOO

SOUTHEAST

American
GUINEA HOG

US ORIGIN OR
MOST PREVALENT IN
Southeast United States

CHARACTERISTICS
*Small, compact, black,
mild-tempered, fat,
umami*

OTHER NAMES
Piney Woods pig

CLOSE RELATIVE
English Black Essex pig

NOTABLE PRODUCERS
*Lisa and Stephen
Grubb, Victoria Jaffery,
Deborah Niemann-Boehle,
Victoria Rozanski,
Brandi Peerman,
Kirk Fackrell,
Carolina Heritage Farms*

A small hog descended from the English Black Essex pig and other free-range Southern hogs, the American Guinea hog was first recognized as a distinct creation in the late 1870s. Once common on homesteads, it emerged in several places in the South, including the Carolinas, Florida, and Louisiana. Unique to the United States, it evolved in the American landscape in the decades after the Civil War when the Black Essex mated with the other hogs and evolved to deal with the often sparse food landscapes of the sandhill pine forests. Sometimes called the Piney Woods pig, it diminished in size and grew more efficient in setting fat to see it through the lean seasons.

In 1917, a Cajun farmer characterized the breed: "It was remarkable for its short legs, compact, well-rounded body, mild docile nature, easy to keep and seldom straying from home. Par excellence, they were 'grease hogs' easily fattened and having very little lean meat, they rendered up a large amount of lard. For some reason this useful breed is now almost extinct."

Given the preoccupation of American consumers and the meat industry with lean pork, it's understandable how the Guinea hog has almost disappeared over the course of the 20th century. In the 21st century it was listed as critically endangered—that means fewer than 200 annual registrations. Yet small populations of Guineas endured, because they are easy to keep, their lard is sumptuous, and their chops and hams are wonderfully flavorful.

In the past decade, the Guinea hog has been taken up by small livestock operations across the United States. It became the fastest-expanding heirloom pig population monitored by the Livestock Conservancy, its status having shifted from endangered to threatened (fewer than 1,000 annual registrations). Because it is a placid breed, hardy and adaptable, it wins converts from livestock farmers who have tried more temperamental heirloom varieties, such as the Ossabaw Island hog. It generates flesh as quickly as modern industrial pigs, but the way the American Guinea hog sets fat makes for a distinctive depth of flavor.

The American Guinea hog was discovered by the "lardcore" movement of Southern chefs—a group of culinarians who shared in the European appreciation of fat quality and flavor in traditional pig breeds. Chefs such as Craig Deihl, Sean Brock, Frank Stitt, and Ashley Christensen have turned their backs on the industrial pink pig and championed heirloom breeds. The Guinea hog stands conspicuous among those heirloom breeds and, in addition to its coveted fat, has a savor that sets it apart from other pork.

Chef CRAIG DEIHL

ON THE GUINEA HOG

A chef-butcher with a broad experience with heirloom pigs, Chef Craig Deihl has championed the Guinea hog, which he writes, "has a small frame and is easy to work with in the kitchen without lots of equipment. You barely need a handsaw to even get the chine bone off for [a] rack of pork. . . . The flavor profile is great and the fat tastes incredible. . . . The meat has great marbling and fat cover, with rich red muscle and dense flavorful fat. It is similar in size and yield to a lamb carcass; the smaller cuts, especially the chops, are great for a tasting menu." For fresh pork, Deihl prefers an 8- or 9-month-old hog—about 55 pounds (25 kg). For charcuterie, Diehl favors a year-old pig of approximately 150 pounds (68 kg). He also highlights one unique attribute of the Guinea hog: "huge jowls, twice as thick as other pigs."

MOJO-ROASTED *American* GUINEA HOG

KURT D'AURIZIO, *chef*
ASHEVILLE, NORTH CAROLINA

The American Guinea hog is ideal for a variety of applications, including traditional porchetta, charcuterie, ham, and barbecue. The hog is a smaller breed, making it easier to handle whole. The meat is red (darker than commercial pork), and the flavor is sweet, buttery, and rich with a generous amount of fat. This recipe accentuates the succulent and flavorful nature of the American Guinea hog.
This dish is delicious with rice and beans or plantains, or as a filling for tacos. If you are lucky enough to find sour oranges, use 1 cup (240 ml) sour orange juice in place of the orange and lime juices.

MAKES 1½ TO 3 POUNDS OF PULLED PORK

3 to 5 pounds (1.4 to 2.2 kg) American Guinea hog pork shoulder (bone-in or boneless; bone-in will take longer to cook)

Salt and freshly ground black pepper

FOR THE MOJO MARINADE

¾ cup (180 ml) extra-virgin olive oil

¾ cup (180 ml) freshly squeezed orange juice

¼ cup (60 ml) freshly squeezed lime juice

2 ounces (60 g) cilantro, stems and leaves

1 cup (15 g) fresh mint leaves

5 tablespoons (5 g) fresh oregano leaves

2 tablespoons chopped garlic

2 teaspoons ground cumin

1 teaspoon sea salt

½ teaspoon ground white pepper

TO MAKE THE MARINADE

Blend all the marinade ingredients together until smooth in a blender.

TO MARINATE THE SHOULDER

Rinse the pork shoulder and pat it dry. Cut 1 to 2 inches into the thick muscles to allow the marinade to better penetrate the meat. Season with salt and pepper. Place the shoulder in a large, nonreactive dish (such as glass, plastic, or stainless steel; do not use aluminum as it will react with the acid in the marinade). Pour the marinade over the shoulder and rotate in the dish until the meat is evenly coated. Cover the dish with plastic wrap and refrigerate overnight or up to 2 days.

TO COOK THE SHOULDER

Preheat the oven to 275°F (135°C). Remove the shoulder from the marinade and place it in a roasting pan. Roast until fork-tender and the internal temperature is 190°F (88°C), about 4 to 6 hours depending on size and cut. The roast will take about 80 minutes per pound; boneless meat tends to cook faster. Shred or pull the meat, spoon pan drippings over the meat, and serve hot.

NOTE: Do not cover the shoulder while roasting it if you want it to form a crust. The shoulder can be turned halfway through cooking if desired.

Kurt D'Aurizio is based in Asheville, NC and is on the leadership committee for Slow Food USA's Cooks' Alliance.

APIOS Americana

A native North American pea vine, *Apios americana* has collected many names: Indian groundnut, Hopniss, Potato bean, and at least 14 designations in Indigenous languages. The vine was widely cultivated by Indigenous tribes in forest landscapes from southern Canada to the Gulf Coast, Maine to Minnesota, Florida to Texas. Wherever ample moisture was available in semi-shade, mats of Indian groundnut vines might carpet the ground in the wild. Native cultivators maintained these wild nurseries, protecting and expanding a versatile food source. Certain Native groups—the Muskogee and Cherokee—transplanted wild plants into cultivated beds near their settlements.

Nearly every important colonial-era report about Indigenous land noted plantings of Indian groundnut vines in proximity to Indigenous communities. It became popular among settlers as both a forage and fodder plant. In his 1585 *A Briefe and True Report of the New Found Land of Virginia*, Thomas Hariot noted its presence in coastal North Carolina. He commented: "Openauk: a kind of root of round form, some of the bigness of walnuts, some far greater, which are found in moist and marish grounds growing many together one by another in ropes, or as though they were fastened with a string. Being boiled or sodden they are very good meat."

The vine has distinctive features: Indian groundnut twists counterclockwise and stretches to as much as 10 to 12 feet in the wild. The vine bears colorful flowers that range from reddish brown to purple to crimson, and that form into edible bean pods. Nonetheless, the beans have always been a subsidiary food source compared to the tubers, even among the Cherokee, who confess a great fondness for the beans. The tubers form on long linear root filaments and can vary in size from a pea to spud. One quirk of its growth habit is that some tubers set in the soil at some distance from the plant stalk above the ground.

The flavor of the raw tubers resembles that of green peanuts. When cooked, they have a floury quality not entirely unlike a Russet potato, though with more minerality. Chefs have experimented with the tubers, commonly slicing and frying them like potato chips. Others boil, mash, and form them into cakes that are then sautéed or fried. The steamed pods taste like most other green beans, and the seeds when left to mature taste like field peas. The Indian groundnut is a perennial vine, and the tubers take two years to fully form. The blossoms smell like violets.

Because the Indian groundnut tubers contain three times more nutrition (protein and micronutrients) than the standard commodity potato, there has been enduring interest in the tuber as a valuable food source. Over time, it has been improved by horticulturists in the hopes that it would develop a rare root vegetable following similar to the Jerusalem artichoke. After the global outbreak of potato blight in 1840, agronomists tried to improve Indian groundnuts even further, but the tubers were still significantly smaller than the Jerusalem artichoke and all of the crop tubers, and they did not grow conveniently bunched around the plant. In 1985, the Louisiana Agricultural Experimental Station initiated a project to select Indian groundnut plants with larger tubers. Before the project was shut down, they had developed a number of strains that produced tubers ranging between the size of a walnut and a human fist, which are now successfully propagated by Southern nurseries.

The importance of Indian groundnut as a Native food source has remained in the cultural memory of several First Nations, and has led to a revived interest in the plant in the past decade. Cherokee, Muskogee, Catawba, and Lumbee people have all inaugurated rematriation efforts for the plant. These groups have intermittently collaborated with local horticulturists and growers—for instance, George-Warren DeLesslin of the Catawba with Chris Smith of the Utopian Seed Project and Nat Bradford of Bradford Family Farms worked together to secure the most robust and productive strains that will enable parts of the Carolinas to once again be carpeted with Indian groundnut vines.

ARKANSAS BLACK
Apple

US ORIGIN OR MOST PREVALENT IN
Arkansas

CHARACTERISTICS
Large, dense, reddish-purple to matte black skin, golden to pale yellow flesh

USDA PLANT HARDINESS ZONES
5b–8a

CLOSE RELATIVE
Winesap apple

NOTABLE PRODUCER
Vanzant Fruit Farms

Apples can be very particular about where they'll grow and when they'll ripen. Some struggle to adapt to soils and climates that differ greatly from that in their places of origin. This is particularly true of apples with complex flavors such as Appalachia's Black Limbertwig and New England's Blue Pearmain apples. The Arkansas Black apple is one of those complex and flavorful apples, but it has proven uniquely adaptable to many environments. Wherever it goes, it never seems to lose its sumptuousness or its sweet-tart taste. The Arkansas Black delivers an initial cherry kiss followed by an acidic bite, rounding out quickly to a faint but satisfyingly fitting coriander or anise flavor.

The figure, versatility, and flavor of the Arkansas Black suggest that it may have been a seedling of the Winesap, a colonial-era apple variety that entered the mainstream market in the early 19th century. There is some debate around when the Arkansas Black seedling came into being, but it's clear that propagation of the variety began in the 1870s. The Arkansas Black was one of two locally developed apples, alongside the Clivens apple, around which the apple industry in northwestern Arkansas developed after the Civil War.

England-born brick mason and orchardist John Braithwaite cultivated the Arkansas Black alongside Winesap and Ben Davies apples in his orchards lining Arkansas's Bella Vista highway. Braithwaite's Arkansas Black apple became a local sensation. For 50 years, it reigned as the most popular apple in the state and a 1917 article claimed that 10 million trees had been planted. Stark Brothers Nursery adopted the apple and gave it national distribution.

The variety was known for its culinary quality, piquant juice, suitability for pies and cakes, and superlative storage qualities. So what spurred the sudden decline of the Arkansas Black apple in the 1920s? The late-season apple variety was passed over when breeders became preoccupied with bringing ripe fruit to market in the summertime. The Arkansas Black was heavy for its size, which drove up shipping costs when freight began to be calculated by weight instead of volume. Perhaps more consequentially, the apple was not red. The flashy Red Delicious had come to dominate the popular imagination as the exemplar of a "classic" apple.

As the name suggests, the Arkansas Black has a reddish purple to matte black skin. The flesh contrasts in a golden to pale yellow, and it is crisp and juicy. The Arkansas Black is a crunchy and dense apple when ripe and picked fresh. If left to mellow in a cool, dark place, the flesh becomes more tender and the flavor takes on notes of vanilla and clove. The unique depth of flavor of the apple is great enough to endure drying and rehydration. Sliced, it bakes wonderfully well, not dissolving to sauce or becoming bitter when caramelized by heat. Few apples produce more lively juice or contribute more sturdy body to hard cider.

Despite its great taste and culinary appeal, the Arkansas Black appeared increasingly rarely at fruit stands in the 20th century. As aesthetics began to drive consumer demand and affect marketing in the mid-1920s, nursery sales of the tree declined. Many suppliers ceased to stock it by the 1930s, but several factors kept the tree from functional extinction. One was the sheer multitude of trees that were planted at the beginning of the 20th century. Also for many people, the Arkansas Black had become the paradigm of apple flavor. It is distinct from other North American apple varieties in almost every way, and for some of the apple-consuming public, it holds value in its novelty.

In the late 1970s, growing awareness of the loss of traditional foodways inspired an effort to recover ingredients and dishes that were once glories of regional cookery. California led the effort, and the first attempt at replanting Arkansas Black apples took place there in the 1980s when orchardist Carroll Barclay began planting dwarf Arkansas Black apple trees in Guy, California. Barclay's apples stimulated intense West Coast demand and a national revival of the Arkansas Black apple. The craft cider revival of the 21st century accelerated the demand for the variety and intensified the appreciation for this all-purpose gem.

Caramel ARKANSAS BLACK APPLE PIE

KURT D'AURIZIO, *chef*
ASHEVILLE, NORTH CAROLINA

The Arkansas Black apple is a wonderful fit for fall pies due to its complex flavor profile, which is sweet-tart with hints of cherry, cinnamon, vanilla, and coriander. The flavor develops as the apple ages, making it perfect for Thanksgiving pies.

MAKES 1 PIE

FOR THE CRUST

2½ cups (315 g) all-purpose flour, plus more for dusting the work surface

2 tablespoons cane sugar (we always use Florida cane sugar for its superior flavor; granulated sugar can be substituted if needed)

½ teaspoon fine sea salt

8 ounces (225 g) unsalted butter (preferably a high-fat European style), cold and cut into small cubes

½ cup (120 ml) ice-cold water

FOR THE CARAMEL

1 cup (200 g) cane sugar

6 tablespoons (85 g) unsalted butter

½ cup (120 ml) heavy cream

¼ teaspoon fine sea salt

FOR THE FILLING

6 large Arkansas Black apples, peeled and thinly sliced

1 tablespoon fresh lemon juice

2 tablespoons all-purpose flour

½ teaspoon ground cinnamon

½ teaspoon freshly grated nutmeg

¼ teaspoon ground allspice

¼ teaspoon fine sea salt

FOR THE EGG WASH

1 large (50 g) egg

Splash of heavy cream

Turbinado sugar, for sprinkling (optional)

SPECIAL EQUIPMENT

9-inch deep-dish pie pan

MAKE THE CRUST

In a mixing bowl, combine the flour, sugar, and salt. Add the butter and toss until evenly coated. Cut the butter into smaller pieces using a pastry cutter, or transfer the mixture to a food processor and pulse until the butter is pea-sized. Add half the cold water and mix just until incorporated. Add the remaining cold water and mix just until incorporated. The dough should be crumbly with visible pieces of butter, not homogenous; do not overprocess. Shape the dough into a ball and flatten it into a disc; it will be stiff and slightly crumbly. Wrap the dough airtight in plastic wrap and let rest in the refrigerator for at least 1 hour, overnight if possible.

MAKE THE CARAMEL

In a heavy-bottomed medium saucepan, heat the sugar over medium heat until completely melted, swirling the pan about every 20 seconds. The sugar will form clumps before melting slowly. Keep swirling to ensure the caramel does not burn around the edges. Once the sugar is fully melted and dark golden brown, remove the pan from the heat and stir in the butter. The mixture will violently bubble, so be cautious of the steam. Add the cream and salt, and stir until thoroughly combined. Let cool, and set aside in the refrigerator.

PREPARE THE PIE PAN

Preheat the oven to 375°F (190°C). Unwrap the chilled dough disc and cut it in half. Lightly dust the work surface and the dough with flour as needed. Roll out each dough half to a circle measuring 12 inches (30 cm) in diameter. Brush off any excess flour. Grease a 9-inch (23 cm) deep-dish pie pan. Fold one dough circle over to make it easier to transfer and carefully unfold it, centered, onto the pan. Tuck it gently against the sides and bottom of the pan.

MAKE THE FILLING

Toss the apple slices and lemon juice together in a bowl. Combine the remaining ingredients in a separate bowl and stir to combine. Add the dry ingredients to the apples and toss to coat evenly.

ASSEMBLE AND BAKE THE PIE

Carefully scrape the apple mixture into the dough-lined pan and distribute the caramel evenly over the top (use two spoons to scoop and scrape off in teaspoon-sized dollops). Make an egg wash by lightly beating the egg and cream together. Brush the edges of the dough with the egg wash. Gently fold the second dough disc in half, pick it up and unfold it, centered, over the top of the apple and caramel filling. Trim off any excess dough and crimp the edges into a decorative pattern.

Using a paring knife, cut three or more 1-inch slits in the top of the dough for vents, making an attractive pattern. Brush the top crust with the egg wash and sprinkle with turbinado sugar, if desired.

Place the pan on a baking sheet (to catch drips) and bake for 45 to 60 minutes, or until the crust is browned and the filling is bubbling. Let cool slightly before serving. The pie can be refrigerated if not eaten the same day. Bring to room temperature or warm it just before serving.

NOTE: You can make the caramel sauce in advance, store in the refrigerator, then bring it to room temperature when adding it to the apples. You can also make the pie dough a day ahead, wrap it airtight, and let it rest in the refrigerator.

Kurt D'Aurizio is based in Asheville, NC, and is on the leadership committee for Slow Food USA's Cooks' Alliance.

BELLE OF GEORGIA
Peach

Stone fruit enthusiasts had their first taste of the Belle of Georgia in the summer of 1870. The sunset-colored, white-fleshed peach reached its peak of popularity in the early 1900s and was heralded in 1932 as having "a richer, yet more delicate flavor than the yellow-fleshed peaches." Fervor for the Belle of Georgia peach was inspired by its rare combination of the sweetness expected of a white peach with a dash of tartness and a singular play of floral perfume. Nowadays, while there are some commercial sources for the fruit, most people enjoying Belle of Georgia peaches harvest them from their own backyard trees. The Belle of Georgia is the only one of the old white peach varieties with the mystique, flavor, and surviving acreage to stage a comeback.

A seedling of the yellow Chinese Cling peach pollinated by an unknown white peach, the Belle of Georgia was discovered and named by Lewis A. Rumph of Marshallville, Georgia. Rumph was a fruit breeder of some eminence and uncle to Samuel Rumph, the creator of the Elberta peach—the leading peach on the consumer market in the final decades of the 19th century and the first half of the 20th. The Mountain Rose peach, first bred in Morristown, New Jersey, in 1851, was considered the best-tasting white-fleshed freestone peach prior to the introduction of the Belle of Georgia. Though an excellent tasting peach, the Mountain Rose was not a prolific bearer of fruit, so the robust production of the Belle of Georgia made it the preference of orchardists interested in taking the fruit to market.

Fervor for the Belle of Georgia peach was inspired by its rare combination of the sweetness expected of a white peach with a dash of tartness and a singular play of floral perfume.

In the period after its introduction, the Belle of Georgia's chief rival on the market was the Amelia, another white-fleshed freestone peach of excellent flavor. The Amelia, however, was prone to bruising and splitting during railroad transit, so the firm flesh of the Belle of Georgia soon made it the preferred variety for transit. Shortly before 1900, it became the number two peach in the New York market, next to the Elberta, both of which established Georgia peaches as national treasures. By 1910, they were being shipped by rail from coast to coast.

The demand and reported profitability of Georgia peaches led growers nationally to plant the newly popular stone fruit in quantity. The Stark Nursery in Missouri reported in 1895, "A grower from Arizona saw Belle of Georgia growing and saw the market returns, then wanted 100,000 trees." Yet the general public began to favor yellow peaches. Yellow peaches contain significantly more acid than white peaches, offering a more complex flavor experience of sweet and sour. White peaches simply taste sweet. From the 1940s until the early 1980s, the consumer preference for yellow peaches became so pronounced that hundreds of acres of Belle of Georgia trees were repurposed or replanted with yellow-fleshed varieties. In the 1980s, though, consumers began to show an increasing interest in the white varieties.

Visually one of the most pleasing of peaches—large and luminously white with a regal crimson cheek on the sun side—the freestone Belle of Georgia is regularly shaped. Its flesh is white and firm, ripening in August. For peaches to thrive, the trees must undergo periodic durations of cold. The Belle of Georgia has a chill requirement of 800 hours between 32°F (0°C) and 45°F (7°C). The tree is prolific but vulnerable to nematode pests. Saplings grafted on nematode-resistant rootstocks are currently available from dozens of suppliers specializing in heirloom trees since it is a fruit of legendary quality. The variety is self-fertilizing. The trees grow from 18 to 25 feet tall, form a round crown, and bear profuse numbers of blossoms that become the peaches. Belle of Georgia trees bear fruit four years after planting and produce brilliant red blossoms. The noble-looking, dark green, lance-shaped leaves change to a deep yellow in fall.

Belle of Georgia peach orchards are now rare in the fruit's original home region of Georgia and South Carolina. More trees are grown in California, in large part because Asian consumers on the West Coast have a marked preference for peaches without pronounced acid. Indeed, this preference led Zaiger Genetics of Modesto, California, in 1986 to launch a white peach, White Lady, with even less acid than the Belle of Georgia. The White Lady has supplanted the Belle of Georgia as the most desirable white peach in the United States and thus has contributed to the Belle's current imperiled status.

Belle of Georgia peaches are divine in myriad traditional peach dishes, but really stand out in beverages. Take the Bellini, for example, a cocktail that mixes Champagne and white peach juice. Savvy mixologists emulsify peeled wedges of Belle of Georgia peach flesh in a blender, strain the liquid into a cocktail glass with ice, and top with Champagne for a simple and sublime cocktail. A worthy addition to any orchard and a complex flavor for your cocktail repertoire, the Belle of Georgia is a taste of Southern history.

SPARKLING
BELLE OF GEORGIA
Peach & Thyme
SORBET

JENNIFER HILL BOOKER, *chef and author*
GEORGIA

This sorbet showcases bright lemon, fragrant thyme, and sweet Belle of Georgia peaches. The Belle of Georgia peach has a big aroma and a firm flesh, which makes it ideal for sorbet. Like a Bellini in a bowl, the splash of bubbles elevates this sorbet to a real winner. Peach lovers should make a double batch to enjoy these seasonal beauties all year round. The sorbet will keep in an airtight container in the freezer for up to 30 days.

SERVES 8

6 to 8 fresh Belle of Georgia peaches, peeled and sliced (about 8 cups/ 1.2 kg), plus more for serving

⅔ cup (135 g) sugar

2 tablespoons honey

2 tablespoons freshly squeezed lemon juice

1 teaspoon lemon zest

1 teaspoon fresh thyme leaves

1 cup (240 ml) sparkling wine

Dark brown sugar (optional)

In a large saucepan, combine the peaches and sugar. Add 2 cups (480 ml) of water. Stir or toss gently to combine until the sugar is completely dissolved. Bring to a boil, reduce the heat, and simmer for about 15 minutes.

Remove from the heat and stir in the honey, lemon juice, lemon zest, and thyme. Set aside for 10 to 15 minutes to cool.

Transfer the cooled peach mixture to a blender or food processor and purée until smooth. Transfer to a container, cover, and refrigerate for at least 4 hours but preferably overnight. Once chilled, stir in the wine.

Pour into a cold ice cream maker and churn for about 20 minutes, or according to the manufacturer's instructions.

Cover and freeze overnight. Serve topped with diced Belle of Georgia peaches and a sprinkle of dark brown sugar, if desired.

Jennifer Hill Booker is a Georgia chef, cookbook author, and member of Slow Food Atlanta.

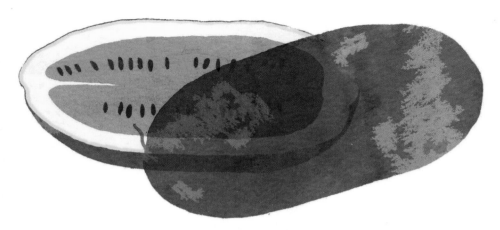

BRADFORD
Watermelon

US ORIGIN OR MOST PREVALENT IN
South Carolina

CHARACTERISTICS
Thick tender rind, sugary meat

USDA PLANT HARDINESS ZONES
7a–10b

CLOSE RELATIVES
Lawson watermelon, Carolina Long watermelon, Georgia Rattlesnake watermelon

NOTABLE PRODUCER
Bradford Watermelon Company

The tale of the Bradford watermelon is as much a survival story as an ode to good taste. The variety falls into the category of "picnic melon," which you can still find on the shelves of some grocery stores in the American South. Picnic melons tend to be oblong and weigh from 10 to 30 pounds, many of them with seeds. They are so named because they were large enough to satisfy all the attendees of a church or family picnic. Now the picnic melon is in the distinct minority when it comes to the commercial market. Nearly every surviving pre-1970 variety of watermelon, of which the Bradford watermelon is one, remains thanks to a handful of devotees committed to older ideals of flavor, the summer backyard romance of spitting seeds, and the ritual of cracking open a chilled behemoth of a melon on a hot summer day.

Nathaniel Napoleon Bradford bred the variety during the late antebellum period in Sumter, South Carolina. The Bradford watermelon is a dark green, sutured (grooved) picnic melon that matures to an impressive size and weight, possessing a fork-tender rind, red flesh, and cream-colored seeds. When it's ready to harvest in August, it can look like a gargantuan cucumber lying in the field. To create his namesake melon, Bradford crossed the splendid-tasting but irregularly shaped and unproductive Lawson watermelon of Georgia with the oblong and dark green Carolina Long watermelon. By careful seed selection over a number of years, Bradford stabilized a melon that consistently merged the shape, regularity, and productivity of the Carolina Long with the desirable flavor and rind of the Lawson. The flavor of this new watermelon was immediately recognized as something special.

Along with its cousin, the Georgia Rattlesnake watermelon (a cross between the Lawson and the Mountain Sweet watermelon), Bradford watermelons were shipped north in 1866 by Southern farmers hoping to win the favor of city markets in the North and bring cash to the Civil War–ravaged countryside of Carolina and Georgia. The farmers succeeded beyond their wildest dreams. Consumers in New York and Philadelphia had never tasted watermelons as splendid as the Bradford and the Rattlesnake, and demand exploded. In fact, this demand spurred the truck farming revolution that would become the South's most lucrative form of agriculture in the Reconstruction Era (about 1865–1877). Truck farming—growing early-season vegetables and trucking them to sell in the city markets of the North—sustained the economies of Virginia, North Carolina, South Carolina, and Georgia after the war's destruction of these states' infrastructure.

The subsequent history of the Bradford watermelon is a textbook example of how superb and hard-won flavor gets overrun in commercial production by agronomic concerns such as disease resistance, days to maturity, drought resistance, and ever-changing consumer taste. The current market ideal for watermelon is a fruit many of us know well: seedless, sized to fit easily in a refrigerator, tough skin to withstand shipping, round and uniform in shape and size, and high sugar content, with a Brix rating of 12 or higher.

How did the picnic melons of the 19th century transmute into the basket-ball-sized refrigerator melons of the 21st century? The first changes began in the 1870s and 1880s. The tender rind of the Bradford caused it to be crushed when transported by boxcar to New York. To increase its viability, Southern farmers transformed both the Rattlesnake and the Bradford, crossing them with the tough-skinned and untasty Scaly Bark watermelon to produce the ideal shipping variety, named Kolb's Gem. The farmers knew that the Kolb's Gem wasn't nearly as delicious as the Bradford or the Rattlesnake, but they also knew that Northerners were happily eating them. It wasn't long before entire counties were dotted with Kolb's Gem watermelons.

Then the inevitable disasters that attend monocropping—pestilence and pathogens—showed up. Fusarium wilt exploded across Georgia in 1893, and farmers pleaded for disease-resistant melons that would ship well. Those came in time, with the Congo and the Charleston Gray watermelons. Increasingly fewer growers kept the superlative-tasting Bradford in their gardens and on their farms, and the last commercial crops of the variety were planted in the 1920s. The decrease in average family size over the course of the 20th century also forced changes in melons. Few families needed 20- or 30-pound melons. Something less than 10 pounds would better serve modern households.

Despite the marginalization of the Bradford watermelon in commercial agriculture, its distinctive flavor held its place in the minds and palates of Southern melon breeders. When grown in good soil, the Bradford blooms with sugar as much as a modern refrigerator melon, yet unlike modern melons, it has a complex flavor that calls forth nectar, raspberry, and mineral notes. The rind has the taste of cucumber, making it perfect for pickling.

When the Carolina Gold Rice Foundation began its campaign to restore the most important food crops of classic Southern cookery, the Bradford watermelon came to its notice. The surviving rhapsodies in 19th-century print sources set the foundation searching for the variety while publishing articles bemoaning its loss. One such article came to the attention of the one person in North America still growing the Bradford watermelon, landscape architect Nat Bradford—a seventh-generation descendent of the original breeder, Nathanial Napoleon Bradford. Nat contacted David Shields, the chair of the foundation, and together they reintroduced the Bradford watermelon to the culinary world.

The love of convenience that characterizes the food industry of the 21st century precludes any large-scale revival of large seeded picnic melons, regardless of taste. So when the Bradford watermelon made a comeback, Nat Bradford knew that the application of the melon into traditional products highlighting its flavor would be the thing to keep it alive. The 2013 revival and availability of the Bradford watermelon was greeted with immense interest by restaurants and consumers.

The almost-extinct Bradford watermelon was soon incorporated into Southern favorites such as watermelon molasses, pickled rind, watermelon brandy, and melon juice for flavoring beverages. Chef Sean Brock's Husk restaurant in Charleston used the fruit to create watermelon molasses, the Culinary Institute of Charleston processed pickled rind, and High Wire Distilling undertook the creation of a Bradford watermelon brandy. The publicity generated by these efforts led to a growing demand for seeds from the public. After some hesitation, Nat Bradford agreed to make the seed available through Sow True Seed in Asheville, North Carolina. Today, Nat Bradford advertises a pickup day each summer when people longing for a fresh, sweet Bradford watermelon visit the farm from as far away as New York and Arizona to acquire the prized fruit.

Bradford WATERMELON Shrub & Club COCKTAIL

DANNY CHILDS, *mixologist*
THE FARM AND FISHERMAN TAVERN, NEW JERSEY

The rich, exceptionally sweet flavor of the Bradford watermelon, combined with the mysterious and deadly history of the varietal, join forces in this alcohol-free cocktail. Feel free to take this drink into a boozier direction; adding mezcal would let the smoky minerality of the spirit interplay with the mellow melon flavor notes.

MAKES 1 COCKTAIL

FOR THE WATERMELON SHRUB

2¼ cups (455 g) organic cane sugar

2 cups (480 ml) white balsamic vinegar

2 pounds (910 g) Bradford watermelon, rind removed

FOR THE BRADFORD WATERMELON SHRUB AND CLUB COCKTAIL

2 fluid ounces (60 ml) Bradford watermelon shrub

Soda water, for topping off

1 mint sprig, for garnish

MAKE THE SHRUB
In a medium saucepan, heat the sugar and vinegar over medium-low heat, stirring until the sugar dissolves. Transfer to a heatproof container and set aside in the refrigerator to cool.

Add the watermelon (don't worry about the seeds) and vinegar syrup to a blender and blend until liquified. Strain through a fine-mesh strainer. Watermelon shrub will keep for a year or more in the refrigerator.

MAKE THE BRADFORD WATERMELON SHRUB AND CLUB COCKTAIL
In an ice-filled highball glass, add the watermelon shrub and top it off with soda water. Garnish with the mint sprig. Serve.

Danny Childs is a mixologist at the Farm and Fisherman Tavern in New Jersey, a cocktail columnist for Edible Jersey, and a member of the Slow Food Northeast chapter, the New England Ark of Taste Committee, and the Cooks' Alliance.

NAT BRADFORD: A WATERMELON THAT CAN CHANGE YOUR LIFE

South Carolina

The Bradford name has been tied to the South's best watermelons since the 1850s. Eight generations later, Nat Bradford is carrying on his family's farm legacy in South Carolina, where he grows an array of place-specific products without chemical inputs and with special attention to preserving and improving the region's essential food products. Nat is an expert seed saver, a thoughtful steward of the environment, and, unsurprisingly, a watermelon lover.

Nat Bradford planted the first crop he remembers growing when he was just five years old—a watermelon patch in his family's garden, right alongside the road. As the fruit slowly neared maturity, young Nat checked the single, already-gargantuan watermelon daily for what seemed like an eternity, patiently waiting for his father to confirm its readiness. On one of his daily checks, he found the watermelon had disappeared. Someone had picked it and, upon realizing it was still not ripe, pitched it into a nearby trash can. Luckily, the disappointment of Nat's first attempt at watermelon did not deter him from trying again, many years later.

Nat knew from his time as a high school member of the Future Farmers of America that he wanted to pursue the homestead style of agriculture he'd learned from his grandfather. By then, the industrial agricultural system had overtaken much of the farmland around him, and there wasn't a clear path to doing it differently. So Nat went into landscape architecture after high school and worked successfully in that world for 15 years until the whole industry took a hit in 2008. Then Nat turned back to agriculture, figuring he'd learn what he could from sustainable and organic farming and then return to landscape agriculture with a different approach. But Nat was made for farming. After about five years of difficult and diligent work, he created a good living and a beautiful life farming in his grandfather's example.

It wasn't long before Nat recalled the story of his family's famous watermelon. He'd found it referenced in articles written by David Shields about American heritage vegetables. When Nat called David to tell him that he was pretty certain that he and his family still had this watermelon, David told him he'd been looking for the variety for 10 years. It was very clear that "if there was one watermelon he could bring back from extinction, the Bradford would be it." Finding an old heirloom doesn't necessarily mean that it will be the best version of itself right away, as there's often a lot of room for improvement with these old varieties. But in the right hands and with the skill to overcome years of inattentiveness, it's possible to revive the genetics of a once-great variety, and that is precisely what Nat did.

"The stuff that is really special to me that I learned growing up was seed keeping," says Nat. "How to not just grow the crop but save the seed and pass them down." Instead of selling the biggest and best watermelons, the Bradford family saved them for seed. As a result of the diligence with which his forebears completed the task and Nat's careful seed saving, the watermelon variety is hearty, delicious, productive, and well adapted to its environment with no chemical input. "If you work hand in hand with nature, you can tease those genetics back out and get it productive," he says. Nat has used this approach to seed saving to restore varieties of okra, peanuts, and other Southern gems. "I'm amazed by the abundance, the adaptability, the resiliency that's already hardwired into nature," says Nat.

As for the taste of the Bradford watermelon, Nat calls it "change-your-life good," without hesitation. It's not an easy crop to grow—it's big and fragile—but as Nat says, "who doesn't love watermelon?"

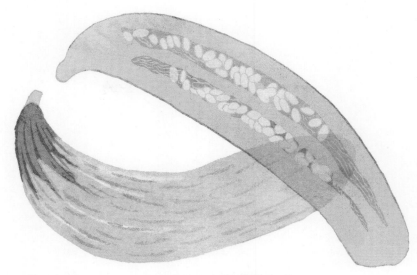

CANDY ROASTER
Squash

**US ORIGIN OR
MOST PREVALENT IN**
Appalachia

CHARACTERISTICS
*Large, pinkish-orange,
verdigris-streaked skin*

**USDA PLANT
HARDINESS ZONES**
5–12

CLOSE RELATIVE
Kentucky squash

NOTABLE PRODUCERS
*Southern Exposure Seed
Exchange, Johnny's
Seeds, Sow True Seed,
Rareseeds.com, True
Love Seeds, Fedco*

You may have encountered on farm Instagram accounts the image of a smiling Southern farmer, probably in jeans and a plaid shirt, cradling and gazing at a noticeably large, pinkish-orange squash in the crook of their arm like an infant. There is something profoundly endearing about the Candy Roaster squash, with its verdigris-streaked skin, as wide as Popeye's forearm and as long as yours, with a name that promises pleasure.

Introduced to the world at the Cherokee School Indian Fair of 1925 in North Carolina, the hardy vegetable was so named "because of the sweetness of its taste when baked into pies or prepared in other ways for the table," according to the *Charlotte Observer*. The Wild Potato Clan of the Cherokee have since been closely associated with the cultivation

Ashton Chapman said in 1958,
"Pies made with Candy Roaster pulp
require less sugar than pumpkin pies, and
such spices as ginger, nutmeg or cinnamon
may well be omitted." He likened the flavor
to a particularly fine sweet potato,
particularly when baked, boiled or mashed.

of the Candy Roaster squash. At some point, Cherokee seedswomen brilliantly transformed the crude Kentucky squash into the elegant and more vividly colored Candy Roaster squash. That ancestor variety, which still survives, is longer than the Candy Roaster, with a rough and almost corrugated skin, sometimes subject to twists and swells and faint longitudinal sutures in the hide. But one can see the blush of orange peeking through the corrugated gray skin, hinting of the Candy Roaster to come.

Ashton Chapman said in 1958, "Pies made with Candy Roaster pulp require less sugar than pumpkin pies, and such spices as ginger, nutmeg or cinnamon may well be omitted." He likened the flavor to a particularly fine sweet potato, particularly when baked, boiled, or mashed.

There are two forms of Candy Roaster. The popular North Georgia strain is more compact and cylindrical. The North Carolina form tends to be larger, heavier, and prone to swelling at the bud end. Both share a rich orange flesh and large beige seeds that are roasted and used as a source of food and oil. Both versions are recognized in the Ark of Taste.

If stored well, the Candy Roaster will cure, concentrating its natural sugars over time, and not spoil until it is cut open.

The Cherokee have prioritized the preservation of the indigenous strains of the Candy Roaster, and it is cultivated at the nursery maintained by the Eastern Band in North Carolina. Since its boarding on the Ark of Taste, the Candy Roaster has enjoyed a burst of popularity among Southern seed and vegetable growers. Small farms have added it to their crop lists, supplying the squash not just to consumers but also to local breweries for specialty beers and to local chefs for seasonal menu favorites.

CANDY ROASTER

SQUASH

AND

Apples

STEVEN SATTERFIELD, *chef*
MILLER UNION, ATLANTA

The Candy Roaster squash possesses qualities that take well to roasting: a firm, rich flesh with pumpkin and butterscotch notes. The red onion and fall herbs serve as a counterpoint to the sweetness of the squash and the dry heat of the oven brings out the natural sugars of both the diced squash and apples, caramelizing the corners and sealing in the flavors. Roast the squash and apples separately because they cook at different rates, and combine them later when finished. The inherently large size of this squash makes it an ideal accompaniment for a group gathering, such as Thanksgiving or a Slow Food potluck.

SERVES 4 TO 6

1 Candy Roaster squash
(around 10 pounds/4.5 kg)

1 red onion, cut into ½-inch
(1 cm) dice

1 teaspoon roughly chopped
fresh thyme leaves

1 teaspoon roughly chopped
fresh rosemary leaves

1 teaspoon roughly chopped
fresh sage leaves

¼ cup (1.15 oz) extra-virgin olive oil

Kosher salt and freshly ground
black pepper

4 large, or 5 small, crisp sweet-tart
apples, such as Pink Lady or
Honeycrisp

3 tablespoons unsalted butter,
melted

Position one oven rack in the lower third of the oven and a second rack in the top third of the oven. Preheat the oven to 375°F (190°C). Line two rimmed baking sheets with parchment paper.

Using a Y-peeler, peel the squash. Using a long knife, cut off about ½ inch (1 cm) of the stem end and the base end and cut the squash crosswise in thirds. Working with one piece at a time, place the widest end down against a work surface. Carefully insert the blade of the knife across the width of the squash at the top and slowly rock the knife until it is fully inserted.

Using both hands, carefully push down through the squash until the blade reaches the cutting board and the squash sections are cut lengthwise in half. Repeat these steps with the other squash sections. Scoop out the seeds and save them for another use or discard them into the compost bin.

Cut the squash sections into 1-inch (3 cm) pieces, cutting them as uniformly as possible so that they roast evenly. Place the squash cubes in a large mixing bowl. Add the onion, thyme, rosemary, sage, and olive oil. Season liberally with salt and a few turns of a pepper mill. Toss well to combine and transfer to one of the prepared baking sheets. Roast for 25 to 30 minutes, or until the squash is tender and the onions are a little caramelized.

While the squash is roasting, peel the apples and slice them into equal quarters starting from the top. Place each quarter cut side down onto a work surface. Holding the knife blade at a 45-degree angle, slice away the core and the seeds from each quarter. Slice each quarter lengthwise into three pieces, then cut the pieces crosswise in half. Transfer the apples to a bowl, toss with the melted butter, and season lightly with salt.

Turn the apples out onto the second prepared baking sheet and roast for 10 to 12 minutes, or until tender. When both the squash mixture and the apples are finished roasting, combine them and adjust the seasoning, if desired, before serving.

Steven Satterfield is the James Beard Award–winning chef of celebrated Atlanta restaurant Miller Union. He serves on the board of Slow Food Atlanta.

Carolina
AFRICAN RUNNER
Peanut

US ORIGIN OR MOST PREVALENT IN
Carolina Low Country

CHARACTERISTICS
Small kernel size, extensive nut mats, oil quality

USDA PLANT HARDINESS ZONES
8a–10b

CLOSE RELATIVES
none

NOTABLE PRODUCERS
Southern Exposure Seed Exchange, Sow True Seed

Once called the African peanut, the Carolina African Runner peanut exemplifies the first peanuts to arrive and be widely consumed in the American South. In 1691, the London physician Hans Sloan collected a peanut from a slave ship newly landed in Jamaica. Sloan was botanizing on behalf of the Royal Society, collecting specimens for his *Catalogus Plantarum quae in Insula Jamaica* (1696) and noted that peanuts were transported on these ships to feed enslaved people on the long journey from Guinea to Jamaica. That solitary pod containing two nuts that Sloan collected survives in the Hans Sloan collection in London. Its configuration is significant, for it is substantially shorter in length than the Virginia peanuts that dominate American cultivation nowadays.

The Carolina African Runner peanut originated in South America and was transported to West Africa in the 1500s as part of the triangular trade among Europe, Africa, and the Americas. For

Despite its superior flavor, its potential as a confection peanut, and its oil quality, the variety's inconveniences of harvesting and vulnerabilities to disease doomed the Carolina African Runner peanut in the 1920s.

much of the 1700s, the peanut grew covertly in gardens tended by Africans and enslaved African Americans, sometimes alongside the single-kerneled Bambara groundnut—the other subterranean legume prized by the Yoruba, Ngere, Ibo, Fon, Cormanti, Ashanti, and Mende peoples. Africans embraced it because it offered twice as much "nut" per pod as the Bambara, and they prepared the peanut in the same manner that they did the Bambara, which was to boil the pods. The practice of boiling (and growing, for that matter) peanuts came to the United States with African people. Peanuts were also parched, or dry roasted, in a skillet (much like benne seed) or ground into meal and made into a kind of peanut coffee drink. In the West Indies, the parched peanuts were combined with molasses to form peanut candies in the early 19th century—the original forms of what would become treats such as peanut brittle, peanut caramels, and groundnut cakes.

The Carolina African Runner peanut was largely supplanted by the Virginia peanut, created from Bolivian landraces in the mid-1800s by a Dr. Matthew Harris and Thomas B. Rowland. The Virginia peanut was larger in size and favored as a roaster. It became easier to harvest than the spreading Carolina African Runner peanut when breeders developed a bush configuration for the Virginia peanut. Daniel R. Shafter laid out the differences between the two important peanut varieties grown in the United States in 1875, stating that "The Virginia is cultivated almost exclusively for eating, while the Carolina is principally used for the manufacture of [peanut] oil, which cannot be distinguished from olive oil, and is, accordingly, sold as such. The standard weight of the Virginia peanut is twenty-two pounds to the bushel; that of the Carolina twenty-eight pounds." The Carolina African Runner peanut was also more prolific than its counterpart and sweeter in taste, and its oil quality was deemed superior as well. The oil was so fine that it became the foundation for castile soap in France. Growers in North Carolina exported half of that state's crop to supply French soap makers in the latter half of the 19th century.

Despite its superior flavor, its potential as a confection peanut, and its oil quality, the variety's inconveniences of harvesting and vulnerabilities to disease doomed the Carolina African Runner peanut in the 1920s. Additionally, it faced fierce competition as other peanuts entered commercial markets. In the latter half of the century, giantism entered the world of peanut breeding with the fierce desire to create the largest peanut one could, so the Jumbo came into being—a roasting peanut intended as snack food at circuses. The small Carolina African Runner peanut would have survived as a hog peanut, but the even smaller Spanish White peanut was introduced and proved more prolific, making it the typical feed peanut of the early 20th century. The last commercial crops took place in the early 1930s. The ancestral peanut of the South became functionally extinct during the Great Depression, but not before P. H. Kime collected 100 plants from farmers' fields in 1929. This would become part of North Carolina State University's peanut breeding collection. From that collection, Clemson University's Brian Ward secured 20 seeds, from which he rebuilt the seed stock for the South's ancestral peanut to reestablish the variety as a crop.

The Carolina Gold Rice Foundation, of which Ward is president, exerted a decade of effort to find and restore the peanut. Nat Bradford, known for his work on the Bradford watermelon, conducted rigorous culling for disease resistance, drought resistance, and productivity over the course of four years, producing a strain of the Carolina African Runner peanut largely free of the vulnerabilities to disease that sidelined the variety 80 years ago. As it is an important African diaspora crop, seed has been restored to the Gullah Geechee people in the Low Country, and cooks are reclaiming its flavor for traditional dishes like peanut perloo, groundnut cakes, and peanut and chicken stew.

CAROLINA GOLD
Rice

**US ORIGIN OR
MOST PREVALENT IN**
South Carolina

CHARACTERISTICS
*Golden hulls, wholesome
starch, medium
grain size*

**USDA PLANT
HARDINESS ZONES**
8b–9a

CLOSE RELATIVES
*Charleston Gold rice,
Santee Gold rice*

NOTABLE PRODUCERS
*Carolina Plantation
Rice, Marsh Hen Mill,
Anson Mills*

A gold-hulled, subtropical Japonica rice, Carolina Gold rice became a global culinary commodity in the middle of the 19th century. Treasured for its pearly translucence when milled and cooked, the variety has a hint of hazelnut and butter in its flavor. It blooms starch on the tongue, flooding the mouth with wholesome flavor. Carolina Gold became a fixture in Southern cooking and the base grain in quintessential one-pot meals such as jambalaya, shrimp creole, Hoppin' John, shrimp pilau, chicken bog, and crab rice. The credit for its global success, its culinary prevalence in Southern food, and its successful adaptation to the Low Country growing environment is owed to the genius and labor of the enslaved Africans who tended the rice fields and first cooked the aforementioned Southern dishes.

Carolina Gold was the second commodity rice to have been grown in the South Carolina Low Country. The first, Madagascar

Its mild flavor, lack of pronounced fragrance, and plush starch made it an ideal foundation upon which to marry ingredients and mix flavors.

White, had been brought to the colony shortly before the end of the 17th century. It became an export staple early in the 18th century, shipped to Great Britain for sale to consumers in Europe by English brokers. The American Revolution disrupted seed production for Madagascar White, so that at the end of the war planters had difficulty finding rice to plant. But one enterprising planter, Hezekiah Mayham of Berkeley County, found a new kind of rice seed in 1785. It produced more tonnage per acre, milled to a more refined and flavorful product, and, when ripe, filled fields with beautiful golden panicles of grain. When Mayham secured this rice is not recorded. It is genetically South Asian, but is likely to have been grown in West Africa. Planters who saw Mayham's rice wanted the seed, and by the end of the 18th century, "Gold Seed Rice" monopolized the rice fields of the Lowcountry.

The Gullah cooks who created the rice-centered cookery of the Lowcountry, or what historian Karen Hess called "the Carolina Rice Kitchen," found Carolina Gold a useful medium upon which to build stews and pilaus. Its mild flavor, lack of pronounced fragrance, and plush starch made it an ideal foundation upon which to marry ingredients and mix flavors. Many cooks noticed the quality of the variety. In his famous *Physiology of Taste* (1825), Jean Anthelme Brillat-Savarin included a dialogue between two stout gourmands incapable of doing without their Carolina Gold rice, despite its fattening quality.

The European demand for Gold Seed rice intensified when grower Joshua John Ward brought a long-grain version of Carolina Gold (a medium-length grain) to market in the 1840s. It was this "Long Gold" version of Carolina Gold that soon won gold medals in expositions in London and Paris, where it also commanded the highest price on the world rice market. Long Gold would become extinct during the Civil War when the conflict thwarted seed production. No seed remained in storage for Long Gold after the Civil War.

The conquest of the Confederacy that freed the enslaved labor force revealed the true and increasing financial cost of growing Carolina Gold rice in the region. The capital expenditures were great for excavating and tending the huge water impoundments where rice was grown. The costs of hiring field laborers on top of infrastructure costs made rice planting costly. Despite its splendid flavor, its global reputation for quality, and its suitability to the style of cooking that came to be in the South, increasingly less Carolina Gold rice was grown after the end of the Civil War until the outbreak of World War I. Cheap white rice from Honduras and other cheap rice varieties being produced in Louisiana, Texas, and then Arkansas began to replace Carolina Gold rice on grocery shelves. Finally, a series of hurricanes along the South Carolina coast breeched the dikes of several major plantations, and the cost of repair was too great to undertake with any hope of future profit. Carolina Gold rice ceased to be a commercial crop in the 1920s, rendering the most famous rice ever grown in the United States virtually extinct by the Great Depression.

The USDA and other entities, however, preserved the seed for breeding purposes. Carolina Gold had been the standard of quality for so long that any subsequent long-grain white rice was judged in comparison to its form and qualities. It was from this USDA germplasm that Richard Schulze replanted Carolina Gold at Turnbridge Plantation in the 1980s. Merle Shepard of Clemson University; Glenn Roberts, CEO of Anson Mills; and Campbell Coxe of Darlington, South Carolina, became the catalysts of the restoration of Carolina Gold rice to American fields and tables early in the 21st century. The Carolina Gold Rice Foundation was formed in 2004 to research the rice and its role in the agricultural system and food culture of the South. Since its reintroduction, it has become a highly regarded specialty rice sought after for classic American rice dishes. Southern restaurants that value authenticity of flavor and quality ingredients reintroduced the classic rice to the restaurant scene. The restaurants created a public demand for the rice, and it became available regionally on grocery shelves in the 2010s. From a cultural, historical, and now culinary perspective, it has become the most important heirloom rice variety of American cooking in this century.

CAROLINA GOLD
RICE and
COCONUT
Pudding
WITH
TUPELO HONEY-ROASTED
GEORGIA PEACHES

PIERRE THIAM, *executive chef and co-founder*
TERANGA, NEW YORK

The nuttiness and chew of the grains make Carolina Gold a great rice pudding stand-in, plus the Tupelo honey brings rich flavor and health benefits to this phenomenal end-of-the-meal treat. It has a much higher fructose-to-glucose ratio content than regular honey. As a result, it is healthier and doesn't crystallize. The green, pear-like flavor complements the tropical ripple of the rice-and-coconut pudding and interplays with the bright sweetness of the peaches.

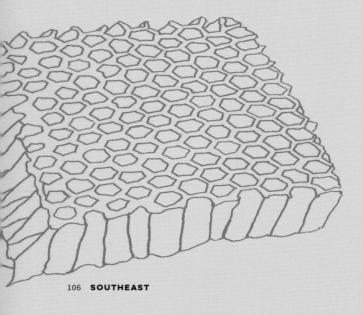

SERVES 4

4 cups (1 L) coconut milk

½ cup (120 ml) plus 2 tablespoons
Tupelo honey, divided (see page 142)

1 teaspoon pure vanilla extract

1 cup (195 g) Carolina Gold rice

2 tablespoons unsweetened
shredded coconut

1 cup (155 g) pitted and diced
Georgia peaches (1-inch/3-cm pieces)

In a saucepan, bring the coconut milk,
½ cup (120 ml) of the honey, and vanilla
to a simmer over low heat for 10 minutes.
Stir in the rice and bring to a boil over
medium-high heat. Let boil for about
1 minute. Reduce the temperature to
low and cover tightly. Adjust the heat to
maintain a simmer; it will take about 20
minutes for the liquid to be absorbed
but the rice to remain soft and creamy
and loose. Remove from the heat and
stir in the shredded coconut. Set aside.

Meanwhile, in a sauté pan, heat the
remaining 2 tablespoons of honey over
medium-high heat until the honey starts
to bubble, about 1 minute. Add the
peach pieces and let cook, undisturbed,
until the mixture begins to brown
around the edges, about 2 minutes.
Carefully stir and continue cooking
until the liquid has almost evaporated.
Remove from the heat.

To serve, divide the pudding among
small bowls and top with the honey-
roasted peaches. Serve cold or at room
temperature.

Pierre Thiam is a chef, award-winning author,
and social activist best known for bringing West
African cuisine to the fine dining world. He is
the executive chef and co-founder of Teranga,
New York; the executive chef of Nok by Alara in
Lagos, Nigeria; and the signature chef at the
Pullman Hotel in Dakar, Senegal.

GROWER PROFILE

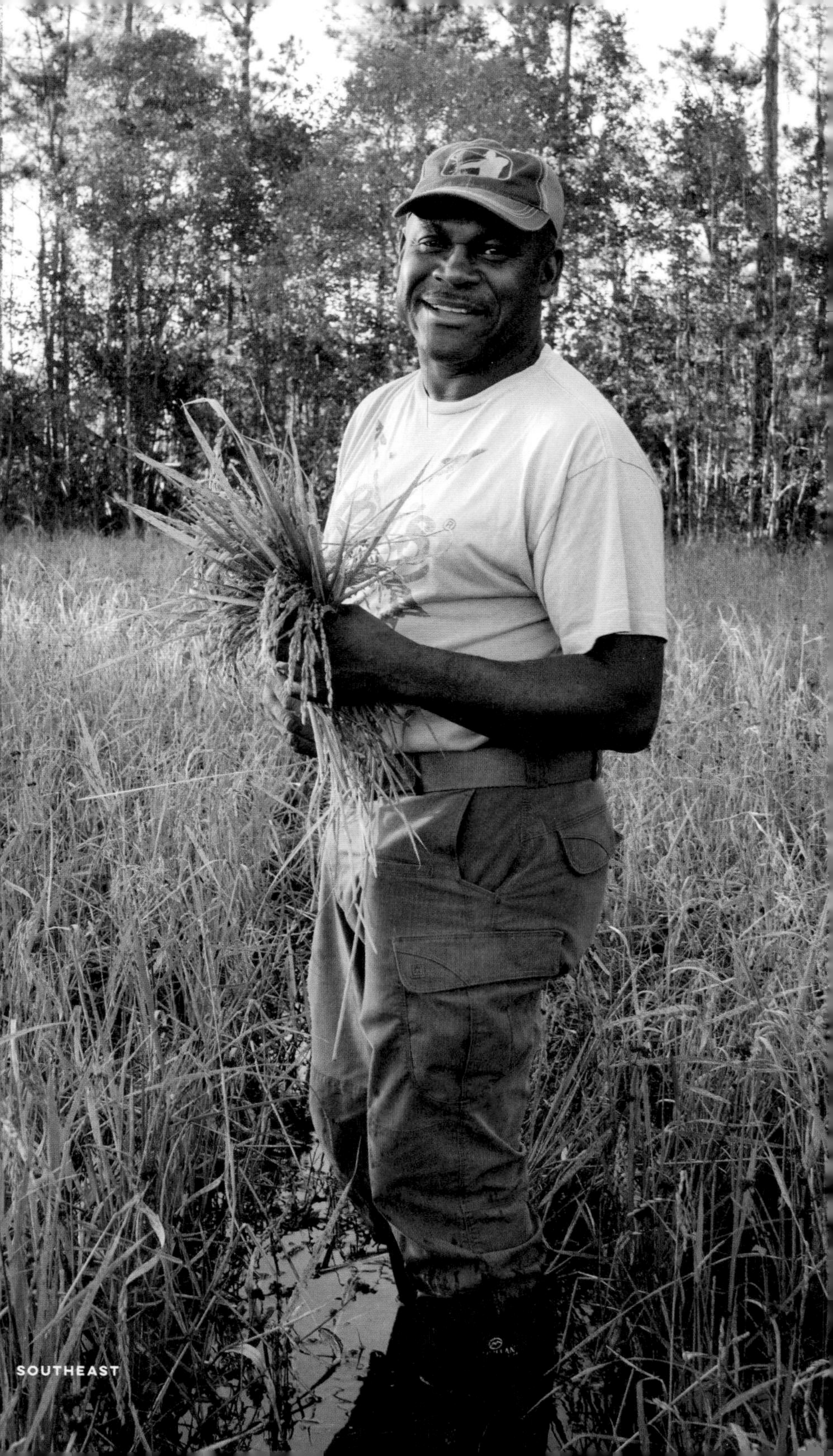

ROLLEN CHALMERS:
CAROLINA GOLD RICE AS LEGACY

South Carolina

A third-generation farmer growing Carolina Gold rice in South Carolina, Rollen Chalmers learned most of what he knows from his mother, who at 93 years old still checks in with him about tasks and timing. He tells his story of family, home, and purpose with immeasurable warmth and energy: "The things that my mom was telling me growing up as a kid, all these different things about the rice field, it's almost like I'm reliving it right now. It really gives [me] a good drive." His grandparents grew rice alongside other keystone foods that enabled their family and community to survive the dire conditions of the enslaved people of the South. Rollen wields the wisdom of his ancestors to tend his rice fields for the consumer market, but his trade is still deeply rooted in notions of both self-sufficiency and community.

Rollen grows Carolina Gold rice at Turnbridge Plantation, where the variety was originally restored due to the efforts of Richard "Doc" Schulze Sr. When Doc took over the administration of the plantation, he turned to Rollen and Glenn Roberts of Anson Mills to keep the rice growing, proclaiming, "If anybody can do this thing, I know it's you—have at it." And Rollen has been at it ever since.

While no longer hand harvested, the fields are kept by methods as close as possible to the traditional way of growing the African rice variety. "These fields are just like the original fields that were grown here in the South where the slaves would work because you got all your palmetto trees around, your pine trees, your live oaks," says Rollen. "You got your alligators, you got your snakes . . . everything [in the landscape] is there like it was 200 years ago when this rice came over here." At Turnbridge, Rollen grows Carolina Gold and Charleston Gold rice in 5- to 10-acre fields separated by embankments. When Rollen's mom was growing rice, canals ran through everyone's fields and provided the water needed to flood the paddies. Now that those canals are gone, Rollen relies on well water to do the necessary flooding, one of the few differences outside of tractors in the way that he grows rice now.

Though these crops have been successful, he's all too aware of the new challenges he's facing today due to climate change. "If you are growing a crop down here, you can really see what's going on," says Rollen. "Some people are not paying attention, but people like me out in these fields, we can see what's happening." For example, as the ocean creeps slowly inward and the well water is more saline than ever, the rice struggles to thrive.

The trees and wild vegetation on the rice farm are complemented not just by the alligators and snakes that populate the unique Southern landscape. The hard labor of planting, tending, and harvesting the rice must also be done in the company of mosquitoes, deer flies, and yellow flies. He says, "There are very few people who would get out in these environments to grow this rice. . . . This rice is always a challenge." But Rollen also revels in how beautiful the fields are at dawn, when the sun rises over the hill and bathes the fields in a sharp golden light.

"Come out in the morning and catch that sunrise," he says. "It casts a halo on the field—a field of gold."

Though many of Rollen's neighbors grow rice to support wildlife and cultivate grounds for recreational hunting, no other farmers in Rollen's community grow Carolina Gold rice for commercial production. But Rollen's fields are productive and have given him a well-earned reputation as the region's premier Carolina Gold rice grower. Rollen also has a small research field at Wormsloe Plantation in Savannah for the University of Georgia. He takes his rice to the seed house at Anson Mills, where it is milled and processed for retail sale as three separate products—whole grain, long grain, and middling, which has a texture similar to grits. The rice is nutty and nutritious, with a light golden color that sets it apart from the other rice found in most pantries.

Respected and beloved in their community, Rollen and his wife play a vital role in reviving Carolina's signature rice, as well as other signature products of the region. They are part of the Carolina Gold Rice Foundation, of which David Shields is the chairman. The members are close-knit and rightly proud of this one-of-a-kind rice. They are the stewards of their history, their culture, and their culinary traditions, and they are bringing this quintessential variety back to Southern fields and tables, one grain at a time.

CHEROKEE PURPLE
Tomato

No ingredient quite conveys the charm of heirloom vegetables like the Cherokee Purple tomato. At the end of the 20th century, grocery store produce sections were filled with tasteless tomatoes that were harvested green and ripened with the aid of bananas and their ethylene gas. That's when the Purple Cherokee came onto the scene, reminding tomato lovers of just how luscious, juicy, and versatile a tomato could be. It began as a home gardener's specialty, circulated by tomato expert Craig LeHoullier through a handful of heirloom seed companies. Before too long, it became a breakout star on produce stands with its distinctive dark purple and rosy skin, its unique shape, its robust and ripe heart, and the dynamic flavor for which it is now known.

The Cherokee Purple tomato was added to the Ark of Taste as a recently discovered heirloom. At the time of its boarding, it had only a small and select community of growers. In the decades since, the Cherokee Purple tomato has been taken up by great numbers of market gardeners and small farmers, and it has become anything but an endangered variety. Some think it is the most successful of the revived heirlooms, and Slow Food considers it a success story as the Ark label drew attention to a worthy ingredient, contributing to the demand that would take it from being imperiled to a widespread and beloved summer treasure.

The flavor that makes the Cherokee Purple special, even among heirloom tomatoes, is a smoky umami that gives it a deeper, more resonant flavor than the Brandywine, arguably the market standard of heirloom tomatoes.

The origins of the Cherokee Purple tomato are something of a mystery. In 1990, Craig LeHoullier received a packet of seeds from John D. Green of Sevierville, Tennessee, with a story that the seed was procured by an unnamed neighbor who had received it decades ago from Cherokee neighbors. Cherokee horticulturists have inquired in the community about any familiarity with the variety to no avail, and so it is simply a tale of sharing and the serendipitous survival of one highly desirable tomato. The color is unusual, with the distinguishable purple-pink coloring of the Buckeye tomato from Ohio, but with an added green tinge when fully ripe. It is also darker, not unlike the Black Krim tomato, grounding the tomato's color palette in what looks like a deep purple. It's a beauty.

While this novel coloration suggests a relatively recent genesis, much about the Cherokee Purple tomato suggests an origin in the late 1800s, particularly in its structure. The Cherokee Purple's occasional lobes, shoulders, and striations date from an era prior to the 1880s, when Alexander Livingston normalized the shape and skin texture of the mass market tomato. The dense and nearly seedless heart is also a feature of late 19th-century tomatoes and has the meaty density of the Ponderosa tomato, and the fact that the core ripens at the same time as the areas closer to the skin indicates careful breeding. But the feature that matters most is that it has the highly celebrated lusciousness and flavor that made the tomato the favorite vegetable in the United States at the end of the 19th century.

The flavor that makes the Cherokee Purple special, even among heirloom tomatoes, is a smoky umami that gives it a deeper, more resonant flavor than the Brandywine, arguably the market standard of heirloom tomatoes. The Cherokee Purple tomato boasts a solid balance between sweetness and acidity, with no bitterness. The tomato's chemistry gives it a pronounced retronasal effect that furthers the potency of its perceived flavor, bringing the smoky, fruity, and floral notes to every bite. When fully ripe, the sugar becomes a touch more prominent than the acid, but the meat of the Cherokee Purple never degenerates to a mushy or soupy texture. It remains solid, tender, and juicy.

While the Cherokee Purple tomato remains a garden favorite, it carries the same liabilities as most heirloom tomatoes for the commodity market. The irregular shape makes packing and shipping difficult. The plants are vulnerable to viral diseases and watery growing seasons. The vines can be overburdened if the fruit grows too large. The plants are not as productive as conventional field tomatoes.

Chinese and American geneticists are attempting to isolate the genes that govern the flavor of the Cherokee Purple (and other fine-tasting heirlooms) in contemporary field tomato cultivars, though it may be a futile exercise. The kinds of agronomic tomatoes that geneticists seek to plant are designed to be grown in mass quantities on sterilized soils supported by chemical supplements. Much of the flavor of the Cherokee Purple and other heirloom tomatoes derives from their being cultivated on healthy, living soil, with the microbiome and microrhizome populations supporting the uptake of micronutrients into the plant. That would be lost in any engineered tomato incorporating Cherokee Purple flavor genetics. Perhaps it is better suited for home gardens and small farms, which can take the legendary tomato from garden to kitchen or farm to market, and maintain its unquestionable taste and splendor.

FOR THE Love OF TOMATOES

Craig LeHoullier's love of heirloom tomatoes began in 1986, when he joined the Seed Savers Exchange. During his tenure there, he named and popularized a number of varieties, including the Cherokee Purple. A gardener as well, LeHoullier began breeding tomatoes in 2005. He now co-leads the Dwarf Tomato Project for space-challenged gardeners, which has introduced more than 125 new compact growers.

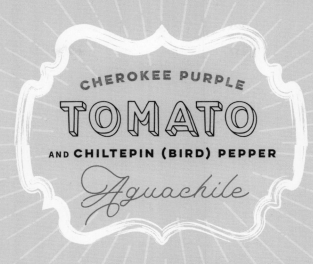

CHEROKEE PURPLE
TOMATO
AND CHILTEPIN (BIRD) PEPPER
Aguachile

DREW DECKMAN, *chef and owner*

DECKMAN'S EN EL MOGOR, VALLE DE GUADALUPE, MEXICO

Chef Drew Deckman chose the Cherokee Purple tomato for this dish to highlight a beloved and beautiful tomato that originates in Mesoamerica, underscoring the Mexican origins of this refreshing and spicy entrée. This dish is vegan, but you could easily add ceviche, tempura tofu, poached shrimp, or fried oysters.

SERVES 4

6 Cherokee purple tomatoes
(100 g per person)

2 Persian cucumbers, 1 julienned,
1 roughly chopped

1 bunch freshly picked cilantro,
roughly chopped

1¾ ounces (50 g) freshly picked
edible flower petals

1 shallot, roughly chopped

1 Chiltepin pepper, ⅛ ounce (2.5 g)

Juice of 10 key limes, divided

Sea salt

3 tablespoons high-quality
extra-virgin olive oil, divided

1 tablespoon freshly ground
fennel seed

1 ripe avocado, cubed

Freshly fried tortilla chips or grilled
bread, for serving

CONTINUED >>

Slice the tomatoes and divide them evenly among four plates (one and a half tomatoes per plate), slightly overlapping them in a circular pattern.

In a separate bowl, toss together the julienned cucumber, the cilantro, and the flower petals. Set aside in the refrigerator.

In a blender, blend together the chopped cucumber, shallot, chile pepper, and lime juice (setting aside approximately 1 teaspoon of the lime juice for seasoning the salad). Season with salt to taste. Blend on high until smooth. Remove from the blender and taste to adjust the seasoning, if desired. Be careful: the chiles are very spicy.

Toss the cilantro mixture once more and season with salt, a tablespoon of the olive oil, and the reserved lime juice.

Season the sliced tomatoes with salt and sprinkle them with the fennel seed. Spoon the chile mixture over the sliced tomatoes in the quantity desired according to your spice tolerance. Top with the avocado cubes and the remaining olive oil, then arrange a small "nest" of the cilantro mixture on top.

Serve immediately, accompanied by freshly fried tortilla chips or grilled bread.

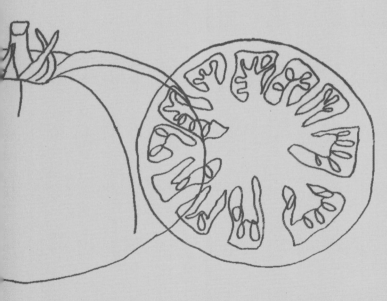

Michelin-starred chef Drew Deckman continually strives to run a zero-kilometer, sustainable community with Deckman's En El Mogor, where the majority of the ingredients come from the ranch and nearby sea. He served as a regional governor for Slow Food International.

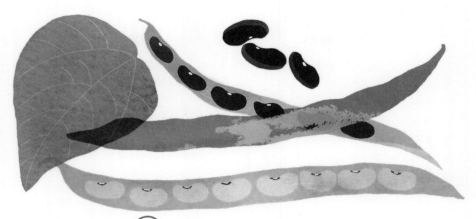

Cherokee TRAIL OF TEARS Bean

US ORIGIN OR
MOST PREVALENT IN
*North Georgia,
Oklahoma*

CHARACTERISTICS
*Drought resistant,
stringless, purple-black
beans*

USDA PLANT
HARDINESS ZONES
7a–10b

CLOSE RELATIVES
None

NOTABLE PRODUCERS
*Seed Savers Exchange,
Victory Seeds*

Before his death on July 19, 1985, John McCord Wyche, a retired dentist in Hugo, Oklahoma, forwarded an envelope filled with the shiny black seeds of a pole bean to the Seed Savers Exchange. He included a letter in which he indicated that his forebears had carried the seeds from the Eastern homeland of the Cherokee westward on the Trail of Tears. The genealogical evidence and Wyche's family history lend credence to both the provenance and the path of the seeds. Wyche's great grandfather, George William Wyche, a full-blooded Cherokee, was born in north Georgia in 1837, months before General Winfield Scott forcibly marched the Cherokees westward from that region. The Wyches were resettled in Cherokee County, Texas, and evaded the displacement of Indigenous people into Oklahoma in 1839. John McCord Wyche's grandfather, John William Wyche, moved from Texas to Oklahoma after the Civil War, and the beans that the family had carried with them from

Georgia to Texas accompanied John William to Hugo, Oklahoma.

When the Seed Savers Exchange received Wyche's seeds, it was a relatively new organization, and its dissemination of the variety became one of its early successes, demonstrating that superb flavor linked to valuable cultural history are what's needed to popularize a rare vegetable and consequently preserve heritage varieties. It was among the earliest items to be boarded onto the Ark of Taste, and the number of companies making seeds available has multiplied since that time. Enthusiasm among home growers has expanded enough to take the bean out of the realm of endangered. Rather, the Cherokee Trail of Tears bean is now an emblem of the care that gardeners manifest to storied and delicious plants.

The variety grows prolifically, requiring 10-foot poles and 20-inch spacing to accommodate its expansion. The bean blossoms into beautiful pink flowers verging into purple. The plant is drought resistant and robust in the face of diseases and pests, and not much preferred by the garden slugs that afflict other beans. The green pods grow about 7 inches long, turn purple-red, contain 6 to 10 beans, and are stringless, making them convenient to hand-process into snap beans, though some prefer to shell the beans. When the beans are mature (from 65 to 85 days, depending on growing zone), they are glossy purple-black and dry down well. With a remarkable delicacy of taste, the beans combine wholesomeness with extraordinary vitality, cooked as a snap bean or dried down and reconstituted. Gardeners who have grown the Cherokee Trail of Tears pole bean understand that it is a treasure to be preserved.

A FEW BEAN CATEGORIES

Snap Beans: Also called green beans or string beans, these can be either bush or pole beans in terms of growth habit. The former grow in a compact hump; the latter range and require support (poles, strings, trellises). They are usually harvested when the pods have attained a length between 5 and 6 inches. If the pods have a seam string, it is removed before cooking. Otherwise, the green bean is snapped into sections (if they are full bodied) or put into the pot whole to be steamed or boiled.

Shelly Beans: Also known as shuck beans or fall beans, these are long pod beans between the immature green bean stage and the dried bean stage. In many areas this stage is reached in August when the individual beans have grown fat in the pod. Lima beans and snap beans can belong to the category of shelly beans.

Soup Beans: The dried mature bean seeds of any large sized kidney, lima, or pod bean. The dried beans are soaked as preparation for cooking, whether baking, boiling, or incorporating into soups and stews.

CHEROKEE TRAIL OF TEARS

AND

GREEN BEAN *Salad*

FERNANDO AND MARLENE DIVINA,
authors of Foods of the Americas: Native Recipes and Traditions

Combining snap beans with cooked Cherokee Trail of Tears beans
is a great way to fold last season's dry beans into your menus along with
in-season fresh beans. Oils such as olive, sunflower, and avocado work
wonderfully, as do most vinegars and citrus juices, so feel free to riff on
this basic salad. Spring and summer will bring loads of greens from your
garden or wildlings, so try blending some mild and astringent greens to
replace the cress. Bitter greens blanched in salted water are nice with this
salad as well. While the mustard adds a punch to the relatively mild-
flavored beans, freshly grated horseradish and apple cider vinegar make
a nice alternative. The level of sweetness is your call, so consider using
maple, birch, agave, or prickly pear syrup if your tastes run regional.

CONTINUED >>

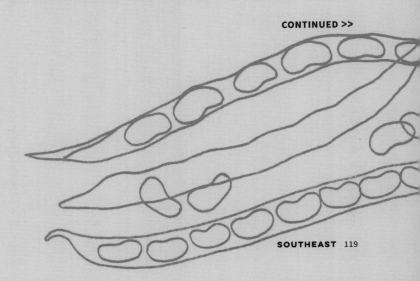

2 tablespoons camelina, olive, sunflower or your favorite oil, including nut oils

1 tablespoon sherry vinegar or your favorite vinegar

Juice of ½ lemon

1 tablespoon Tupelo honey or your favorite regional honey or birch syrup

¾ teaspoon Dijon mustard

⅛ teaspoon dry mustard

⅛ teaspoon sea salt

Freshly ground black pepper

4 ounces (115 g) fresh green beans, cut into 2-inch (5-cm) pieces, blanched in salted water, shocked in cold water, and drained

1 cup (195 g) cooked Cherokee Trail of Tears beans, Rockwell beans, or your favorite regional dry bean

1½ tablespoons chopped fresh herbs (tarragon, chives, and fennel all work well with this recipe)

1 to 2 ounces (30 to 60 g) fresh spicy greens like watercress, wild arugula, or young wild mustard greens (about 1 cup/240 ml, loose, torn, leaves and tops)

In a small bowl, whisk together the oil, vinegar, lemon juice, honey, Dijon mustard, dry mustard, salt, and a few grinds of pepper until thoroughly combined. Add the fresh and cooked beans and toss to coat with the dressing. Spoon the beans into a serving bowl, leaving a few teaspoons of dressing and a few tablespoons of dressed beans in the mixing bowl. Add the herbs and watercress to the mixing bowl, toss to coat, and top the beans in the serving bowl with the bean and herb mixture. Serve immediately.

NOTE: You can prepare this bean salad up to a day in advance, but wait to add the herbs until just prior to serving.

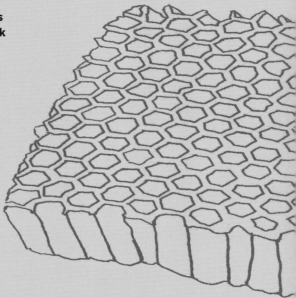

Fernando and Marlene Divina are the founders of divinAmerica, a consultancy service for the hospitality industry, and members of Slow Food Cooks' Alliance.

Cocke's PROLIFIC Corn

US ORIGIN OR MOST PREVALENT IN
Virginia

CHARACTERISTICS
Prolific, mountain taste, good meal for recipes

USDA PLANT HARDINESS ZONES
7b–9a

CLOSE RELATIVES
Tuscarora White corn, Rare Ripe corn

NOTABLE PRODUCERS
Marsh Hen Mill, Colonial Milling

Horticulturists and seed savers keep lists of fruits, vegetables, and grains believed to be extinct. For many years, Cocke's Prolific corn, a white dent variety, topped the list of desirable lost corn varieties, but in November 2017, seedswoman Angie Lavezzo spotted a craigslist ad for "Cox Prolific corn" being sold in Landrum, South Carolina. She bought some and called David Shields to see whether the corn she had purchased matched the historic Cocke's Prolific. Her kernels looked precisely like the ones depicted in century-old state experimental station reports.

So begins one of the most heartening crop rescue stories of the 2010s. Shields joined Angie to meet 94-year-old Manning Farmer, who had been growing Cocke's Prolific corn since 1947. He had secured his seed from his uncle, who had purchased it from Hastings Seed Company in Atlanta in the early 1930s and kept the strain pure for 70 years, growing it apart from any other corn variety. Seed for Cocke's Prolific ceased being offered commercially in 1941, and in 2017 Manning Farmer was the sole individual on the planet growing what had once been the classic field corn of Virginia and a favorite Southern white dent.

A lively cultivator and seed saver, Manning Farmer maintained his strain of Cocke's Prolific because its qualities were precisely suited to his needs. Farmer milled his own meal in a shed he built with boards he milled at his own sawmill. (The shed also serves as a wagon wheel workstation.) He savored the flinty texture of the grits he ground there. He continued planting into his 90s, but had to make allowances for dialysis sessions, and Manning's friend Clarence Gibbs offered to sell some of the corn seed on craigslist for money to defray the medical expenses. Angie Lavezzzo had just read David Shields's description of Cocke's Prolific on a "most wanted" vegetable list and serendipitously noticed the ad for "Cox Prolific" that Gibbs had posted.

Cocke's Prolific was the first of the prolific white dent corn varieties. Most of the landrace flint corns, flour corns, and gourdseed corns would set one or two ears per stalk. A prolific corn set at least two ears and as many as five, depending on the richness of the soil and the spacing of the corn hills. John Hartwell Cocke of the Bremo Plantation in Virginia had crossed a white eight-row flint corn—Rare Ripe corn—with a long-eared White Virginia gourdseed variety to create his namesake corn variety. Once he stabilized these hybrids, he had a 14-row corn whose ears sometimes attained 18 inches in length and

MAJOR TYPES OF CORN

Dent, also known as field corn, is the most commonly grown variety. It is typically milled for cornmeal and used to feed animals and make products such as corn syrup.

Flint has rounded kernels and dense starch and can be white or colored. It is the classic hominy and grits corn.

Flour is composed of soft starch and is easy to grind.

Pod is a wild precursor to modern corn.

Popcorn has a hard exterior and starchy interior that expands when heated.

Sweet is the type typically eaten off the cob.

bore multiple ears per stalk. The tall stalks produced much foliage—ideal fodder for livestock. It was a superb roasting ear in the milk stage and made a winning meal corn for cornbread, grits, and spoonbread.

It was a superb roasting ear in the milk stage and made a winning meal corn for cornbread, grits, and spoonbread.

Cocke belonged to the Albemarle Agricultural Society, an association of Virginia farmers that included Thomas Jefferson and James Madison and formulated many of the early critiques of exploitative practices in farming. The group championed contour plowing, crop rotation, fallowing, and crop diversity over monocropping cash crop staples, manuring fields, and experimental agriculture. The society provided a vehicle for disseminating the best creations of its members, and Cocke's Prolific corn spread through the countryside as "Virginia Field corn." The variety did not go by the name Cocke's Prolific until the 1870s when other prolific strains—Comanche corn, Dorrance Prolific, Champion Prolific, Wyandoot/Hick's Prolific—clamored for attention. It was then that Virginians decided to honor the famous agronomist, military leader, and temperance crusader by attaching his name to his corn.

Word of the rediscovery of Cocke's Prolific corn spread throughout the heirloom grain world during the winter of 2018. Farmers from Texas to Maine contacted Clarence Gibbs for seed, and articles began appearing about the extraordinary devotion of one man—Manning Farmer—in keeping a classic variety viable for seven decades. Greg Johnsman of Marsh Hen Mill favored the "authentic mountain taste" of Cocke's Prolific and began cultivating the variety after visiting Farmer to buy a substantial amount of seed. Colonial Milling in upstate South Carolina offered grits from a stand of Cocke's Prolific corn grown by the Hyder family.

Manning Farmer died at age 99 in the autumn of 2021. He had harvested his last crop of Cocke's Prolific some months earlier. He enjoyed a measure of fame before his death, and his corn will continue to be sown by the many farmers who have taken up his cause. Cocke's Prolific corn now grows at Monticello, and also at Bremo Plantation, planted by the descendants of John Hartwell Cocke. In 2019, it was boarded onto the Ark of Taste, the same year that South Carolina Legislature honored Manning Farmer for his contributions to Southern agriculture.

DYEHOUSE
Cherry

US ORIGIN OR
MOST PREVALENT IN
Kentucky

CHARACTERISTICS
*Tart, orange-red
translucent skin, used in
pies and preserves*

USDA PLANT
HARDINESS ZONES
7b–9a

CLOSE RELATIVES
*May Duke cherry,
Red Morello cherry*

NOTABLE PRODUCER
Dan Dutton

In the 1860s, a seedling sour cherry appeared in Lincoln County, Kentucky, in the orchard of George W. Dyehouse Jr. It had a fine tang on the sugary side and a translucent orange-red skin, and it thrived in the many below-40-degree days that Kentucky offered. The Dyehouse cherry quickly became the signature pie and preserves jelly of Appalachia in the 1800s, and it took that same standing in the South in the 1900s. It was grown from Alabama to Virginia, from Georgia to Texas. Trees were available for sale by Stark Bros and other nurseries until the Second World War.

The Dyehouse became virtually unavailable in the 1950s, when the cherry industry of the Great Lakes and the Pacific Northwest converted consumers to their Montmorency, Bing, and Rainier cherries. The two regions have dominated the market since the second quarter of the 20th century. These Northern states abound in the chilly temperatures that cherries need to thrive. American sour cherry cultivation is concentrated in Michigan and Wisconsin, and sweet cherries are mostly found in Oregon and Washington. The Dyehouse cherry was functionally extinct by the end of the 20th century, and the dream of a Southern cherry was half remembered by the oldest orchard keepers and farmers. But all hope was not lost.

When the Appalachian Food Summit sought the revival of key regional foods in 2014–2015, it called on the Ark of Taste committee of the Southern states to name items besides corn that might be renewed. The extinct Dyehouse cherry was high on that list, and the Ark Committee encouraged the Summit to explore the cultivation of this famed pie cherry. With the aid of Alan Cornett, host of the *Eat Kentucky* podcast, the committee blanketed the state with wanted posters for the cherry, old photos of the fruit, and descriptions. Among the descriptions was a copy of the first horticultural identification of the Dyehouse cherry published by Henry T. Harris in 1870: "The tree is almost a semi-dwarf; or rather, not a full standard, growing bushy, stocky, and the branches not so pendant and willowy as the common old red Morello. The fruit is a clear, transparent dark pink; the skin and pulp almost opaque, and begins to ripen, in this latitude, about the first days of June; and the crop is fully gathered before the old Morello red is fairly blushing. . . . Both tree and fruit are exceedingly hardy, and enormously prolific—rarely failing to mature a full crop even when all other varieties fail."

In order to enlist a serious public effort to find the cherry, various descriptions of the Dyehouse cherry's taste from the 1870s to the 1930s were republished, impressing upon people the quality of this lost stone fruit: "It is exceedingly juicy, tart and pleasant when fully ripe, but is much too acid to eat from the tree. As preserves, and for tarts, however it has no equal in the cherry kingdom." While the final claim may be hyperbolic, the broad adoption of the fruit as a pie cherry inspired a strong following, particularly in Appalachia and the American

PERFECT FOR *Pies*

The flavor of the Dyehouse cherry is quite tart, so it is used primarily for preserves and baked goods rather than fresh eating. When it was popular, the dark red variety was considered one of the very best pie cherries, superior to the Red Morello, May Duke, and Early Richmond.

"It is exceedingly juicy, tart and pleasant when fully ripe, but is much too acid to eat from the tree. As preserves, and for tarts, however it has no equal in the cherry kingdom."

South. The notoriously prickly horticulturist U. P. Hedrick was favorably impressed with the taste: "flesh light yellowish-white, with pinkish juice, tender, sprightly, tart; of very good quality; stone nearly free, ovate, slightly flattened, with smooth surfaces; somewhat ridged along the ventral suture."

The Ark of Taste committee's effort bore fruit, if you will. Word of the search reached artist Dan Dutton of Somerset, Kentucky, not too far from the place of origin of the Dyehouse cherry. Dutton had a tree on his old family land that he suspected might be the Dyehouse, so David Shields traveled there in early June 2016, saw the tree, ate a pie, and celebrated the discovery that one Dyehouse cherry tree had, in fact, survived. When word spread that the Dyehouse cherry was not extinct, Dutton planted an orchard of saplings to meet the demand for trees from Southern growers. On the fifth anniversary of the discovery of Dutton's tree, an episode of the *Eat Kentucky* podcast celebrated the find and alerted listeners to other lost Kentucky fruit such as the Red Kentucky crab apple. A listener contacted Melanie Hutti of Lincoln County, Kentucky, asking if her yard tree might be a Dyehouse. Hutti sent photographs, and sure enough, a second Dyehouse survivor was confirmed.

It will be 2027 before enough Dyehouse cherries can be harvested to serve the bakers and jam makers of the region. But they will have what they had desired—the cherry of their region. The demand for trees now outstrips supply . . . but there is little doubt that the South's signature cherry will have a future and a tasty one at that.

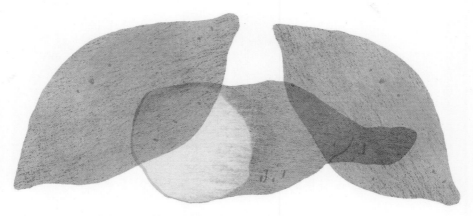

HAYMAN
Sweet Potato

US ORIGIN OR MOST PREVALENT IN
North Carolina

CHARACTERISTICS
Oblong, smooth, large, and blunt at the ends with greenish-yellow flesh

USDA PLANT HARDINESS ZONES
7a–9b

CLOSE RELATIVE
West Indian White sweet potato

NOTABLE PRODUCER
Red Horse Creek Farm

The Hayman sweet potato is the signature vegetable of the Eastern Shore of Virginia. The potato takes its name from Captain Dan Hayman, who transported it in 1856 from the West Indies to Elizabeth City, North Carolina, aboard his coffee schooner, the *Harriet Ryan*. A Methodist clergyman bought the potatoes from Captain Hayman and popularized the variety in the coastal counties of North Carolina, Virginia, and Maryland. The Hayman sweet potato spread through the dense networks of Methodist ministers and laymen along the coast. During the first half of the 20th century, sellers offered the Hayman under a variety of names: Southern Queen, Californian yam, Cuban yam, Kentucky White, McCoy, Carolina Lee, and Catawba White.

Of all the differences in regional taste preferences and habits, the most inexplicable outcome may be the aggressive wrangle that took place over sweet potatoes between the North and South in the latter half of the 19th century. Southerners craved baking potatoes—richly textured sweets that wept sugar in the oven like the Hayman sweet potato. Northerners favored boilers—firm-textured potatoes like the Nansemond or Jersey potatoes that kept their shape when steamed. These tended to be not as sweet as baking sweet potatoes. Much of the agricultural and culinary press was dominated by Northern writers who tarred the sugar-weeping potatoes with the term *turpentine potatoes* on account of the look of the caramelized sugar coming from the potatoes. Those in the know recognized that the dark syrup was a sign that the potato had cured to perfection, but this did not convince people unfamiliar with the Hayman. Those unfamiliar with those sweet potatoes saw the sugar secretions as suggestions that the potato had gone bad and was only good for stock feeding. In the period from 1900 to 1910, Northern agronomists and culinary writers systematically denounced the Hayman potato and other sugar-exuding white-skinned varieties, leading to a dire drop in Hayman sweet potato cultivation north of Maryland.

Before the bad press, the Hayman sweet potato was heralded as a keeping potato, able to resist rot over winter if properly cured. Prolific both in vining and setting tubers, the Hayman sweet potato is oblong, smooth, large, and blunt at the ends or spindle shaped. The raw flesh is greenish-yellow. When baked it turns a matte yellow or greenish-gray. The flavor is delicate and sweet, with a minty note. Flavor is a point of distinction with the Hayman: "[It] is never mealy, and when at its best in mid winter, is, when baked with the skin on (the only way any sweet potato should be cooked), as soft as custard and as sweet too."

Even more consequential than the North-South sugary sweet potato debate for the destiny of the Hayman sweet potato was the growing preference for orange-fleshed sweet potatoes like the Porto Rico or the Georgia Pumpkin yam. When sweet potato pie became the favorite dessert of the South, a reddish-golden pie delighted more than a yellowish-gray pie, regardless of the

CURING SWEET POTATOES

When freshly picked, the body of the sweet potato is largely composed of starch compounds. These begin to break down and naturally convert to sugars within the first week out of the ground. Since the sweeter the potato, the more desirable, farmers "cure" their sweet potatoes. They first store them in a warm, dark place with high humidity (80°F to 90°F/ 27°C to 32°C at 90 percent humidity) for 1 to 2 weeks. Then they are stored at cool temperatures (60°F/ 16°C maximum) for up to 2 months so the conversion of the bulk of the starches into sugars can take place.

". . . when baked with the skin on (the only way any sweet potato should be cooked), as soft as custard and as sweet too."

Hayman's splendid flavor. A community of devotees of the white West Indian potatoes remained, however, finding their flavor unusual and pleasing. Alas, the red pumpkin yams made increasing inroads on the white sweet potato fan base. Finally, cultivation fell to under 500 acres in the 21st century, all on the Eastern Shore.

Its extreme locality became its salvation, though, with the rising recognition of regional foodways and ingredients that express locality. In 1999, the *Baltimore Sun* marked the change in attitude, publishing "Sweet Potatoes Gain Wider Appeal," a piece explaining the expanding interest in the Eastern Shore's Hayman sweet potato. Robert Gustafson's article "On the Trail of the Elusive Hayman Sweet Potato" in *Chesapeake Bay Magazine* documented the growers and outlets found on the Eastern Shore of Virginia. While there are probably still less than 500 acres of Haymans now under cultivation, awareness of and demand for this variety has expanded greatly since its boarding on the Ark of Taste. While you still may not want to use it for your autumn pies, you will find that it makes a fantastic and simple side to many savory dishes of the season.

HEWES
Crab Apple

US ORIGIN OR MOST PREVALENT IN
Virginia

CHARACTERISTICS
Astringent flavor, ideal for hard cider production

USDA PLANT HARDINESS ZONES
6a–8a

CLOSE RELATIVE
North American native wild crab apple

NOTABLE PRODUCERS
Trees of Antiquity, Oranepippintrees.com, Raintree Nursery, Rockbridge Trees, Big Horse Creek Farm (saplings); Albemarle Cider Works and Blue Bee Cider (Hewes cider)

A simple and undeniable truth known to expert cider makers of yore is that the best cider comes from apples whose flavors and textures are too pungent or unappealing for fresh eating. In 1888, a cider maker in Illinois declared, "of all the cider apples known, none are better than those called the Virginia or Hewes crab. This is a small apple, a little larger than the common wild crab, and perfectly destitute of any of the good qualities of an apple to be eaten." But when crushed, pressed, and fermented, "crab cider is highly esteemed for its good body and sparkling qualities, and large quantities are no doubt manufactured and sold as champagne." The Hewes crab apple was a king among crab apples when it came to achieving the desired qualities of a good cider.

Crab cider is hard cider predominantly made of crushed crab apples, while hard cider as we know it is generally made from common apples, perhaps with crab apples added as an accent. Crab

For makers of fine hard cider, juice of the Hewes was added to the must formed from the pressing of crushed common apples. It imparted a clear, tart edge to the liquid and the juice of the Hewes crab apple had a brightness of taste, a mouth-filling presence, and an ideal effervescence when fermented.

apples were categorized as either jelly crabs—Yellow Siberian, Transcendent, and Montreal Beauty—or cider crabs—Hyslop, Kentucky Red, Martha, and Hewes. The Hewes was the most universally esteemed of the latter category. For makers of fine hard cider, juice of the Hewes was added to the must formed from the pressing of crushed common apples. It imparted a clear, tart edge to the liquid and the juice of the Hewes crab apple had a brightness of taste, a mouth-filling presence, and an ideal effervescence when fermented.

Horticulturists believe that the Hewes was a natural cross between the native wild crab apple of North America and an undetermined European variety. The first Hewes apples were borne by a seedling tree on the edge of a colonial farmstead in northern Virginia in the early 18th century. The Hewes crab apple was recognized and celebrated from its early days, and it was planted throughout the upper South throughout the 18th and 19th centuries, though its Virginia origin begot an alternate name, the Virginia crab.

This once ubiquitous cider apple became a victim of Prohibition in America in 1919. The ban on alcohol sales led to the collapse of the commercial cider-making industry, and the Hewes crab apple proved too pungent in its unfermented form to be used for the apple juice that began to be marketed as "sweet cider" in the 1920s. As each decade of the 20th century passed, the old knowledge about mixing crab apples with sweet apples in cider making evaporated. So-called all-purpose apples, or the old Winesap variety, went into the cider crush instead.

By the time of Prohibition's repeal in 1933, cider had become passé. For the remainder of the 20th century, cultivation of the Hewes crab apple relied on the private maintenance of old orchards for domestic cider production. Historic sites concerned with the preservation of heirloom varieties of apples—Monticello in particular—maintained orchards. The Hewes crab apple survived because of about a dozen or so plantings in the upper South. Thanks to those conservationists, plant material was available for the planting of new orchards when the 21st-century cider boom took off. In the early 2000s, cider making began to emulate craft brewing, pushing producers to reclaim old ingredients and manufacturing methods, and once again pay attention to the old Hewes crab apple.

The great collector of heirloom Southern apples Creighton Lee Calhoun Jr. describes the Hewes crab apple in his book, *Old Southern Apples*, as "Fruit very small, about one and one half inches [4 cm] in diameter, round; skin green, usually neatly covered with dull or purplish red; dots numerous, large, whitish, stem long, slender, and red in a yellowish cavity; calyx closed; basin shallow and small; flesh firm, fibrous, acid astringent. Ripe September/October." In the Deep South it ripens in mid-August. An observer in the 1810s noted, "The trees bear abundantly, the fruit ripens late and is free of rot of any kind. The fruit is small and hard and therefore bears the fall from the tree without bruising. It grinds small and the pulp is remarkably tough, yet parts with its juice readily, and the must runs from the press very fine and clear."

There are aspects of the Hewes crab apple's growth—its tendency toward biennial bearing, for example—that inhibit large-scale mass market cideries from adopting it, so the variety remains a niche product. But because it is propagated by cuttings or grafting, the Hewes crab apple can be replicated true to type. It is old and hardy but has susceptibility to fire blight and certain viral diseases that afflict apples. Cider apples do not have to have the perfect configuration needed to market table apples, so the marring of fruit is not an issue, and the Hewes crab apple is productive when it bears. As a biennial harvest, its productivity cannot be credited for its existence. Instead its distinctiveness of flavor and historical importance have ensured its survival.

OSSABAW ISLAND *Hog*

US ORIGIN OR MOST PREVALENT IN
Canary Islands, Georgia

CHARACTERISTICS
Low growth, extraordinary fat production

CLOSE RELATIVE
Spanish Black pig

NOTABLE PRODUCERS
Amy Ross Manko, Simeon Edmunds, Joel and Cheryl DiTomasso

Sailors cruising the northern coast of South America during the colonial age frequently confronted storms, reefs, and pirates. Getting marooned on one of the multitude of islands in the West Indies was a fate sailors feared, for often the sandy isles had no fresh water and no edible meat except turtles and birds—both of which posed challenges to catch. So in the 16th and 17th centuries, Spanish colonial officials began dropping pairs of hogs on deserted islands—two males and two females. These island hogs would eventually populate the limited landmass to provide protein for anyone shipwrecked. One of the northernmost islands so equipped was Ossabaw

Island, off the mainland coast of Georgia, and the hogs may have been placed there as early as 1521. When making an eastward transit across the Atlantic, Spanish ships sailed up the coast of the Western Hemisphere, off the Carolinas, to ride the southeastern leg of the Gulf Stream back to Spain.

The hogs left on the islands were derived from species on the Canary Islands, an Atlantic way station of Spanish ships engaged in trade and the colonization of the Americas. DNA research indicates that the Canary Island species were primarily descendent from hogs originating on the Asian continent.

Ossabaw Island was hot and humid and held a scarce food supply in certain seasons, even for an omnivore such as the hog. When acorns were plentiful, the population would explode, quickly draining the very resource that caused the population rise and leading to die-off. But the population adapted to the conditions on the island over centuries. They decreased in size to better ensure survival and became extremely efficient in setting fat during bountiful seasons to tide them over the leaner seasons.

The Ossabaw Island hog population underwent intensive study in the 1960s and 1970s, and some startling findings were made. The species has the smallest adult body size of any feral hog in the world, with pregnant females weighing less than 100 pounds. They contain higher levels of body fat than any other species of terrestrial wild mammal and tolerate extraordinary levels of salt in their diet. Ossabaw Island hogs have a unique hormonal system that allows them to quickly use stored body fat, but when taken from their habitat and subjected to conventional feeding, they develop type 2 diabetes. Physicians began using the Ossabaw hog as an experimental breed for obesity and diabetes studies in the 1970s, when herds of Ossabaws were taken off the island.

Overpopulation on Ossabaw Island by the hogs led to their attacking important nesting sites of endangered Loggerhead turtles, and rigorous population management of the herds has been practiced since the beginning of the century. The island population was also infected with brucellosis, which led to the prohibition of any attempt to breed island hogs with herds descended from those taken off the islands in the 1970s and 1980s. Ossabaw Island is now owned by the state of Georgia and is maintained as a nature preserve.

But the Ossabaw Island hog persists on the mainland, largely stewarded by those who champion its culinary qualities, despite the challenges it presents. It is certainly a unique breed and likely the closest manifestation of pig genetics of four centuries ago. Indeed, it has an aggressive disposition, and many of its characteristics seem atavistic—the hogs circle with snouts out and rumps together at signs of danger, it is relatively small but the head is large with dark coloring and white brindles, and the bristles around the face are stout and

There isn't much place for an undersized, slow-growing, overly fatty, and ornery pig in 21st-century commodity livestock processing.

strong. It also takes two years to become fully mature.

There isn't much place for an undersized, slow-growing, overly fatty, and ornery pig in 21st-century commodity livestock processing. So where does the Ossabaw fit into our modern world? Fat is where flavor resides, and the Ossabaw shares that quality that makes the Iberian Black pig the most valued in the world. The rendered lard and cured back fat of the Ossabaw are sublime. Its meat is divine when expertly barbecued. In the artisanal world of cured pork, the flavor profiles of the finest charcuterie are grounded in breed distinctiveness and terroir, and the Ossabaw delivers. Industrial pig types have average flavor and act more as a carrier for seasonings and spices in sausage and other highly processed products than as a flavor source. In turn, an Ossabaw Island hog fed on mulberries and peanuts, and finished on barley or apples, is revelatory.

The Heritage Breed Conservancy has listed the Ossabaw Island hog as critically endangered, but increasing numbers of small livestock operations have begun raising Ossabaws over the past decade. Some use them for breeding, crossing them with the Mangalitsa hog to create a super sumptuous form of pork that will mature in a year. Others wish to preserve examples of the oldest forms of pigs in the western hemisphere. The most visionary effort to connect the Ossabaw with the contemporary culinary world has been Marc and Lydia Mousseau's farming operation, which raises one of the largest herds of purebred Ossabaw Island hogs in the world, at around 70 animals. Because Ossabaw Island hogs lived as feral animals on their home island, the Mousseaus took care not to make their domestication akin to factory-style captivity. They gave the animals free range of Island Creek Farms near Milledgeville, Georgia, and ample access to natural forage and supplies of non-GMO feed. Recently the herd moved, and now thrives in the Kentucky countryside north of Louisville.

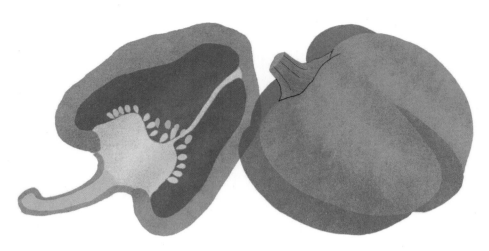

PERFECTION PIMENTO
Pepper

US ORIGIN OR MOST PREVALENT IN
Georgia

CHARACTERISTICS
Glossy red skin, smooth, thick walls

USDA PLANT HARDINESS ZONES
7a–10b

CLOSE RELATIVE
Valencia pimento

NOTABLE PRODUCER
Georgia Coastal Gourmet Farm

Pimento is an Americanization of the Spanish *pimiento,* the name for a fleshy pepper that began to be imported from Europe by North Americans in the mid-19th century. Pimento peppers share the intense red skin of their relative Red Bell peppers, but have more fragrance, flavor, and sweetness. After the Civil War, olives stuffed with tiny spears of bright red pimento began to appear in groceries as a novelty. Growers began breeding for a locally adapted American pimento pepper, one that didn't carry the exorbitant prices of the imports. Breeders aimed for ideal size of 4 inches long by 3 inches wide and wished the skin to be smooth, curved rather than ridged, and almost glossy in its redness. Canners wished for a glossy skin that peeled easily when the flesh was heated.

Early experiments at creating American pimentos undertaken by the Moore and Simon Seed Company of Philadelphia unfortunately faltered. The American product was undeniably mediocre in contrast with the splendid canned pimentos offered by producers in Valencia, Spain. Agronomist S. D. Riegel of Spalding County, Georgia, secured seed for the Valencian variety and began growing them in 1911. Sometime around 1912, Riegel found a spontaneous mutation growing among his Valencia pimento, a plant bearing a pepper with decidedly thicker walls. It had perfectly smooth contours and glossy red skin to boot. He called the line he propagated from this sole plant the Perfection pimento, as it carried many of the traits originally sought after by fans of the pimento.

It was from this pepper that the Southern craze for pimento cheese would arise. After World War I, a generation of home cooks created the cooked and canned form of the Perfection pimento that was used to make pimento cheese,

The PIMENTO CHEESEBURGER

Pimento cheese was invented in New York a decade after the end of the Civil War using cream cheese as its base. It became Southern in the second decade of the 20th century when Duke's brand mayonnaise and pepper breeders in Georgia contributed two fundamental components of the mix we now know: the Perfection pimento pepper and mayonnaise that was "absolutely pure and uncooked." Cheddar cheese (a non-Southern ingredient that also appears in Southern mac and cheese) was part of the mix prior to the naturalization of the dish to Southern climes. The great question for pimento cheese makers is how spicy the mix should be. How much cayenne, jalapeño, or Carolina Reaper you incorporate becomes a signature of your own unique vision.

In the 1950s a restaurant in midtown Columbia, South Carolina, created the pimento cheeseburger. Known as the Dairy Bar, this luncheonette became a way station for statehouse politicians and students at the University of South Carolina, and its signature burger became a matter of local lore. After the Dairy Bar closed, its creation was kept alive by other eateries. Finally a national writer chanced upon the version sold by Rockaway Athletic Club in Columbia in 2013, igniting regional interest in the burger. Now versions appear on menus throughout the South, and every regional newspaper or magazine has offered up a recipe.

Pimento peppers share the intense red skin of their relative Red Bell peppers, but have more fragrance, flavor, and sweetness.

which became a fixture on buffet tables throughout the region. S. D. Riegel's son, Mark, a breeder at the Georgia Experimental Station in Griffin, invented a roasting and peeling mechanism that enabled the large scale processing of Perfection pimentos for canning. The machine was patented in 1914, the same year that S. D. Riegel released seed for the Perfection pimento commercially. Quickly, the counties around Macon, Georgia, became the heartland for pimento cultivation (and pimento cheese) in the United States.

Seed maintenance for the pimento pepper fell into the hands of big growers around Macon, and selecting and improving seed stock began to lag among farmers fixated on production in the face of increasing demand. In the 1930s, the number of fruits setting on plants began declining and the shape became increasingly irregular. H. L. Cochran began rigorously selecting seed from 1936 to 1943 with the best lines of the pepper grown in the state. He restored most of the original qualities and improved the productivity of Riegel's Perfection pimento to over 10 fruit per plant. He also bred disease resistance into the strain. Cochran named the improved strain "Truhard Perfection Pimento pepper," and this became the standard cropping pimento after World War II. In the latter decades of the 20th century, disease resistance became a preoccupation among plant breeders concerned with commodity-scale production. The Perfection pimento had a vulnerability to nematodes. Richard Fery and Judy Thies bred the Truhard-NR variety (*NR* stands for *nematode resistant*), which now dominates Southern fields. This strain and the original Perfection pimento are covered in the Ark of Taste listing. Despite their culinary excellence and historical importance, the older strains have been sidelined, but pimento cheese and all its derivative culinary products are here to stay!

PURPLE RIBBON
Sugarcane

US ORIGIN OR MOST PREVALENT IN
St. Eustacius, Georgia

CHARACTERISTICS
Cold tolerance, used for syrup and sugar production

USDA PLANT HARDINESS ZONES
8a–10a

CLOSE RELATIVES
Louisiana Purple sugarcane, Blue Ribbon sugarcane

NOTABLE PRODUCER
Dixon and Thomas's Coastal Georgia Gourmet Farm

Purple Ribbon sugarcane found its North American home on Sapelo Island in Georgia, a maritime forest preserve off the coast of the Peach State that is as large as Manhattan Island. Since the downfall of the Confederacy, it has remained a largely undisturbed semitropical enclave. The island is owned and maintained by the state of Georgia, except for some private holdings by the Saltwater Geechee inhabitants of Hog Hammock. The history of the sugarcane plantations on the island is fraught, but the revival of the crop is a promising story for the people whose ancestors once cultivated the land and rightfully wish to keep hold of it in the face of development.

These African American islanders, who numbered less than 100, were mostly descendants of enslaved people who had worked the Spalding sugar plantations prior to the defeat of the Confederacy. They were disinclined to sell their holdings to land-hungry developers, so the developers orchestrated a sharp rise in property taxes. Cornelia

It was the primary sugarcane grown throughout much of the South until the end of the 19th century, when it was supplanted by varieties of its own offspring that had more cold tolerance.

Bailey, Sapelo Island's matriarch, realized that the islanders needed a source of revenue to pay the new taxes. She looked to Sapelo's agricultural heritage and encouraged growing and selling the famous Sea Island Red peas that thrived in the region. With the support of William Thomas and chef Linton Hopkins, the peas were well received, but they did not generate sufficient income to pay the taxes. In 2014, Bailey called upon the Carolina Gold Rice Foundation to explore other products that could be grown on the island. As the ruins of old sugar plantations and the foundation of the Spalding Mill still stood conspicuously on the landscape, the group began exploring the idea of reviving and using the sugarcane that had brought no uncertain misery upon the residents' ancestors to save them from the schemes of modern land developers.

Historical research shows that two varieties of sugarcane had been grown there—Otaheite (Tahitian) sugarcane and Purple Ribbon. The former has been long extinct, and the latter is significant in American history. Purple Ribbon sugarcane allowed for the cultivation of sugar on a commodity scale on mainland North America in the early 1800s. It came originally from India, but the Dutch had found it in Batavia and planted it in their West Indian colonies of St. Eustatius, Curacao, Guinea, and Suriname in the 1750s. In 1814, sugarcane was brought from St. Eustatius by Thomas Butler King of Savannah for planting at St. Simons. Alexander Spalding soon planted it in spades on Sapelo Island. Word of its success spread quickly. It was the primary sugarcane grown throughout much of the South until the end of the 19th century, when it was supplanted by varieties of its own offspring that had more cold tolerance, such as the Louisiana Purple or Blue Ribbon sugarcane. The cold tolerance of those varieties allowed for large-scale planting of sugarcane in the South that made American sugar production in 1824 sufficiently cheap and accessible to consumers who used it to preserve fruit harvests. Purple Ribbon sugarcane ushered in the age of jams, jellies, preserves, conserves, and berry wines in the United States.

Cornelia Bailey, William Thomas, Jerome Dixon Sr., and the Carolina Gold Rice Foundation officers were convinced in 2014 that a sugarcane variety as influential as the Purple Ribbon was worthy of restoration, particularly if it could be used to help the descendants of the enslaved people on Georgia's sugar plantations. But they quickly discovered it did not exist in any cane collection or germplasm repository in North America, so they sought to reconstruct its agricultural trajectory. After consulting with West Indian horticultural collections, the revivalists concluded that they would have to reverse engineer Purple Ribbon from its descendent cane varieties. To perform the back-breeding, they enlisted Stephen Kresovich, the Coker Chair of Genetics at Clemson, and a search was undertaken in herbariums and at historical societies for a surviving specimen of Purple Ribbon to provide a genetic target.

In the midst of this effort, David Shields chanced upon a surviving population of Purple Ribbon sugarcane kept by a syrup brewer in southern Mississippi. From this cane, Kresovich and his students laid out the initial beds in Townsend, Georgia, with Dixon and Thomas. Cane was planted on Sapelo the next year. Kresovich's pro bono aid ensured that populations in both places would survive the hurricanes that threatened its destruction in 2016. Cornelia Bailey died in October 2017, during the week when the first batch of Sapelo Island Purple Ribbon syrup was brewed by Dixon and Thomas. Cornelia's son Maurice Bailey brewed his own batch of syrup using island-grown cane in 2020. Despite challenges posed by coastal storms and the COVID-19 pandemic, plantings of the cane have been consistently expanding on Sapelo Island. As of this writing, developers have not secured land on Sapelo Island.

TUPELO *Honey*

US ORIGIN OR MOST PREVALENT IN
Florida and Georgia

CHARACTERISTICS
Resistance to granulation, floral flavor

CLOSE RELATIVES
None

NOTABLE PRODUCERS
Savannah Bee Company, L. L. Lanier and Son's Tupelo Honey

We owe this most distinguished of American honeys to the enterprise of one person, Sidney Smith Alderman (1835–1922), born in Mariana, Florida, just as the Second Seminole War broke out. As an orange grower, he required bees to pollinate his groves in Calhoun County. In 1872, he built 70 hives at the Old Fort Place outside of Wewahitchka on the margins of the swamps that straddle the Chipola River, a tributary of the Apalachicola. It so happened that this area housed the largest wild stand of White Tupelo Trees (*Nyssa ogeche*) in North America. When they were not pollinating the oranges, Alderman's honeybees harvested the nectar of the white-flowered Tupelo. The honey they produced had several remarkable virtues—it was a light, cloudy, greenish-white color; it did not granulate; and it had a distinct and charming flavor.

After 1872, Alderman began selling both Orange Blossom and Tupelo honey under his Orange Bloom brand. He hired a young apiarist to oversee the expansion of the enterprise to 1,400 stands at six sites. By the 1890s, he was shipping 84,000 pounds annually to Boston and New York. The steep rise in demand in 1898 forced

When they were not pollinating the oranges, Alderman's honeybees harvested the nectar of the white-flowered Tupelo. The honey they produced had several remarkable virtues— it was a light, cloudy, greenish-white color; it did not granulate; and it had a distinct and charming flavor.

Alderman to change his business model, and he hired several Northern apiarists to come and harvest honey on contract, taking a cut of the proceeds. One of these contract beekeepers, A. L. Swinton, reported that Alderman terminated his contract the moment the harvest was complete, despite the provisions that called for several more weeks of employment. Swinton was both the beneficiary and victim of a new world of beekeeping. The beekeeping industry went mobile, thanks to the mass scale of the citrus and truck vegetable industry, combined with the short six-week harvest window each spring in Florida and Georgia. Bee hives were carted from farm to farm throughout the Apalachicola Tupelo forest to land briefly on temporary wooden platforms high enough to keep hives dry during the wetlands' spring floods. Alderman and his fellow producers, including J. K. Isbell, pioneered the mobile pollination and beekeeping force that the industry would rely on for the next century.

From the beginning, Tupelo honey commanded a premium on the market. Circa 1900, Alderman and Isbell organized the honey market, making sure that White Tupelo, Black Tupelo, and Orange Blossom honeys were strictly segregated and their purity policed. The late 19th century was the heyday of adulterating honey with simple syrup, and the promise of pure Tupelo honey became a commercial article of faith.

Naturalist William Bartram encountered White Tupelo Trees on the banks of the Ogeechee River in Georgia in the late 1700s, where they grew up to 40 feet high. The limbs of female trees tend to grow out horizontally from the trunk, and males perpendicularly, and mature trees often have flat crowns. The ovular, deep-green leaves are noteworthy for their whitish undersides, giving the tree the nickname White Tupelo. The trees bloom profusely with white blossoms from March to May, the fruit ripens pale to reddish, and the autumn foliage is gaudy and parti-colored from yellow to purplish-red. The Tupelo has a decided preference for moisture and grows most densely in and around the margins of swamps.

The stands that grow along the Altamaha and Ogeechee rivers are not as extensive as the Apalachicola forest, but as prices for Tupelo honey rose over the course of the 20th century, hives were placed throughout Georgia. As climate change and hurricanes have disrupted the Apalachicola basin, Georgia honey has taken on greater prominence in the national marketplace. Because of scarcity and price, bogus Tupelo is sometimes offered for sale, but pollen analysis quickly determines whether the honey is authentic.

The reason for the exalted prices—$14 to $29 a pound in 2022, depending on quality—is rarity and flavor. In 2015, Samantha Rachelle Gardiner of the University of Illinois at Urbana-Champaign undertook a physicochemical analysis of Tupelo honey. Besides the expected high fructose level, she discovered pronounced levels of rose-scented phenylacetaldehyde and citrus-scented nonanol; there was also vanillin, eugenol (clove), and (E)-β-damascenone (cooked apple). This chemistry explains the sensory impressions of generations of honey lovers who detected elements of spice, citrus, vanilla, and fruit in Tupelo honey. Interestingly, Gardiner found that the levels of White Tupelo pollen in different samples of honey did not affect the sensory perception.

Presently, demand exceeds supply for the honey. There are between 210 and 230 beekeepers who produce pure Tupelo honey. In addition, there is an unregulated group of small-scale producers who find vacant Tupelo stands and settle hives in their vicinity. The number of hives varies from year to year. To counter the fly-by-night supply of undocumented Tupelo, major producers in Florida have organized into the Tupelo Beekeepers Association. Membership in this association by your supplier is a guarantee of authenticity and quality.

ARKANSAS BLACK
APPLE
DOUGHNUTS
WITH
Tupelo Honey

FERNANDO AND **MARLENE DIVINA,**
authors of Foods of the Americas: Native Recipes and Traditions

Fruity, spicy Tupelo honey joins forces with notes of cinnamon and almond from the Arkansas Black apples used in this recipe. This late-ripening apple improves in flavor and texture when refrigerated for several weeks to a couple of months after harvest. Typical apple filling flavorings such as cinnamon seem unnecessary in this yeast-raised stuffed doughnut; when omitted, the natural flavors of the apple and honey shine through. The apple skins can be waxy, but we prefer leaving them on rather than peeling the apples to retain as many nutrients as possible. Served with sparkling cider or wine, these doughnuts are great at brunch. They also make for a memorable dessert with more sliced apples, sweet grapes, or ripe fruit, and even with ice cream.

CONTINUED >>

FOR THE ARKANSAS
BLACK APPLE PURÉE

**6 to 8 ounces (170 to 226 g) aged
Arkansas Black apples (see page 80)**

1 to 2 tablespoons Tupelo honey

FOR THE DOUGHNUTS

**5¾ teaspoons (18 g) active dry yeast
or ¼ cup (85 g) fresh yeast**

½ cup (120 ml) warm water

½ cup (120 ml) warm milk

**¼ cup (60 ml) Tupelo honey,
plus more for drizzling**

**3 tablespoons (40 g) unsalted butter,
melted**

2 large (100 g) eggs

1 teaspoon pure vanilla extract

1 teaspoon table salt

**3½ to 4 cups (420 to 480 g)
all-purpose flour**

**Neutral-flavored oil such as canola,
for coating a bowl and for frying**

**½ cup (120 ml) Arkansas
Black apple purée**

**Confectioners' sugar, for coating
(optional)**

SPECIAL EQUIPMENT

Heavy pot

**Standard hot-temperature
thermometer**

MAKE THE ARKANSAS
BLACK APPLE PURÉE

Core and coarsely chop the apples
(set aside the cores to make pectin or
compost). Taste a piece of apple to
determine how much honey to add,
to taste, based on their sweetness.
Place the apple pieces in the jar of a
blender or in a food processor with the
honey and process until liquefied.
Transfer the purée into a small, lidded
saucepan. Bring the purée to a simmer
over medium-high heat, then reduce
the heat. Stir from time to time, and
cook until the mixture is cooked
through, about 8 to 10 minutes.
Let cool completely.

MAKE THE DOUGHNUTS

In a bowl, whisk together the yeast,
water, milk, and honey. Place the bowl
in a warm spot near the stovetop away
from direct heat for about 5 minutes to
activate the yeast. In the bowl of a stand
mixer fitted with the paddle attachment,
beat the butter on medium speed while
adding the eggs one at a time until fully
incorporated. With the mixer off, add
the vanilla and the yeast mixture to the
bowl. Beginning on low speed, mix until
thoroughly combined. Gradually add
the salt and flour, beating until a smooth
dough is achieved. Thoroughly coat a
large bowl with a thin layer of oil. Transfer the dough into the bowl, cover with
a clean, dry kitchen towel and set aside
to proof in a warm spot for about 1 hour,
or until the dough doubles in volume.
Punch down the dough and turn it out
onto a lightly floured work surface.

SHAPE AND FRY THE DOUGHNUTS

Divide the dough into 8 pieces. Using a rolling pin, roll out each piece into a disk measuring about 5 inches (8 cm) in diameter and ½ inch (1 cm) thick. Spoon a scant tablespoon of the purée into the center of each disc and pinch the edges of the dough together in the center to seal it into a ball. Place the doughnuts on a sheet pan lined with parchment or wax paper or on a lightly oiled plate and cover with a clean, dry towel. Set aside for about 15 minutes to rise a second time. You may place them in the refrigerator to slow the speed of the rise and to keep them for a few hours or up to a day before frying.

Add at least 2 inches of the frying oil to a large pot, and heat to about 325°F (163°C). Fry the doughnuts in batches, adding only a few at a time to avoid overcrowding the pot, until brown, about 2½ minutes per side. Transfer the doughnuts to a rack or onto paper towels as they are finished frying. Generously drizzle the doughnuts with additional honey or dust with confectioners' sugar, if desired. They are best when served immediately.

Fernando and Marlene Divina are the founders of divinAmerica, a consultancy service for the hospitality industry, and members of Slow Food Cooks' Alliance.

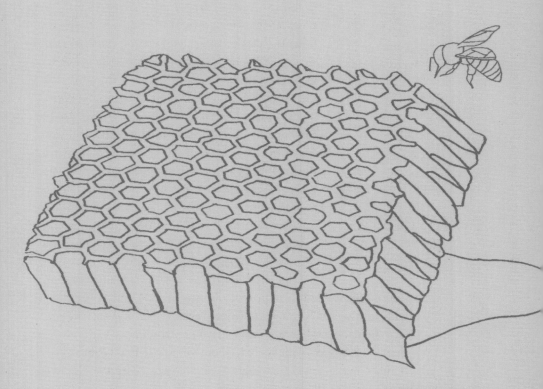

WHIPPOORWILL
Pea

US ORIGIN OR MOST PREVALENT IN
Virginia

CHARACTERISTICS
Speckled skin, creamy texture

USDA PLANT HARDINESS ZONES
7a–10b

CLOSE RELATIVE
Asparagus bean

OTHER NAMES
Shinney Pea, Cowpea

NOTABLE PRODUCERS
Southern Exposure Seed Exchange, Truelove Seeds

Of all the seeds carried across the Atlantic by enslaved peoples during the middle passage, the Cowpea *(Vigna unguiculata)* was unmatched in its variety and versatility. As many as 20 different pea varieties traveled to North America from the Gold Coast and Slave Coast of West Africa in the period before 1820—ancestors of the Clay pea, Brown Crowder, Black-Eyed pea, Sea Island Red pea, Lady pea, Black pea, and Speckled pea, once known as the Shinney pea, now called the Whippoorwill pea. Each of these legumes proved to be highly valuable as portable protein, but of the many varieties of Cowpea that arrived at that time, none inspired quite such vocal and insistent championing as the Whippoorwill pea.

Robert Chisolm of Beaufort, South Carolina, first published a description of the pea in 1850 and undertook a comparative trial of the pea for productivity and health. The next year, he declared that he would suspend planting any variety other than the Whippoorwill. The Whippoorwill was so important as a soil builder and as a culinary ingredient that it became the object of much breeding experimentation. One effort at its improvement crossed it with the Lady pea to create a plain, white Whippoorwill, which belies its resemblance to the spotted Whippoorwill bird. The original Ark of Taste designation for this pea is associated only with the spotted pea. Once the standard for Southern peas, the Whippoorwill is still available as seed and grown widely in the gardens of Southern heirloom enthusiasts.

The naming and categorization of the variety and adjacent members of the entire plant family is confounding. Articles published in the first decade of the 20th century clarified that the Shinney and the Whippoorwill were one and the same. Some descriptions, such as this one from 1875's *Southern Planter and Farmer*, suggest that the Shinney was simply a speckled Whippoorwill "of a light brownish color, thickly streaked or mottled with deeper brown." The first records of the speckled Shinney pea being called a Whippoorwill date back to the late 1870s. The new and popular name was inspired by the mottled wings and body of the Whippoorwill bird, which resemble the pronounced speckling on the pea. By 1900, Whippoorwill entirely supplanted Shinney as the name of this beloved pea.

The Whippoorwill had many enthusiastic fans and few vocal detractors. The naysayers objected to the unappealing dark gray color of its pot likker or pea gravy. But champions of the pea embraced its wholesome taste, deep earthy flavor, and creamy texture, and the absence of the chalkiness that makes many cowpeas mediocre. The same flavor arises from a dried, reconstituted Whippoorwill pea as from the fresh shelled pea.

The Whippoorwill pea grew more vigorously than other varieties and could be plowed under as natural fertilizer or dried and cured as fodder. The variety was easier to cook than others, swelled larger when hydrated, and tasted better. Another major attraction of the Whippoorwill pea was its ability to generate two crops per year. Planted on the first of April in Southern farms and gardens, the first crop of the year ripened in mid-July. A second seeding would then take place to harvest around the time of the year's first frost, usually mid-November. In 1887, P. M. Edmondston added even more attributes when he declared before the Virginia State Agricultural Society that the pea was "the most valuable variety of field pea [because] it produces a very heavy crop of vines, as much as any pea I know, and for this reason is very valuable as a fertilizer. It matures early and continues to bear until frost, and thus will admit of early or late planting." Yet another driver for its broad appeal was the popular conviction that the variety had particular potency as a natural soil renovator. The vines grew in a manner convenient to be plowed into the soil as a green manure, and grain growers used it as a rotation crop. By the turn of the century, the many-splendored pea was grown as far west as Texas and as far north as Maryland.

WILSON POPENOE
Avocado

US ORIGIN OR
MOST PREVALENT IN
Florida

CHARACTERISTICS
Tannins, strong umami notes, and a much creamier flesh than other avocados

USDA PLANT
HARDINESS ZONES
9a–10a

CLOSE RELATIVE
Zutano avocado

NOTABLE PRODUCER
Pine Island Nursery

In the 1910s, the US Department of Agriculture dispatched a plant hunter to Central America with the mission to locate as many avocado varieties as could be found. The USDA's goal was to create new commercial crops by growing out plant products found in other parts of the world on American soil. The plant hunter's name was Wilson Popenoe, and the California Avocado Growers Association formed in part to fund Popenoe's expedition. Of the dozens of avocados that he collected, only one was named after Popenoe.

Before he had even brought back what would become his namesake avocado, the Fuerte variety that Popenoe collected became the focus of intense cultivation (see page 254). The Fuerte possessed the requisite size, durability, and productivity of a mass-market product. In 1923, after the success of this variety, Popenoe predicted that "the culture of avocados will someday become even more than citrus culture in Florida and California." He soon returned to Central America to secure more varieties, including a large avocado that he shipped from Honduras to Florida in 1925. It was tapered like a semi-deflated football and sometimes assumed even stranger and more extenuated shapes. The productivity was modest, a defect that might have relegated the variety to history. However, it had a complex flavor unlike any other avocado—with tannins, strong umami notes, and a much creamier flesh. In 1966, the stock was replenished by a second shipment of young trees to Miami from Lancetilla Botanical Garden and Research Center in Tela, Honduras.

The Floridian who nominated the Wilson Popenoe avocado to the Ark of Taste wrote, "The Popenoe avocado is an enormous (up to half a kilogram), oval shaped avocado. It has shiny, green, smooth skin. The texture is firm, yet juicy, described as almost melon-like. This avocado has an unusual flavor, described as having a tannic effect on the palate. It has also been described as having a 'rubber or canvas scent.' The texture is creamier than most avocados and it is good for use in chopped salads." For nearly a century, a small community of avocado savants kept individual Wilson trees for themselves. The fruit would be shared only with those who were knowledgeable about the variety.

AVOCADOS EVOLVED TO FEED SLOTHS

Back in the Cenozoic period, when monster mammals roamed the Western Hemisphere, the avocado co-evolved with giant ground sloths—huge solemn creatures that extended the plant's range by eating the fruits whole and excreting the seeds. Numerous distinct avocado varieties developed, each manifesting a different quality of fat and a different mix of micronutrients to make ground sloths, or gomphotheres, desire the fruits more avidly. And in places like Guatemala, Honduras, and Mexico, ancient avocados survived the sloths that went extinct millennia ago.

. . . it had a complex flavor unlike any other avocado— with tannins, strong umami notes, and a much creamier flesh.

Today, just a few avocado varieties dominate the market, and you might say that, in this age of avocado toast, creaminess is king. But that has not always been the case, and folks (particularly in avocado-growing states) have long known and appreciated other varieties for their divergent flavors and textures. Descriptions of the Wilson Popenoe avocado promise a more tropical taste with the same desired creaminess of texture that could be ideal for spreading on toast, but the variety never quite took hold in the commercial market. Pine Island Nursery is a reliable source of the scion wood needed to grow a tree, though the growers at the nursery have commented that it has "fantastic flavor" but "mediocre production." The latter characteristic points to why the variety remains a great rarity. By 2020, there was no substantial commercial production in Florida.

A Wilson Popenoe tree is on exhibit at the Fairchild Tropical Botanic Garden in Coral Gables, Florida. Notices of plants for sale periodically appear on Etsy or eBay and are snapped up very quickly. One must beware when purchasing plant material, though, for a number of long-necked avocado varieties are passed off as the Wilson Popenoe. One challenge of the variety is that it can be difficult to graft, even if you do manage to secure scion wood. If you do come across a true Wilson Popenoe avocado, take it home with you and try it on toast, in honor of one of the great plant hunters of our time and the unique pleasure of a tropical-tasting avocado.

YELLOW CREOLE
Corn

US ORIGIN OR MOST PREVALENT IN
Louisiana

CHARACTERISTICS
Dark orange, small cob, used for breakfast grits in Cajun New Orleans cush cush

USDA PLANT HARDINESS ZONES
8b–10a

CLOSE RELATIVE
Guinea Flint corn

NOTABLE PRODUCER
Inglewood Farm

This ancient landrace of the Island Tropical Flint corn of the West Indies adapted well to similar climates in the American South when it was conveyed northward sometime before the colonial era. Indigenous people cultivated the legendary small-eared yellow flint corn long before French and Spanish settlers arrived. It had all the nutrition, flavor, and beauty of a landrace maize, having been improved by Indigenous islanders for hundreds of plant generations before arriving in North America.

Yellow Creole corn quickly became installed among the essential ingredients of the developing and distinct cuisine of the region. It was lye processed—nixtamalized—into hominy and ground into grits to become the signature ingredient in the quintessential breakfast grits of Cajun New Orleans. A correspondent wrote a letter to the *New Orleans Bulletin* in 1875, observing how adamantly Louisianans preferred "the oily yellow creole corn, for the rich hominy of the breakfast table, against the white flint of Ohio and Kentucky."

While boiled hominy grits made of Yellow Creole corn enjoyed a following in New Orleans, in the countryside, it was the hominy fried with lard and salt—called cush cush, couche couche, or kush kush—that was the decidedly preferred preparation. Yellow Creole corn was also favored to make a very typical Louisiana cornbread, or pain de mais, a preparation that finds its history in Haiti.

Though Yellow Creole corn held fast for a time as a center point of Louisiana country cooking, it was also in favor for other benefits and uses. George DuBlanc's Pelican Grist Mill, a commercial processor of Yellow Creole corn in 1890s Lafayette, Louisiana, declared that their "clean, healthy Creole corn [was a] sure cure for dyspepsia and all affections of the stomach." A curious consequence of Yellow Creole corn's extraordinary reputation for healthfulness was its widespread use as chicken feed. Fowl were subject to an extraordinary range of illnesses in Louisiana, and it was thought that Creole corn countered some of the ailments.

So how did the corn most fit for the region's most beloved breakfast slowly disappear from produce shelves in the 1970s? Despite its culinary stardom, commercial farmers only seemed to see its shortcomings as a crop—it was not prolific and needed a minimum of 120 days to mature. Growers began to see higher profits in cultivating the softer, more productive, yellow dent corns, which were ready for harvest in as little as 85 days. As early as 1911, agronomists began discouraging farmers from growing Yellow Creole corn in newspaper stories, assuring them that they had "found two varieties which will mean thousands of dollars to our farmers in increased yield, if they will plant this seed instead of the native, or creole corn so long used in this section." With yields per acre four times that of Yellow Creole corn (a flint corn), the yellow dent meal corn common in the American Corn Belt brought more revenue to the farm and rendered a much cheaper grocery product. It took over a half century before the agronomists succeeded in their appeal, but farmers eventually went the way of generating dollars with more bushels per acre and all but abandoned the corn that was the culinary linchpin of Louisiana cookery.

Nowadays, when you see "Creole corn" on a menu, it likely doesn't mean you're getting Yellow Creole corn. It's the name commonly used for a dish called maque choux, combining any yellow sweet corn with peppers and tomatoes.

In 2018, a group of Black culinarians in Louisiana—including Howard Conyers, Zella Palmer, and Elisabeth Keller—arranged for the rematriation of Yellow Creole corn to its homeland. After securing germplasm from James Holland of North Carolina State University and from the Carolina Gold Rice Foundation, the group planted seed plots at Inglewood Farm in Alexandria, Louisiana, with the intention of restoring the corn as an ingredient in local foodways.

YELLOW CREOLE
Corn
SOUP
WITH
ROASTED TOMATOES
AND GARLIC OIL

CAROLINE GLOVER, *chef*
ANNETTE, COLORADO

This recipe embraces whole-vegetable cooking, turning the cob cores into a charred, creamy stock that makes a great backdrop for the other flavors in this dish. Yellow Creole corn tends to be less sweet than other yellow corns, which allows the more savory corn notes to shine through.

SERVES 8

FOR THE CORN STOCK

8 ears Yellow Creole corn, kernels removed and set aside (about 4 cups/ 580 g; reserve the cobs for the stock)

FOR THE ROASTED TOMATOES AND GARLIC

1 cup (145 g) cherry tomatoes

4 garlic cloves

1 cup (240 ml) extra-virgin olive oil, plus more for drizzling

1 tablespoon salt

2 sprigs thyme

FOR THE SOUP

8 tablespoons (1 stick/115 g) unsalted butter

2 shallots, thinly sliced

3 garlic cloves, thinly sliced

Salt

4 cups (580 g) fresh corn kernels (reserved from the 8 ears of corn)

2 cups (480 ml) cream

2 to 3 cups (480 to 710 ml) corn stock (recipe on page 157)

Freshly chopped chives, for garnish

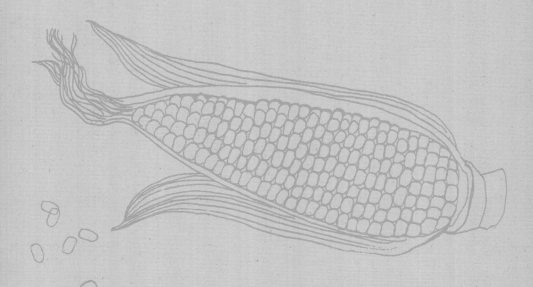

MAKE THE CORN STOCK

Grill four of the stripped corn cobs until nicely charred. Place all (a total of eight) of the corn cobs in a medium pot. Add just enough water to cover them. Bring to a boil, then reduce to a simmer. Let simmer for 30 minutes. Strain, reserving the liquid for the soup. Discard the cobs.

MAKE THE ROASTED TOMATOES AND GARLIC

Preheat the oven to 250°F (120°C). Place all the ingredients in a deep oven-safe dish, toss, and roast for about 45 minutes, or until the tomatoes begin to release their juices and the garlic is soft (see note).

MAKE THE SOUP

In a large pot, melt the butter. Add the shallots and garlic with a pinch of salt. Cook over medium-low heat until softened; do not let them brown. Add the corn kernels and stir to coat with the butter. Add the cream and corn stock, reserving some of the stock for finishing. Season with salt. Let simmer for about 20 minutes. Allow the soup to cool slightly, so that it is not too hot to blend safely. Transfer the corn mixture to a blender in two batches and blend until completely smooth (it is important that the mixture be very smooth). Adjust the consistency using the reserved corn stock, if needed. Season with salt.

Top with the roasted tomatoes, a drizzle of olive oil, and chives.

NOTE: Save the roasted garlic cloves for anything you want. Consider smearing the garlic on some toast to go alongside the soup!

Caroline Glover is chef of the award-winning Annette in Aurora, Colorado, and the 2022 James Beard Award winner for Best Chef, Mountain. She also headlined at the Slow Food Nations food festival in 2019.

RABBIT AMERICAN WILD PERSIMMON A
AD TOMATO BEAVER DAM PEPPER **BOUR**
PICKLED RED WATERMELON GIANT CHIN
HOG **HIDATSA RED BEAN** INCIARDI TOMATO
SCO'S BIRD EGG BEAN **LIVINGSTON GLOBE**
OMIN MILWAUKEE APPLE MULEFOOT HOG
PURPLE STRAW WHEAT SALZER'S FERRIS
PIMIENTO STAGHORN SUMAC THELMA SA
TE CORN **AMERICAN PADDLEFISH** ARIKAR
ERICAN CHINCHILLA RABBIT AMERICAN
UNDERGROUND RAILROAD TOMATO BEA
EN **BUTTERNUT** FRESH-PICKLED RED WAT
FISH HEREFORD HOG **HIDATSA RED BEAN**
RENCH PEAR LINA CISCO'S BIRD EGG BEA
N QUEEN TOMATO **MANOOMIN** MILWAUKE
GOOSE PLUMB CIDER APPLE **PURPLE STR**
N TOMATO SHEEPNOSE PIMIENTO STAGH
HEAT **TUSCARORA WHITE CORN AMERICA**
ELDERBERRY AMERICAN CHINCHILLA RA
O AUNT LOU'S UNDERGROUND RAILROAD
Y BUCKEYE CHICKEN **BUTTERNUT** FRESH
BIT **GREAT LAKES WHITEFISH** HEREFORD
O JESUIT PEAR, OLD FRENCH PEAR LINA
IVINGSTON'S GOLDEN QUEEN TOMATO M
N GRAPE PILGRIM GOOSE PLUMB CIDER
EEL TOMATO SHEBOYGAN TOMATO SHE
RS SQUASH **TURKEY RED WHEAT TUSCAR**
W BEAN AMERICAN BLACK ELDERBERRY
MON **AMISH PASTE TOMATO** AUNT LOU'S
R **BOURBON RED TURKEY** BUCKEYE CHICK
CHINCHILLA RABBIT **GREAT LAKES WHITE**
ATO IVAN TOMATO JESUIT PEAR, OLD FR
N GLOBE TOMATO LIVINGSTON'S GOLDE

SH PASTE TOMATO AUNT LOU'S
ON RED TURKEY BUCKEYE CHICK
HILLA RABBIT GREAT LAKES WHITEFISH
IVAN TOMATO JESUIT PE OLD
TOMATO LIVINGSTON'S GOLDEN
NORTON GRAPE PILGRIM G
HEEL TOMATO SHEBOYGA
DERS SQUASH TURKEY RED W
YELLOW BEAN AMERICAN BLAC
LD PERSIMMON AMISH PASTE TO
R DAM PEPPER BOURBON RED T
MELON GIANT CHINCHILLA RAE
CIARDI TOMATO IVAN TOMATO
LIVINGSTON GLOBE TOMATO LIV
APPLE MULEFOOT HOG NORTO
W WHEAT SALZER'S FERRIS WHE
RN SUMAC THELMA SANDERS
PADDLEFISH ARIKARA YELLOW
BIT AMERICAN WILD PERSIMMO
TOMATO BEAVER DAM PEPPER BO
CKLED RED WATERMELON GIAN
OG HIDATSA RED BEAN INCIARDI
CISCO'S BIRD EGG BEAN LIVINGS
NOOMIN MILWAUKEE APPLE MU
PPLE PURPLE STRAW WHEAT SA
NOSE PIMIENTO STAGHORN SU
RA WHITE CORN AMERICAN PADDLEFISH
MERICAN CHINCHILLA RABBIT
NDERGROUND RAILROAD TOMA
BUTTERNUT FRESH-PICKLED R
SH HEREFORD HOG HIDATSA RED B
NCH PEAR LINA CISCO'S BIRD E

American PADDLEFISH

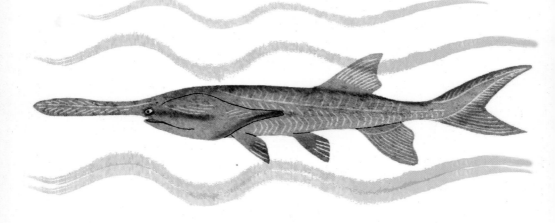

US ORIGIN OR MOST PREVALENT IN
Greater Mississippi Basin
Region: Midwest

CHARACTERISTICS
Spoonbill, shark-like body, smoked flesh, cured roe

USDA PLANT HARDINESS ZONES
5b–7a

CLOSE RELATIVE
Sturgeon

NOTABLE PRODUCER
L'Osage Caviar Company

A most mysterious and strange freshwater fish of the United States, the American Paddlefish maintains its perilous place in American rivers by periodic stocking. With its shark-like body, paddle-shaped rostrum (spoonbill), cartilaginous skeleton, smooth skin, and underdeveloped, independently focused eyes, it reflects features of the earliest known fishes in its nearly 5-foot-long frame. Distantly related to sturgeon, it shares their slow rate of growth and maturation as well as their long life span: 30 years or more, if left undisturbed in their native waters.

The greater Mississippi basin is the home waterway of the Paddlefish, but dam construction, the degradation of water, the invasion of Zebra mussels, and industrial construction on highly trafficked waterways have constricted its natural range. These environmental threats, along with overfishing, would likely have eradicated the American Paddlefish if Missouri had not launched an aggressive campaign in the 1960s to farm the fish and perfect methods of its artificial propagation. Shortly after the turn of the 21st century, the Chinese Paddlefish went extinct in its Yangtze habitat because ichthyologists did not intervene to advocate for and establish aquaculture infrastructures for the species.

Like sturgeon, Paddlefish are esteemed for their cured roe. A subsidiary market exists for the smoked flesh of the Paddlefish, and it is something you can still find at local markets from Oklahoma to Ohio, often sold under names like Spoonfish or Spoonbill. When Iran's Islamic government set itself against Western powers, and the United States in particular, caviar from the Caspian Sea became virtually unobtainable. Russian caviar prices soared. American sturgeon populations had plummeted from overfishing, and attention turned to the Paddlefish. To satisfy the demand for caviar, a culture of illegal Paddlefish harvesting erupted. The law allowed sport fishers to snag catch the fish (as plankton filterers, they don't respond to baits). The law limited how many fish these sport fishers could keep. But poachers blocked estuaries with nets to capture males and females indiscriminately, killing off much of the population. Later, Russian money and the global rise in caviar prices fueled more illegal harvesting, compelling wildlife enforcement officials in Paddlefish states to arrest and prosecute poachers forcefully. Regulations were revised—for instance, imposing annual catch limits rather than daily limits, to forestall sport fishers becoming commodity harvesters.

In addition to a global culinary market for roe, a parallel market for live eggs has emerged from governments wishing to introduce Paddlefish into rivers in China and Ukraine. American buyers tend to be private citizens stocking ponds, lakes, and rivers. The Paddlefish is an imperiled fish, with some sustaining populations in Oklahoma and Missouri, and other populations kept afloat by constant restocking. When Missouri began its propagation program, the intention was to supply stock for wild rivers in keeping with the model of classic fish hatcheries. Other states have followed suit.

It takes 10 years for female fish to sexually mature, so the impetus of the state propagation was not to create a caviar farming industry, or so they thought.

In 1981, Jim Kahrs of Osage, Missouri, saw the future of world caviar supply and began farming Paddlefish to that end. It was a long-range and visionary plan grounded in Kahrs's experience farming catfish. Now, L'Osage Caviar Company is the oldest Paddlefish caviar company in the United States and has served as the model for other aquaculturists determined to establish a sustainable supply of Paddlefish roe. The L'Osage product has been likened in flavor and texture to traditional Sevruga caviar.

In the past decade, efforts have been made to perfect a no-kill surgical extraction of the roe sacks from female sturgeon and Paddlefish. Earlier efforts at C-section extraction have proven only marginally successful because sutures tend not to hold. The Vivace method from Germany has been attempted in the United States, but with no marked success. Perfection of a minimally invasive surgery stands as the best hope for a humane Paddlefish caviar industry.

Eggs to Tail

ON CAVIAR

The market for fresh Paddlefish meat is scarce, but some Midwestern fishermen do catch the fish for food. According to *Kansas City Magazine,* "spoonbills have sections of flakey white flesh and dark reddish-brown flesh. The red meat on the spoonbill is, by all accounts, foul. 'Like motor oil.'" Those who stock their freezers with white Paddlefish meat grill, fry, or pressure-cook it.

After the roe is taken from the fish, traditional culinary use is to smoke the meat. Shuckman's Fish Company and Smokery is one commercial entity that supplies both Kentucky Paddlefish caviar and smoked spoonfish as part of its retail line. Atlanta Smokehouse Products is another reliable source for smoked Paddlefish. Most often, though, fishermen selling Paddlefish caviar to brokers smoke the meat themselves to sell at produce markets and the region's roadside gas and ammo outlets.

AMISH PASTE
Tomato

US ORIGIN OR MOST PREVALENT IN
Pennsylvania and Wisconsin

CHARACTERISTICS
Plum shape, meaty texture, excellent sun-dried tomatoes and tomato jam

USDA PLANT HARDINESS ZONES
6b–9a

CLOSE RELATIVE
San Marzano tomato

NOTABLE PRODUCERS
Heirloom Seeds, Seed Savers Exchange

The Amish Paste was one of the tomatoes saved during the great recovery of heirloom tomatoes that took place in the 1980s, having been secured by Tom Hauch of Heirloom Seeds. The Seed Savers Exchange added the variety to their catalog in 1987 and made it nationally available. The oral history behind the Amish Paste tomato suggests an origin in Medford, Wisconsin, in the 1870s. The seed is said to have been procured from an Amish farmer near Lancaster, Pennsylvania, sometime thereafter.

The genetics of the Amish Paste tomato indicate a southern Italian genesis—far from the Swiss and Alsatian homelands of the Amish. The provenance of the variety is a bit mysterious; its appeal in the kitchen less so.

The first pear-shaped Amish Paste tomatoes appeared in seed catalogs in the Midwest in 1872. The George S. Haskell Co. of Rockford, Illinois, illustrated its listing with an engraving showing its distinctive shape. The 1872 *Phoenix Catalog* described the "Pear

Shaped Scarlet" as "A striking variety; the fruit about the size of a plum." Members of the Amish community likely secured seed from these Midwest catalogs, or from D. M. Ferry in Detroit.

On account of its old age, the Amish Paste tomato has some genetic diversity that manifests in peculiar ways. Some report that the fruit near the stem end ripens after the body of the tomato in clay soil. Others claim that productivity is low when subjected to irregular watering. Odd genetic manifestations aside, the Amish Paste tomato has been reckoned among the most distinctively flavored of tomatoes—a rich earthy sweetness that intensifies when fruits are dried. It is unsurprising, then, that people turned to the Amish Paste tomato as a variety to cook down and pair with sugar, particularly during the vogue for sun-dried tomatoes in the late 1980s and early 1990s.

. . . the Amish Paste tomato has been reckoned among the most distinctively flavored of tomatoes— a rich earthy sweetness that intensifies when fruits are dried.

Pear-shaped or plum tomatoes were not often used for rending into sauce or paste in the 19th century. D. M. Ferry's 1888 catalog stated its original purpose: "Used for preserves or for making 'tomato figs.' Fruit bright red, distinctly pear shaped, and with a peculiar flavor." Tomato figs are sugar-preserved whole tomatoes. The category of a paste tomato only emerged in the United States in the 1940s. It was then that the San Marzano tomato was introduced into general cultivation. Seed catalogs explained that its traditional usage in Sicily was as a paste tomato. Tomato paste was certainly known in the 1800s, but tomatoes suited, bred, or selected specifically for making tomato paste was a new concept. So the old plum-shaped tomato underwent something of a rebranding in the mid-20th century to become a well-understood tomato category today.

After being transplanted into the soil, the Amish Paste tomato ripens from green to orange to bright red in three months. The staked plants can grow up to 6 feet tall. Its fruit ranges from plum shaped to pear shaped, with a solid heart, and weighs between 8 and 10 ounces. Most heirloom seed companies have selected for the distinctive plum or Roma shape, but the genetic makeup is such that it will naturally take on a more teardrop profile. Amish Paste tomato plants respond vigorously to a variety of soils and can grow in the cool climes of southern Canada, provided they have sufficient sunlight.

Its depth of flavor and meaty texture have made the Amish Paste tomato as much a slicing or salad tomato as a sauce and paste variety. But its true glory may lie in its original applications as a preserves variety. When one looks at Amish recipes from the 19th century, tomato ketchup is the closest one comes to a tomato paste, but you will easily find tomato jam—still a signature food if we are to judge by the enduring commercial success of Amish-made Mrs. Miller's Tomato Jam. If it's fair to say there's been a revival of small-batch preserves in recent decades, tomato jam is chief among the favorite recipes to put up, and the sweet and savory jam can be easily found from craft food makers in any tomato-friendly environment.

Sugar AND TOMATOES

Tomato jam remains something of a Pennsylvania signature food. Besides the expected tomatoes and sugar, lemons and ginger root are also often in the recipe. But tomato jam is not the sole survivor of the early, sugary Pennsylvania-Amish foodways. There's also tomato jelly and sugared tomato pie highlighting the appeal of a tomato that marries well with sugar. The Amish Paste tomato partly provided the inspiration behind many tasty tomato preserves and sweet-savory dishes. If you've never had the pleasure of one of the aforementioned tomato delights, seek them out—they're a unique showcase of the unparalleled umami sweetness of a vine-ripened tomato.

BOURBON RED
Turkey

US ORIGIN OR MOST PREVALENT IN
Kentucky

CHARACTERISTICS
Beautiful appearance, great flavor, broad chest

CLOSE RELATIVES
White Holland turkey, Bronze turkey, Buff turkey

OTHER NAMES
Kentucky Red turkey, Bourbon Butternut turkey

NOTABLE PRODUCERS
McMurray Hatchery, Cackle Hatchery

The Bourbon Red turkey is the youngest of the trio of heirloom varieties that have gained stellar reputations for flavor and texture—the White Holland, the Standard Bronze, and the Bourbon Red. It was bred at the end of the 19th century when state fairs and agricultural exhibitions made the beauty of fowl important, and the Bourbon Red competed well in that regard. John F. Barbee of Millersburg, Kentucky, tested a number of crosses between the White Holland, the big-breasted Bronze, and the Buff turkeys to fix the configuration and coloration of the Bourbon Red. The variety was stabilized in 1882 and became immediately popular in Bourbon County. Some escaped into the countryside, and by 1900, a substantial number of Kentuckians and outsiders believed them a wild landrace.

*"The Bourbon Red Turkey
will average nearly as large
as the Bronze, is plumper
when dressed for the table,
and the meat is finer grained,
sweeter and more juicy."*

The flavor of any turkey depends in large part on what the birds eat, so the complex flavor brought about by the diverse diet of a free range bird on varied ground rivals the deep earthy flavor of a wild turkey ranging in a mixed forest-pasture countryside. Still, the intrinsic quality of the flesh does matter in birds. The flavor of the Bourbon Red first inspired comment by the *Colfax Gazette* in 1908, in a comparison with one of its parent breeds, the Bronze turkey: "The Bourbon Red Turkey will average nearly as large as the Bronze, is plumper when dressed for the table, and the meat is finer grained, sweeter and more juicy."

While its flavor was widely praised, its appearance also inspired near universal admiration. The Livestock Conservancy describes the variety: "Bourbon Red turkeys are handsome. They have brownish to dark red plumage with white flight and tail feathers. Tail feathers have soft red bars crossing them near the end. Body feathers on the toms may be edged in black. Neck and breast feathers are chestnut mahogany, and the undercolor feathers are light buff to almost white. The Bourbon Red's beak is light horn at the tip and dark at the base. The throat wattle is red, changeable to bluish white, the beard is black, and shanks and toes are pink. Standard weights for Bourbon Reds are 23 pounds for young toms and 14 pounds for young hens."

The chestnut red coloration derives from a Pennsylvania strain of the Buff turkey called the Tuscarora that existed in the Civil War era. The white flight and tail feathers came from the White Holland, an old out-mutation of the Bronze turkey in which the feathers lacked pigmentation. The broad chest of the Bourbon Red derived from the Bronze turkey, and became the feature that led to its widespread adoption in the early 20th century as a meat turkey.

The American Poultry Association ratified the breed and defined for it an American Standard of Excellence in 1910. This fulfilled the ambition of Barbee, yet he knew that looks were not everything. He immediately began talking about another turkey widely grown in Kentucky, one of the parents of his new turkey: "The White Holland Turkeys are bred in a considerable number, and when prepared for the table are considered the finest flavored turkey we have, but are less hardy than other breeds." One can see the work of the great old-school livestock breeder in using the best-tasting turkey with a notable liability to make a turkey void of that liability with commensurate good flavor and a more strikingly beautiful appearance.

This breeding aesthetic proved entirely different from those of the industrial poultry breeders who took the White Holland turkey and transformed it into a creature so front-heavy it could not breed naturally, fly, walk any distance, or forage. No need to run and forage if your entire life is to be spent relatively immobile in a factory interior, in stark contrast to the rather idyllic circumstances of most Bourbon Reds. In the past half century, industrial turkeys have relegated all of the historic breeds into a narrow niche of production, amounting to less than 1 percent of the total sum of turkeys processed in any given year in the United States. Of the surviving heirloom varieties, the Bourbon Red is lucky to have a group of faithful admirers. Its meat and eggs can be acquired from many farms, and it still turns heads in country fairs and poultry exhibitions. Its numbers are sufficiently robust so as not to be regarded by the Livestock Conservancy as endangered or threatened, though it is on the watch list. Next time you're in the market for a great turkey, even if it's just once a year, be on the lookout for a Bourbon Red and enjoy this uniquely savory heirloom.

BUTTERNUT

US ORIGIN OR MOST PREVALENT IN
Appalachian Ridge

CHARACTERISTICS
Oily and sweet nut used in confections

USDA PLANT HARDINESS ZONES
5b–8b

CLOSE RELATIVES
Kenworthy, Kinneyglen, Buckley, Helmick, Johnson, Sherwood, Irvine, Love, Crax-Ezy, Thill, Van der Poppen

NOTABLE PRODUCERS
Sold by backyard harvesters on eBay

Butternut trees grow along the Appalachian ridge from New England to the North Georgia border, following the northern extent of Tennessee into eastern Missouri and north up to southeastern Minnesota, southern Wisconsin, and Michigan. In the early 1800s, locals called the tree and its nut different names in different regions—New Englanders observed Indigenous people extracting oil from the nut meats by mashing and boiling them, and the fruit came to be known as Oil Nut in Massachusetts, New Hampshire, and Vermont. It was known as the White walnut in Maryland and Pennsylvania, since the light grain of the wood contrasts so starkly with that of the native Black walnut. Finally, in Connecticut, New York, New Jersey, Virginia, and the Carolinas it was called the Butternut, the name that came to designate the tree nationally over the course of time.

The Butternut is the most cold tolerant of the hickories and walnuts in North America, yet its range extends only into southern

The nuts average around 2 inches in length and are egg-shaped with a point at one end. The kernels are oily and sweet, less bitter than walnuts and less aromatic than black walnuts.

Canada. It does not have robust wild populations anywhere in its growing range. Instead, it is generally scarce and grows in clusters of a few individuals in mixed hardwood forest settings. It requires well-drained soils, the more alkaline the better. In almost every habitat, it is the shortest-lived hardwood tree in the forest, rarely reaching 80 years of age. It is also of modest size, rarely growing past 60 feet. The trees begin bearing nut crops at 20 years of age and will bear an ample crop every second or third year until they reach 60 years of age, when the seed bearing declines noticeably. The nuts average around 2 inches in length and are egg-shaped with a point at one end. The kernels are oily and sweet, less bitter than walnuts and less aromatic than black walnuts. They are avidly sought after by wild creatures as a food source. Indigenous Peoples of the Northeast cherished the nut as a food source, boiled the tree's sap, and used the bark to intoxicate fish so they would be easy to catch.

While never as common as any other of the major nut trees, the Butternut inspired great appreciation for its culinary qualities. In the late 19th century, a concerted effort was made to improve the trees by making them taller and knot-free for timber, and more regular in bearing nuts. Nurseries found the Butternut difficult to propagate, and the breeding efforts directed at making it a crop nut had limited success. H. P. Burgart of the Michigan Nut Nursery wrote, "That good old fashioned long nut is going to be a thing of the past unless people take the situation to heart and plant more young trees. Little has been done in the past in the way of propagating this nut as good cracking varieties have been very scarce." Unfortunately, Burgart's introduction of the Crax-Ezy Butternut did not stem the declining fortunes of the nut.

Natives and New England settlers appreciated the keeping quality of the Butternut. It can remain in storage for years without going stale or rancid, so was reckoned an insurance store against famine. The Narragansetts tended to grind the nuts into meal (wussoquat) for porridge and to incorporate meal into baked cakes. The nuts were consumed raw and roasted as well. Because they proved somewhat difficult to extract from the shell, cooks largely used broken halves until the emergence of the Crax-Ezy variety in the mid-1930s. Because the Butternut grows in northern New England, it is often paired with maple syrup in old New England confections. Butternut maple candies were sold at roadside stands in spring in Vermont before 1970. A classic preparation was maple and Butternut cream, made simply with maple sugar, cream, and Butternut meat.

In 1967, fungal canker was first detected on American Butternut trees. In subsequent decades it would prove a scourge, shrinking the wild populations of the tree dramatically. Trees die several years after infection. In the past decades, the native Butternut trees in North and South Carolina have disappeared. The ravages of the canker have been so extensive that American Butternut has been put on the US endangered species register.

Butternut meats are extremely difficult to source in produce markets. There is no inbred resistance to the fungi that devil the tree at present, but the trees are available at some nurseries. The Ark of Taste designation applies to all surviving strains offered by 20th-century nurseries: Kenworthy, Kinneyglen, Buckley, Helmick, Johnson, Sherwood, Irvine, Love, Crax-Ezy, Thill, and Van der Poppen.

Great Lakes
WHITEFISH

Native to the Great Lakes, this cold-loving, deep-dwelling relative of the trout, the salmon, and the char was known to the Ojibwe people as Atikamig. They traditionally netted the fish in the autumn season when the surface waters cooled and the fish rose from the depths to lay eggs. The Ojibwe smoked and dried the split fish, sometimes reducing the dried meat to powder for flavoring soups and stews. The Atikamig was an important dimension of Native foodways of the region.

Great Lakes whitefish are silver-and-white-bodied when mature, with a faintly green-brown back and small head, and range from 17 to 22 inches in length. The weight can range from 1½ pounds up to 4 pounds. The size of the fish and the quality of its flesh, along with its healthy population, made them marketable, and by the 1840s, a fishing industry had emerged in Door County, Wisconsin. By the 1880s, the emerging resort culture in Bay City, Michigan, leveraged the whitefish population in Lake Huron as a culinary magnet that received national publicity. The Great Lakes whitefish soon became a fixture on menus in Milwaukee and Chicago.

In 1878, the economic and cultural value of the local whitefish prompted the state of Wisconsin to instigate a breeding operation at the Milwaukee Hatchery. In 1870, the state's Fish Commission reported distributing 10 million fry into Lake Michigan. A scientific enterprise, the Wisconsin Hatchery segregated populations of whitefish by lake, restocking Wisconsin lakes with offspring of fish taken from its waters. The stocking of lakes that lacked populations had begun in 1849 when Governor Leonard J. Farwell introduced whitefish into Fourth Lake. These lake populations developed distinctive genetic features, including taking the baits of fishermen, while the mother population in Lake Michigan could only be captured by net. Wisconsin proved active in restoring stocks, though Illinois did not and Michigan simply reaped the benefits of Wisconsin's largesse by intensively fishing the eastern shore of the lake. Indiana also took without restoring as well. The result of heavy fishing without restocking was that the population dropped in southern Lake Michigan until it disappeared almost totally in 1890. Fishermen shut down harvesting operations, and their cessation helped the population to rebuild. The whitefish reappeared in spring of 1905.

The Ojibwe smoked and dried the split fish, sometimes reducing the dried meat to powder for flavoring soups and stews.

The Potawatomi fished whitefish for centuries in the modern-day Door Peninsula and Washington Island, Wisconsin, the veritable centers of the fishery in Lake Michigan's watershed. In the second quarter of the 19th century, settlers organized a fishing fleet and processing house to supply Midwestern cities with salted whitefish. At its peak in the first half of the 20th century, Washington Island had 43 boats and over 600 people directly employed by the fishing industry. By contrast, in the early 2000s, there were only two families, two boats, and three commercial fishermen on Washington Island involved in fishing whitefish, none of whom engaged in fishing as their primary occupation.

The decline of the catch has more to do with the degradation of Lake Michigan waters than the decline of the whitefish population. We can point to two causes— one commercial and one environmental. Commercial restaurants, stores, and processing firms that had once used whitefish turned to cheaper farmed and globally sourced fish that flooded the American market, despite the clean flavor, excellent texture, and locality of the Great Lakes whitefish. In an effort to restore favor for the once-beloved local products, Michigan's Sea Grant program inaugurated a campaign to market Great Lakes whitefish in 2006. Fishermen in Lake Michigan and Lake Huron organized a multistate initiative to reacquaint the public with this resource. Since it lacked the visual elegance of salmon and trout, whitefish won favor primarily for its cleanliness, flavor, and texture. The Grand Hotel on Mackinac Island has taken a forward role in drawing attention to the culinary quality of the fish. And yet, as attention turned once again toward the local whitefish, an environmental problem caused a decline in the population—invasive species, Quagga and Zebra mussels, were disrupting the Great Lakes food chain, causing fish populations to decline steadily in the 21st century. In the 1990s, landings in Lake Michigan averaged 4 million pounds a year. In 2017, that number fell to 1.3 million. The decline in Lake Huron was even more dire.

In the face of this decline, longtime champions of the whitefish have labored to keep the species and its foodways present in the minds of the public so as not to lose the native whitefish entirely. Publicity has focused largely on Door County's cycle of outdoor festivals and their whitefish foodways in the past decade. While smoked whitefish remains a feature of Door County's celebrations, the reigning tradition since 1940 is whitefish boiled in kettles with potatoes and onions. According to the *Chicago Tribune*, "when it is done cooking, kerosene is thrown on the fire, creating a 'boil over.' This gets rid of the fish oil that has floated to the top and fish and vegetables can be lifted out of the liquid and eaten immediately." Great Lakes whitefish has also entered a new realm as roe and the yellow eggs are sold as Golden whitefish roe. The hope is to expand the usage of whitefish and improve its environment so that the Great Lakes whitefish will continue to occupy its native waters for years to come.

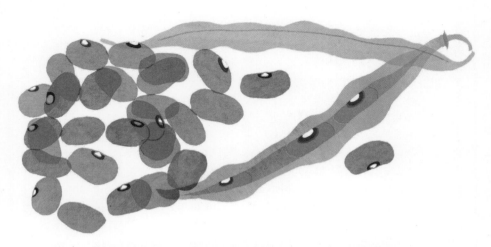

HIDATSA RED

Bean

In 1882, New York horticulturist Oscar H. Will purchased a failing nursery in Bismarck, Dakota Territory, rebranding it as the Pioneer Brand Seed House. Will did as every seed company proprietor did, offering the most up-to-date versions of popular garden vegetables and field crops. But Will also belonged to a small set of American plant breeders who believed that growers neglected and looked down on certain, unfamiliar crops. His lasting fame lies in his collecting native landraces of maize, beans, and squash of the Mandan, Arikara, and Hidatsa peoples. Some of these he bred into commercial cultivars, such as the Great Northern bean or Dakota Gold sweet corn—Will developed the latter from seed given to him in 1907 by James Holding Eagle of the Mandan community—while others he simply presented to the world as perfected native varieties. The Hidatsa Red bean, which first appeared in Will's catalogs as the Indian Red bean in 1915, was one of these.

The Hidatsa are a trading people, and their corn seeds, sunflowers, and beans were exchanged for vegetables from Will's supply. The Hidatsa traded for onions, melons, strawberries, and potatoes, the latter of which would supplant wild turnip in Hidatsa cookery. He also supplied iron hoes and plows with which the Hidatsa cultivated gardens. They maintained a close supervision and stewardship over their seeds. The company introduced its Indian collection of corn, squash, and beans in the 1915 catalog. Buffalo Bird Woman, the matriarch of Hidatsa seed keeping when Will traded with the people, recalled that of the five beans maintained by the tribe at the turn of the 20th century, the red bean Ama'ca hi'ci was the only variety cultivated by the Hidatsa during her girlhood in the mid-1800s. She described traditional gardening in the classic 1917 monograph by Gilbert Livingston Wilson, *Agriculture of the Hidatsa Indians: An Indian Interpretation*. She also described a favorite Hidatsa recipe, "Ama'ca Di'hě, or Beans-Boiled." The beans were boiled in a clay pot, with a piece of buffalo fat, or some bone grease. If the beans were dried beans, they were boiled a little longer than squash is boiled—a half hour or more. Spring salt, or other seasoning, was not used.

The Hidatsa Red bean is hardy and drought resistant, and it makes for excellent baking. It is dark red, kidney shaped, and meaty. It grows in a bush configuration, ranging upward of 3 feet. Though it can be harvested in the pod immature and prepared as a green bean, it is more popularly used as a dried shelling bean. The original form had pink flowers, but now they are white. The beans were dried down in the pod, threshed by treading and beating with sticks, and stored for year-round consumption. To this day, the Hidatsa Red bean is usually used in its dried form and soaked before baking. The bean has a thin skin and, when cooked, a soft, creamy interior. It differs in texture and flavor from the common Red Kidney bean, with a flavor that some have likened to red miso, and makes a more interesting red beans and rice dish when substituted.

Oscar H. Will died in 1917. In subsequent years, his son George Will made a point of acknowledging the Indigenous seedcraft behind the company's products, including, for instance, a photograph of the Mandan agriculturist Scattered Corn in a catalog just as he would any famous plant breeder. He also expanded the Indian Seed Collection in the 1920 catalog. George also renamed the bean that appeared under the name Indian Red in the 1916 catalog as the Hidatsa Red bean, attesting to its provenance.

LIVINGSTON GLOBE
Tomato

US ORIGIN OR MOST PREVALENT IN
Ohio

CHARACTERISTICS
Smooth skin, mild, meaty, medium sized

USDA PLANT HARDINESS ZONES
7b–9a

CLOSE RELATIVES
Ponderosa tomato, Stone tomato

NOTABLE PRODUCER
Victory Seed Company

Irregularity ruled in the world of tomatoes before the 1880s. Large tomatoes tended to be broad and oblate, instead of spherical, and represented a broad spectrum of color that included red, pink, purple, green, and yellow. Lumps, humps, clefts, crenulations, and concavities at the stem were common. The fruits tended to ripen unevenly, with the core of the tomato hard and green when the region beneath the skin was ready. In the late 1800s, a certain vision of the perfect tomato overtook tomato production largely at the hands of one breeder, Alexander Livingston. Livingston thought the ideal tomato should fill a woman's cupped hand. His Paragon tomato, introduced in 1870, was the first draft of the tomato that would come to dominate the market—red, smooth-skinned, meaty, and spherical.

Working in Columbus, Ohio, Livingston pursued his vision of the tomato, releasing a number of new tomatoes, but did not achieve the shape he so desired in breeding in the 1870s and 1880s.

"The fruits are of large size, and a good marketable size is retained throughout the season; always smooth, of firm flesh and has few seeds; ripens evenly; color, a fine glossy rose, tinged with purple, and without the slightest hint of yellow at any stage of ripening."

Their squatness limited the number of slices one could render from a single tomato. A more elongated, globular tomato would maximize the number of slices, which was important since sandwiches were the primary end goal driving the tomato market. Throughout the 1890s, Livingston worked on a tomato that would embody the ideal to which he had devoted his tomato breeding career—enter the Livingston Globe tomato.

In the Livingston Globe tomato, Livingston achieved this combination of desirable features by crossing his Stone tomato, which provided the shape and flesh density, and Peter Henderson's Ponderosa tomato, which contributed size, flavor, and productivity. Livingston laid out the qualities of his new creation in a 1904 prospectus for the general seed market: "The fruits are of large size, and a good marketable size is retained throughout the season; always smooth, of firm flesh and has few seeds; ripens evenly; color, a fine glossy rose, tinged with purple, and without the slightest hint of yellow at any stage of ripening. An exceedingly productive variety, having plants with many short joints at which large clusters containing three to seven fruits are almost invariably formed, so that it can be truthfully stated the plants are literally loaded with fruit. It is a remarkably good keeper, none of the many varieties we grow surpassing it."

The Livingston Globe tomato proved an instant hit. Its uniformity of shape, consistency, and rich red coloring made it ideal for packing, shipping, and displaying on produce stands. It would provide the template for the commercial tomato of the 20th century, when product uniformity became the hallmark of the industrial food market. It reigned in the fields of the Midwest for decades, but monocropping exposed weaknesses in the variety: susceptibility to viral diseases, problems with splitting in rainy conditions, and quick spoilage after becoming ripe. Before too long, many growers abandoned the Livingston Globe for industrially produced tomatoes that lacked in flavor, had a tough texture, and were subject to gas ripening (harvested green and ripened by ethylene in closed chambers). These tomatoes still rule the conventional tomato market today. Thus, the Livingston Globe became scarce, and its place as the most versatile slicing and canning tomato in the United States has largely been forgotten.

In one of the more remarkable rehabilitation projects of modern seed saving, The Victory Seed Company undertook the restoration of all surviving Livingston tomato lines in 1999, with Mike Dunton of Molalla, Oregon, as the moving spirit behind the project. Since the Livingston Globe tomato was largely responsible for the improvement of the tomato in general so that it became the favorite American vegetable in the early 20th century, and because many agronomic breeders defaced the genetics that Livingston had so painstakingly curated, Dunton sought all surviving varieties that Alexander Livingston had introduced during his lifetime. Several have gone extinct, but many of the classic Livingston varieties have been revived and are now available as heirlooms—the Paragon (1870), the Perfection (1880), the Golden Queen (1882), the Favorite (1883), the Beauty (1886), the Stone (1889), and of course, the Globe (1905).

Livingston bred his famous tomatoes, the Globe included, in reaction to the unbalanced acidity of many earlier tomato varieties. Mildness and meatiness were the qualities that typified the Livingston line. Twenty-first-century tomato breeders noted the success of high acid and high sugar and increased the pungency of many contemporary lines. The delicacy of the Livingston Globe is undeniably a contrast to more recent and widely known tomatoes, but also precisely the thing that makes it stand out and worth preserving.

MANOOMIN
(Wild Rice)

Manoomin is the wild landrace *Zizania aquatica* rice, traditionally hand harvested and prepared by the Anishinaabeg (Ojibwe) people each year during the 30 days of the Wild Rice Moon. It is North America's one Native cereal that contributes significantly to food production and grows primarily in the lakes and watercourses of the glacier outwash of Wisconsin and Minnesota, near the Canadian border. Anishinaabeg teachings explain that wild rice was the reason for their migration West and settlement in their homeland. They called the aquatic grass that adorned this watery region Manoomin, meaning "the good grain."

The folklore of Manoomin tells that the hunter Nanaboozhoo had failed to capture game and came home hungry. When he returned to his homeplace, Nanaboozhoo saw a duck perched on the edge of his cooking kettle. As the hunter approached, the duck flew away. Nanaboozhoo looked into the kettle and found Manoomin floating on the surface of the simmering liquid. Though

*The Anishinaabeg believe
that Manoomin supplies spiritual
as well as physical nourishment,
and that the presence of Manoomin
in the lakes of the upper Midwest
ensures their continuance as a people.*

he did not know what it was, he ate from the kettle and proclaimed it was the best soup he had ever tasted. Nanaboozhoo ventured out in the direction the duck had flown, arriving at a lake full of Manoomin. Thus, he had discovered a treasure trove of what would become a staple food for his people.

During the month of the Wild Rice Moon, harvesters go into the fields in pairs. One person impels the canoe from the stern with a pole, while the other faces the stern and uses two handheld wooden poles—one to push panicles of the rice over the boat and the other to beat the rice twice to dislodge the grains into the interior of the canoe. The grains are then spread out and cleaned on a tarp before being parched in a metal pan over an open fire. The Anishinaabeg believe that Manoomin supplies spiritual as well as physical nourishment, and that the presence of Manoomin in the lakes of the upper Midwest ensures their continuance as a people.

Zizania aquatica belongs to a family of wild grass and rice found in North America that includes the imperiled *Zizania texana* and the Southern water plant *Zizania miliacea*. The latter was called "prolific rice" or "wild rice" in early exploration accounts of the region. Indigenous people foraged all of the varieties growing wild in the region, but only Manoomin became a staple of Indigenous foodways.

When explorer and evangelist Jacques Marquette traversed the region in 1673 to convert Native peoples, he encountered the Anishinaabeg and their staple grain. In his 1988 study *Wild Rice and the Ojibway People,* ethnobotanist Thomas Vennum Jr. suggested that Marquette mistook the unfamiliar rice for the European weed Fool's Oats, or *Lolium temulentum*. Marquette described it as such: "The ears [panicles] grow upon hollow stems, jointed at intervals; they emerge from the water about the month of June, and continue growing until they rise about two feet above it . . . in September [when it is harvested]."

Unlike Manoomin, the "wild rice" you might find at your grocery store is an agronomically improved, cultivated form of *Zizania aquatica* grown and processed for commercial sale as a cereal commodity. In an 1837 treaty between the United States and the Ojibwe, the American government recognized the right of the Anishinaabeg to exercise control over their native wild rice. This treaty provision underwrote efforts by the tribal authorities to halt research into *Zizania aquatica* by geneticists at state universities to serve commercial interests. The commercial cultivation of wild rice has led to the takeover of some prime waterways in Michigan, Wisconsin, and Minnesota by commercial entities. The cultivated wild rice had different characteristics than Manoomin—being more intensely black in color with a higher starch content. These deviations from the landrace form are viewed as defacements of a plant regarded as a divine gift. To avoid an adversarial relationship between tribes and universities, a collaborative campaign was created and called Kawe Gidaa-naanaagadawendaamin Manoomin, which made scientists aware of the cultural knowledge and ecological concerns of the Anishinaabeg and gave Indigenous harvesters access to scientific findings about water chemistry and other matters causing a decrease in Manoomin productivity in certain waterways.

The Slow Food USA Manoomin Presidium works with existing conservation and policy initiatives developed by Native Harvest (White Earth Land Recovery Project) to promote consumption of traditionally harvested and prepared wild rice. The primary goal of the Presidium is to ensure that the Anishinaabeg may grow, harvest, and process their rice in traditional ways. The White Earth Land Recovery Project also provides the landrace wild rice for people outside of the Indigenous community on their website as well as incorporating Manoomin flour and grain into cake, fry bread, and soup mixes for sale.

MANOOMIN

WITH GRILLED

Sunflower

AND

ROOT VEGETABLES

ELENA TERRY, *chef and founder*
WILD BEARIES, WISCONSIN

*This recipe highlights the earthy flavor and delicate chew
of the Manoomin. Depending on what's in season, you can use almost
any produce in the recipe, from fresh berries to roasted vegetables.
Seek our hand-harvested Manoomin to get a more delicate hull
than a cultivated version. You may substitute a fresh corn cob
for the sunflower, but the sunflower is highly recommended
if you can access an edible one.*

1 head of garlic

Extra-virgin olive oil, for drizzling

1 immature sunflower head
(green, closed flower head)

2 cups (350 g) Manoomin
(or any wild rice)

7 tablespoons (105 ml) sunflower oil,
divided

Salt and freshly ground black pepper

1 zucchini

1 eggplant

1 onion

1 purple potato

Flat-leaf parsley, chopped for garnish

Heat the oven to 350°F (180°C). Cut off the top of the garlic head, drizzle with olive oil, and bake for 25 minutes. Remove the petals and any other flower parts from the sunflower head. Soak the cleaned sunflower, stem side down, in cold water for 30 minutes.

Put 6 cups of water in a sauce pot. Add the Manoomin and bring to a simmer. Cook the rice until the grains open; you'll be able to see the gray of the rice on the inside of the hull (hand-harvested, about 12 minutes; cultivated, about 35 minutes). Drain and transfer to a large bowl. Toss the rice in 2 tablespoons of the sunflower oil and season with salt and pepper. Cut the zucchini, eggplant, onion, and potato into approximately 2-inch (5-cm) pieces and evenly brush them with 3 tablespoons of the sunflower oil. Season lightly with salt and pepper. Brush the sunflower head with the remaining oil, then rub it with the roasted garlic.

Grill or roast the vegetables to the desired level of doneness. Grill the sunflower head on low heat until the seeds change color. Arrange the vegetables and sunflower on a plate over the Manoomin and serve warm, sprinkled with parsley.

Wisconsin-based Elena Terry is chef and founder of Wild Bearies, an organization that helps heal and educate Indigenous communities through ancestral food. She is the Food and Culinary Program Coordinator for the Native American Food Sovereignty Alliance.

NORTON Grape

**US ORIGIN OR
MOST PREVALENT IN**
Virginia and Missouri

CHARACTERISTICS
*Deep purple color,
blueberry aroma, overt
fruitiness, firm, juicy*

**USDA PLANT
HARDINESS ZONES**
5–8

CLOSE RELATIVES
*Bland grape, French
Meunier grape*

NOTABLE PRODUCERS
*Chrysalis Vineyards
and Horton Vineyards
in Virginia, Stone Hill
Winery in Missouri*

American wine making was built on a short list of grapes that we have largely forgotten: the Herbemont, the Lenoir, the Catawba, the Isabella, and the Norton. All five of these grapes emerged in the first quarter of the 19th century. Daniel N. Norton of Richmond, Virginia, first grew the hybrid that bore his name in 1820. Nicholas Longworth's Sparkling Catawba was the most popular wine of the 19th century, but connoisseurs of fine wine judged red wine from Norton grapes to be the most distinctive of American varietal offerings. Today, the Norton is still considered one of the best American-born varietals and makes for a much-loved red wine.

Throughout the colonial period, American horticulturists planted seeds, roots, and even vines of Europe's *Vitis vinifera* grapes, hoping to replicate the refined wines of France, Spain, Germany, and Italy. These efforts flourished for a moment in Philadelphia, Savannah, New York, and Virginia, and then failed absolutely. An array of plant diseases that included black rot, Pierce's disease, powdery mildew, and phylloxera attacked the roots, leaves, and berries of the grapevines, turning gorgeous green vineyards into tangles of dead plant matter. The native *Vitis aestivalis* grapes were resistant to the disease, but the wine that they produced tasted foxy, musty, or brazenly fruity. Early in the 1800s growers chanced upon natural crosses between imported European *V. vinifera* grapes and the native *V. aestivalis* and *V. labrusca* varieties, which they discovered were disease resistant and offered some of the flavor of those premium European vines.

The variety retains the small size and minimal pulp of its V. aestivalis *parent. It produces an intensely fruity and flavorful red wine with a lively play of tannin, acid, and berry.*

Thus, the 1820s were a period of intense experimentation with wine making in the United States, driven by the work of Nicholas Herbemont and the prospect of turning marginal lands and sandhills in gravelly countryside into highly profitable terrain. Norton, a recently widowed grape grower, assuaged his grief with horticultural experiments. According to his records, he hand-pollinated the Bland grape, a native *V. aestivalis* from the eastern shore of Virginia, with the French Meunier, a *V. vinifera*. The Norton arose from the seed of this cross. The variety retains the small size and minimal pulp of its *V. aestivalis* parent. It produces an intensely fruity and flavorful red wine with a lively play of tannin, acid, and berry. Furthermore, the variety possessed resistance to American diseases that devastated most European varieties.

The Norton grape became nationally famous because it captured the attention of pomologist William Prince II of Flushing, New York. Proprietor of the Linnaean Garden, the most highly regarded stone fruit nursery in the United States at the time, Prince foresaw that wine grapes would be a great cash generator in American farming. Though he championed his own proprietary grape variety, the Isabella, Prince understood the message of Europe wine culture—that a diversity of varieties and wine styles had to exist for there to be an enduring popular demand for locally made wine. He secured vine cuttings from Norton and began selling them to a national clientele. Buyers hailed from most parts of the United States, but the length of time required to ripen the Norton grape made it better suited to the longer growing seasons of the Southern United States.

Every important promoter of grape growing to follow Prince listed Norton in their catalogs until Prohibition. Here is a typical description from one such catalog: "Norton: Black; bunch long, compact, shouldered; berries small, flesh tender, melting, without pulp and vinous. Ripens too late for most Norther[n] localities, but is very highly esteemed at the South and Southwest, and considered their best red wine grape. Vine very healthy, vigorous grower, hardy and productive; very difficult to propagate and does not bear transplanting as well as most varieties."

By the 1860s, one state had embraced the variety with greater zeal than any other—Missouri. Curiously enough, Missouri's love of the Norton was complicated by a controversy. A "strain" of Norton was popularized there under the more mellifluous name of Cynthiana, triggering a 125-year quarrel about whether the two varieties were identical, with some adherents claiming the Cynthiana was more delicate and refined. Missouri emerged as the most energetic promoter of the contested Cynthiana variety, so much so that it became Missouri's state wine and the linchpin of the state's active wine industry. Genetic testing in the 21st century indicated that the two varieties are indistinguishable.

The challenge of making beautiful wine from the Norton grape lies in controlling the intensity of anthocyanin in the skins; this chemical gives the grape a deep purple color, blueberry aroma, and overt fruitiness. Badly managed batches of Norton grapes often assume a too-brash fruitiness. In the 1870s, winemakers in Missouri mastered the cultivation and care of the variety with the creation of a brilliantly balanced red wine from Norton grapes. Stone Hill Winery in Hermann, Missouri, won a gold medal for red wine in the 1873 Vienna World Exposition.

Much of this wine making wisdom was lost during Prohibition (1919–1933), and a great many vineyards were converted to other uses. Revival of American varietals was thwarted by a new doctrine that insisted upon the superiority of European *V. vinifera* varieties. Konstantin Frank indoctrinated American vignerons in this belief in the 1950s. It wasn't until the late 20th century that growers and vignerons began questioning Frank's Euro-purism. The Norton grape would become central to the case that great American wine can be made from non–*V. vinifera* varieties. Important vineyards in Virginia and Missouri can be credited for the revival of the Norton grape variety. The next time you're looking for a red that'll spark some impressive table talk, look for the Norton.

PURPLE STRAW
Wheat

US ORIGIN OR MOST PREVALENT IN	*Virginia and Ohio*
CHARACTERISTICS	*Winter growth, soft grain*
USDA PLANT HARDINESS ZONES	*6b–9b*
CLOSE RELATIVE	*North African Spring wheat*
NOTABLE PRODUCERS	*Clemson University's Pee Dee Agricultural Research Station*

The world of Southern biscuits, fancy cakes, and wheated whiskey emerged from two wheat varieties—White May wheat and Purple Straw wheat—though only the latter persisted in the face of agricultural challenges over the last two centuries. After the American Revolution, the South developed wheats that could be grown over winter to avoid the insect and disease pressures—such as wheat rust and Hessian fly—that imperiled the summer wheat brought from northern Europe.

Two soft winter wheats were discovered as mutations in Virginia grain fields that ripened before the heat of June and the consequent outbreak of insects: White May (also Isbell's Forward wheat, Rare Ripe wheat) and Purple Straw wheat (Blue Stem wheat). Their discoverers, Henry Isbell of Caroline County and Robert Emrey of Fauquier County, nurtured the strains and publicized their virtues, inspiring growers to quickly and readily adopt the seed. White May wheat eventually proved vulnerable and genetically

Purple Straw's ability to thrive on marginal soils and evade rust along with its early harvest, its productivity, and the quality of its flour made it the field preference for farmers in parts of the South throughout the 19th century and into the 20th.

unstable, but Purple Straw wheat remained a field crop in the region from the 1790s to the 1970s, when it was widely replaced with more productive wheat varieties. These high-yield soft wheats may have produced more bushels per acre, but they did not match Purple Straw wheat in flavor or flour quality.

The USDA's small-grain geneticist for the Southeast, Gina Brown-Guedira, had noted genetic similarities between Purple Straw wheat and North African spring wheats, though the variety of wheat Emrey grew in the 1780s cannot be determined. In 1790, agronomist John Taylor of Virginia conducted an extensive comparative grow-out of the variety to test for productivity and realized that Purple Straw wheat was surprisingly productive on poorer soils—a significant discovery, since Virginia had exhausted a great deal of soil fertility by monocropping tobacco for a century without rotating crops. The finding that accelerated the widespread adoption of the variety, though, was Taylor's conclusion that Purple Straw wheat afforded more output per acre than corn.

Purple Straw's ability to thrive on marginal soils and evade rust along with its early harvest, its productivity, and the quality of its flour made it the field preference for farmers in parts of the South throughout the 19th century and into the 20th. Many rival wheats were put forward by farmers with the aim of supplanting Purple Straw wheat—Lawler wheat, Hunton wheat, and Maryland-Pennsylvania Yellow Bearded wheat—but they failed. Agronomist and author Edmund Ruffin spent the 1830s improving the seed and explained why no other wheat could supplant the variety: "Its great advantage consists in the ripe grain being able to bear more exposure to wet weather than any white or bearded red wheat and where we make large crops our wheat is exposed in the field from the beginning of reaping to the end of thrashing. Besides this important ground for preference, this kind of wheat is heavier than the bearded, and makes better flour." Ruffin ensured that enough Purple Straw seed was dispersed throughout the South that the disruptions of seed production in the South caused by the Civil War did not imperil the variety.

A beardless soft red wheat that grows erectly atop stiff straw, which colors from dark red to purple to blue over the growing season, Purple Straw prevailed historically because of its unique conjunction of field resilience and flour quality. Many agronomists asserted the excellence of Purple Straw's flour, well suited for pastry and for biscuits but not for bread or pasta, which requires hard wheat flour. Ruffin wrote: "The grain is supposed by experienced millers to make the richest and best flour—though of course not so white, and therefore not so high-priced as the flour of the thin-skinned and more tender white wheats."

With the recognition that the variety was ideally suited for a particular and ubiquitous preparation like biscuits, it became a fixture of regional cookery. In the mid-20th century, 100,692 acres of Purple Straw were grown in the 11 states of the American Southeast. But by the 1980s, newer winter wheats that borrowed some of the genetics of Purple Straw (but not the alleles governing flavor) had muscled the classic wheat from the landscape. In 2010, when Glenn Roberts and Brian Ward sought to bring back the classic flavor, they found remnant fields of Purple Straw grown by the Amish in Ohio. Since that time Richard Boyle of Clemson University has taken up the cause. Efforts to build a seed stock for Purple Straw expanded with distillers supporting the return of the South's classic wheat variety. We hope it will find its way back to biscuits and into distiller's barrels.

RED TURKEY
Wheat

In 1873, a group of German-speaking Mennonite refugees from Russia settled in Kansas. Until then, they had lived in autonomous religious settlements in the Russian Empire as Mennonite colonies and enjoyed legal privileges, such as owning property and holding office. When a Russian nationalization campaign threatened to compel pacifist Mennonites to serve in the Russian Army in 1870, 15,000 Mennonites emigrated from Russia to the United States and Canada. Underwritten by the Santa Fe Railroad, Mennonite elder Bernard Warkentin negotiated the transport and settlement of 7,000 refugees to Harvey and MacPherson counties in Kansas.

They brought with them a Hard Red Winter wheat from Ukraine, a Crimean landrace miscalled "Turkey." The origin region of this wheat is northeast of the Black Sea and north of the Caucasus Mountains. The variety was used as a bread wheat at a time when the majority of wheat grown in the United States was soft winter wheat better suited for making biscuits

The cold-tolerant variety developed in an area of Europe with scant precipitation and was also singularly drought resistant.

and cake flour. Upon its arrival, Red Turkey wheat proved so hard that mills could not process it well, and the variety earned low prices. Eventually, roller mill technology was developed to process the hard wheat, and a grain industry tailored for hard wheat varieties burgeoned in the last decades of the 19th century.

In the early 1900s, when strains of Red Turkey wheat were imported from Crimea, the productive Karkov and Valakoff strains were the first of many revisions of Red Turkey wheat. Compared to standard soft winter wheats—Purple Straw, Fulcaster, White May—Red Turkey expressed relatively little foliage and thin straw. The cold-tolerant variety developed in an area of Europe with scant precipitation and was also singularly drought resistant. While vulnerable to the standard wheat afflictions of Hessian fly and wheat rust, it was grown in a region where those problems did not prevail. The seed heads were outfitted with spiky awns to inhibit insects, a characteristic referred to as being bearded. Its chaff is white, but the grains are dark red and hard. As a landrace, it grew rather tall and developed a tendency to lodge (blow down) in the windy plains of Kansas and Oklahoma.

One of the issues that developed over decades of growing Red Turkey wheat in Kansas was that it became progressively softer. Seed was sent to Canada, where two years of growing there restored its hardness. The renovated seed was shipped back to Kansas under the name Alberta wheat and would remain the most intensively grown wheat in the United States through the 1930s—the majority of it

HARD VS SOFT WHEAT

Soft wheat describes the modest density of starch in a wheat berry; it is suited to biscuit and cake flour. Hard wheat has great starch density, making it harder to mill but proving more glutinous and useful for bread baking.

employed in baking bread, while its bran and subsidiary products were used as feed. It was the most productive wheat variety in Idaho and Nebraska in the 1950s.

With the advent of industrial scale steel roller mills in the 1880s, the fineness and consistency of the milled flour became a foremost concern in food production. Red Turkey wheat consistently generated 80 percent high-grade flour when qualities deemed superior became standardized. It is a high-gluten, high-protein bread wheat that caramelizes richly in the oven. Ellen King, a baker who specializes in heirloom grains, celebrated Red Turkey wheat for its "tender crumb" and earthy flavor as a whole wheat loaf in her highly regarded 2018 cookbook *Heritage Baking*.

The preoccupation of agricultural companies with productivity of wheat per acre saw the eclipse of Red Turkey wheat in the mid-20th century. Sensory testing of wheat varieties for flavor had essentially ceased, and the final four decades of the 20th century witnessed the culinary decline of wheat. Breeders instead prioritized and tested disease resistance, cold resistance, drought resistance, millability, and even spreadability in cookie dough. Flavor no longer seemed to play into the equation. With every passing year, the amount of Crimean wheat grown in the United States diminished from its 1949 high. Red Turkey wheat became a niche variety kept in fields by a small contingent of growers who remained true to their taste buds and by institutions interested in genetics. Those institutions hoped to make use of the genetic alleles that made Red Turkey wheat the leading commodity wheat in its heyday, and keep it available for use in future wheat cultivars.

Ultimately, the rise of artisanal bread baking at the end of the 20th century served as the catalyst for the revival of Red Turkey wheat. A coterie of farmers in Kansas revived the state's historic wheat. It captured the attention of flavor-driven bakers, and the increased demand for the variety caused many millers to reintegrate Red Turkey wheat into their milling operations. Aside from its renewed prominence in baking, current growers have also observed that, despite its slender stem, Red Turkey wheat has an extensive root structure, and that in a recent drought it outperformed other modern varieties. A variety that is as good for morning toast as it is for our changing ecosystem is certainly one to be preserved, and it's undoubtedly affirming to see bags of flour on the shelves of specialty grocers and tags in artisanal bakery cases proudly asserting their loaves are made with Red Turkey wheat.

THE *Grain Renaissance*

A food renaissance focused on grain is happening around the world. A small and steadily growing segment of farmers across the country are cultivating a whole range of grains that are best-suited to where they are grown and they are not compromising nutrition and flavor for profit.

Not just farmers, but a growing number of links in the grain chain—farmers, millers, bakers, chefs, pasta makers, maltsters, brewers, distillers, scientists, activists and educators—have come together to raise consciousness and appetites in our minds and on our plates. The key players in this renaissance make use of the latest knowledge and technology in regenerative agriculture and employ state-of-the-art food production methods, including a new generation of stone mills, to make lowly grains the flavorful and nutritious stars of our diets.

In the US, the grain renaissance has led to the creation of the Colorado Grain Chain (CGC). Formed to work with grain producers, educators, and consumers to promote "grain literacy," the CGC is working to raise awareness and a sense of urgency about the fact that biodiversity in grain agriculture not only contributes to healthy soil, but to a more diverse and nutritious human diet.

Besides many concerns about health—human health, the health of the earth, and the economic health of local foodsheds—the heart of the CGC's mission is the goal of inspiring producers and consumers to explore the bounty and richness of the world of grains they've been missing. The grain renaissance is also about flavor, creativity, and experimentation in the kitchen, the pleasures of eating good food, and the satisfaction of knowing where, how, and by whom it was produced. The CGC places particular emphasis on heritage and ancient grains, as well as modern "open source" (not patented, and not GMO) varieties that are bred to thrive in particular climate and soil conditions. Two examples of these heritage grains are in this book: the White Sonora and Red Turkey wheats.

Consistent with the core values of the Slow Food movement, the grain renaissance reflects a global rise in sensibilities about food provenance, food safety, human health, sustainability, environmental stewardship, good labor practices, cultural appropriateness, and the aesthetics and pleasure associated with "real food." Chief among the players bringing about these changes are the farmers who are experimenting with growing heritage and ancient grains that do best in Colorado soil and climate conditions.

Rather than relying on excessive uses of water and chemical inputs to grow grains, a new generation of farmers is committed to regenerative agriculture that builds soil and emphasizes the appropriateness of a crop for the environment in which it is grown. Just as wine producers talk of "terroir"—the qualities of climate, soil, and growing conditions that give a unique flavor to wine—we are now seeing a rise in consciousness about how particular types of grain can give us the best and most unique flavor that a particular place has to offer.

CHILTEPIN (BIRD) PEPPER CHEROKEE TRAI
ORANGE APPLE CORRIENTE CATTLE CO
GUAJILLO HONEY HERITAGE TEXAS LONGH
O-CHURRO SHEEP NEW MEXICO NATIVE C
DO RED MCCLURE POTATO RED WATTLE
AT TEPARY BEAN WENK'S YELLOW HOT P
BLACK SPHINX DATE BROWN AND WHIT
PEPPER CHEROKEE TRAIL OF TEARS BEAN
CORRIENTE CATTLE COLORADO ORANGE
HERITAGE TEXAS LONGHORN CATTLE MC
NEW MEXICO NATIVE CHILE PEPPER NEW
RE POTATO RED WATTLE HOG RIO ZAPE
N WENK'S YELLOW HOT PEPPER WHITE S
DATE BROWN AND WHITE TEPARY BEAN
KEE TRAIL OF TEARS BEAN CHRISTMAS LI
COLORADO ORANGE APPLE FOUR CORNE
GHORN CATTLE MOON AND STARS WATE
CHILE PEPPER NEW MEXICO TOMATILLO
HOG RIO ZAPE BEAN SONORAN QUINCE
PER WHITE SONORA WHEAT AMERICAN
TEPARY BEAN CAPITOL REEF APPLE CHIL
CHRISTMAS LIMA BEAN COLORADO ORAN
APPLE FOUR CORNERS GOLD BEAN GUAJI
AND STARS WATERMELON NAVAJO-CHURI
EXICO TOMATILLO PUEBLA AVOCADO R
ONORAN QUINCE SPANISH GOAT TEPARY
WHEAT AMERICAN NATIVE PECAN BLACK
L REEF APPLE CHILTEPIN (BIRD) PEPPER
COLORADO ORANGE APPLE CORRIENTE
BEAN GUAJILLO HONEY HERITAGE TEXAS
VAJO-CHURRO SHEEP NEW MEXICO NATIV
CADO RED MCCLURE POTATO RED WAT
AT TEPARY BEAN WENK'S YELLOW HO

OF TEARS BEAN CHRISTMAS LIMA
RADO ORANGE APPLE FOUR CORNERS
RN CATTLE MOON AND STARS WA
ILE PEPPER NEW MEXICO
HOG RIO ZAPE BEAN SONORAN
PPER WHITE SONORA WHEA
TEPARY BEAN CAPITOL RE
CHRISTMAS LIMA BEAN CO
PPLE FOUR CORNERS GOLD BEA
N AND STARS WATERMELON NAVA
MEXICO TOMATILLO PUEBLA AV
AN SONORAN QUINCE SPANISH
NORA WHEAT AMERICAN NATIVE
CAPITOL REEF APPLE CHILTEPIN (BIRD) PE
A BEAN COLORADO ORANGE APPL
S GOLD BEAN GUAJILLO HONEY
MELON NAVAJO-CHURRO SHEEP
PUEBLA AVOCADO RED MCCLU
SPANISH GOAT TEPARY BEAN WE
ATIVE PECAN BLACK SPHINX DA
EPIN (BIRD) PEPPER CHEROKEE TRAIL
E APPLE CORRIENTE CATTLE CO
LO HONEY HERITAGE TEXAS LON
SHEEP NEW MEXICO NATIVE C
MCCLURE POTATO RED WATTL
BEAN WENK'S YELLOW HOT PEPP
PHINX DATE BROWN AND WHIT
EROKEE TRAIL OF TEARS BEAN CHRI
ATTLE COLORADO ORANGE APPLE FO
NGHORN CATTLE MOON AND STARS
CHILE PEPPER NEW MEXICO T
HOG RIO ZAPE BEAN SONORA
WHITE SONORA WHEAT

ROCKY MOUNTAIN AND SOUTHWEST

CHILTEPIN (BIRD)
Pepper

US ORIGIN OR MOST PREVALENT IN
Southwest United States

CHARACTERISTICS
Very small, red, fiery, used in hot sauce

USDA PLANT HARDINESS ZONES
8b–10a

OTHER NAMES
Chile Pequin (IN SPANISH)
Chile Tepin, Chile Del Monte, Chillipiquin, A'al Kokoli (IN O'ODHAM) Chiltepictl (IN NAHUATL) Amash (IN MAYAN) Bird pepper (WEST INDIES) Bird's Eye pepper

CLOSE RELATIVE
Grove pepper

NOTABLE PRODUCER
Don Enrique Pequin Peppers

Native cultivators spread the small and fiery Chiltepin pepper, indigenous to Mexico, into the West Indies, Florida, New Mexico, Arizona, and Texas. Grown by Indigenous people at the time the Spanish colonized the American Southwest and Florida, the Chiltepin adapted to the warm climates and arid landscapes of the southern United States. The peppers go by names as numerous as the distinct regions where they grow. Chiltepin is the name that's been taken up in the American Southwest, while Bird pepper is the more common English name in Southeastern states and the West Indies.

The Chiltepin is a pungent pepper. A 2015 chemical analysis registered the pepper at 50,000 Scoville units—approximately twice as hot as a serrano pepper and ten times as hot as a jalapeño. That's hot, but there is much misinformation about the heat of the Chiltepin, with some commentators claiming 100,000 Scoville units for the dried fruits. These misimpressions probably arise from the

THE BIRD PEPPER

Birds do not respond to capsaicin, the chemical that provokes humans' sense of heat in peppers. So they are able to eat the fruit, unbothered, and spread the seeds across the countryside. Wild peppers grow in the Sonoran Desert, Southern sand plains, and Florida groves; hence the name Bird pepper. Other world peppers are colloquially called "bird peppers," such as the Brazilian Yellow Bird's Eye pepper and the Peruvian Charipita, but the Ark of Taste designation pertains only to the Chiltepin or Pequin Bird pepper variety.

distinctive shock of the initial taste of the pepper. It flashes heat in the mouth then quickly recedes into a modest burn. To mitigate the heat flash, cooks often process it into sauces.

Harvesting wild Chiltepins is a seasonal ritual in many of the rural communities in its growing areas to this day. Families erect camps in the mountains during September and early October to harvest the wild chile peppers. Wild populations are significantly more prolific than cultivated plants. When grown as an annual for the spice market, the Chiltepin suffers from low germination and greater susceptibility to pathogens. Cultivated plants are quite thirsty, while wild plants are drought resistant. Hence, the Chiltepin has been among the costliest peppers on the world spice market, reaching $128 per pound in the 1990s.

Historically, the kitchen tables of Sonoran, Opata, O'odham, or Yaqui rural homes were more than likely crowned with a jar or bowl of dried Chiltepins. Dried, whole, or crushed Chiltepins are used in a host of Native and Southwestern dishes from salsas to pickles to breads, and a salt-and-red-pepper rub used often to preserve venison and beef. Cooks of the West Indies and the American South preferred to use the pepper wet in a hot sauce, rather than dry as a condiment. Before there was Tabasco sauce (1860s), there was Jamaican Bird Pepper sauce, which was imported into the United States since the country's founding. Piquant and potent, the sauce was composed of sherry vinegar and ripe, pureed red Bird peppers aged in a cask with salt. In the early decades of the 19th century, commercial varieties of the pepper sauce came onto the scene. Regional interpretations emerged, with New Orleans calling theirs "zo-zo sauce."

A substantial market emerged in the 21st century for the pepper as an ornamental pot plant, on account of its glossy green leaves, compact growth habit, and striking red fruit when ripe. While it has an endangered status as a wild foraged item, it is cultivated in Mexico, the West Indies, and parts of Florida as the Grove pepper. The Mexican garden version is sold as the Pequin pepper and is available dried in many tiendas.

CHRISTMAS LIMA
Bean

US ORIGIN OR MOST PREVALENT IN
Southwestern states

CHARACTERISTICS
Large bean, dark red mottling on cream colored skin, creamy texture, umami and sweet flavor

USDA PLANT HARDINESS ZONES
7a–10b

CLOSE RELATIVE
Large White lima bean

NOTABLE PRODUCER
Rancho Gordo

If there ever was a beauty queen in the bean world, it might be the Christmas lima bean. The jaunty red mottling on the cream-colored skin of the large bean stands out from the crowd and makes it immediately recognizable. Originally hailing from Peru, the Christmas lima bean is a slightly waxy pole bean with a rich nutty flavor and starchy sweetness. Also known as the Large Speckled lima, it emerged as a national variety in 1860 when it was advertised as "New Speckled Lima Beans," described by the *Hartford Daily* as "earlier and more productive than the White Lima and sure to ripen—very desirable." It is sometimes called the Chestnut lima on account of its taste, and seed marketers began calling the variety the Christmas lima bean in 1937.

Though 1860 is the year that Red Speckled lima beans entered national consciousness in the United States, they certainly existed before this date. The April 1849 issue of *Working Farmer Monthly*, published in New York, mentions them in a survey of lima beans. There was a great deal of horticultural importation that occurred in the

WHITE Lima BEANS

A bean that would have fit the white food fashion of the 1880s is the buttery-tasting Henderson Bush lima bean, another entry in the Ark of Taste. Thought to have been found along a Virginia roadside in the 1880s and popularized by Peter Henderson Seed Company, this hardy variety has 3 to 4 small, creamy, white beans per pod. The dwarf bush was also one of the first beans that didn't need to be supported by poles, making it popular with gardeners.

antebellum period, and a number of similarly mottled landrace Brazilian beans came from Bahia in Brazil. Thus, it is entirely reasonable to surmise that the Speckled lima beans that arrived in the US from Peru in the 1840s and burst onto the national market in 1860 developed in regions surrounding Peru and are connected to the Brazilian landraces grown on the eastern side of the Andes Mountains.

A classic pole bean, the Christmas lima variety tolerates heat, humidity, and even drought. It sets thick pods containing 3 to 5 beans that can each reach the size of a quarter when mature, which takes about 84 days. In his 1896 book *The Pole Lima Bean,* author Liberty Hyde Bailey described the variety as "An early form of Lima, with handsome, medium-sized flat beans, which are speckled and blotched with very dark red-brown. Pods rather long and slender, tipped, containing three or four beans. A tall grower, ripening about all its crop before frost. A good bean, but the color is objectionable to most persons."

The 1890s were the height of a white food fashion in the US, when White Velvet okra, white cucumber, blanched celery, white asparagus, and white field peas reigned in the consumer preferences and kitchens of some American households. There were popular biases based on associations between white and purity. Bailey noted the disinclination of the public toward colored lima beans, but he performed sensory testing with groups of people judging the flavor and mouthfeel of lima beans. There was no objection to the taste of the colored lima. Food aesthetics shifted in the 20th century, when red and black

It has a complex earthy note as a base flavor and a soft finish. Its combination of umami and sweet notes inspired the comparison with chestnuts.

varieties entered the culinary mainstream with fervor. The Christmas lima bean was taken up as a popular variety in that shift and has been enjoying increasing sales as a dried bean and garden seed for the past 40 years.

Beside the visual appeal of the jauntily decorated beans, the Christmas lima offers a markedly different flavor than other lima beans, worthy of culinary attention. First, it has a sumptuous creamy texture when cooked, a characteristic it shares with its sibling, the Large White lima bean. But the Large White lima can taste undesirably vegetal or feel chalky, depending upon the soil in which it was grown. The Christmas lima bean never takes on either of those features. Instead, it has a complex earthy note as a base flavor and a soft finish. Its combination of umami and sweet notes inspired the comparison with chestnuts. Like chestnuts, the variety lends itself well to being pureed and made into soups or dips.

In the United States, Southwestern cooks have incorporated it into a battery of traditional and regional bean dishes, including chili. The Christmas lima bean arrived in Italy in the mid-19th century and incited the creation of several notable dishes. The first is a fresh but hearty salad of Christmas lima beans, orange segments, and walnuts, drizzled with olive oil and seasoned. A simple soup of farro, Christmas lima beans, and winter squash also took hold, along with another soup of Christmas lima beans, barley, and porcini mushrooms. An even simpler preparation of caramelized onions and Christmas lima beans became popular as a side dish. Christmas lima bean salads often rank foremost in popular appeal as they showcase that unique color and mottling of the ever-stylish bean.

FOUR CORNERS GOLD
Bean

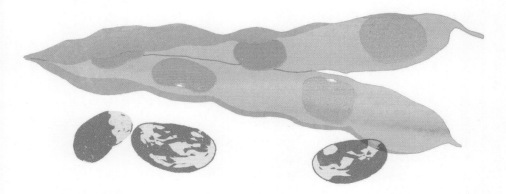

US ORIGIN OR MOST PREVALENT IN
Southwest

CHARACTERISTICS
White base with orange-yellow mottling, pine nut flavor, creamy texture

USDA PLANT HARDINESS ZONES
5–8

CLOSE RELATIVE
Jacob's Cattle bean

NOTABLE PRODUCER
High Desert Seed and Garden

A Zuni landrace bean, the Gold bean is an orange-yellow mottled form of Jacob's Cattle bean (an ancient variety also on the Ark of Taste). The variety now goes by several common names: Four Corners Gold bean, Zuni Gold bean, Prairie Appaloosa bean, Raquel bean. The Zuni people called it Shalako and associated the bean with the winter solstice ritual dances that took place during harvest times. The Shalakos are the giant couriers of the rainmakers that dance in the welcome houses as part of a rite to ensure rain in the coming seasons and bestow beans to the Zuni. The Gold bean's features match those of many Southwestern landraces: it is a bush bean with high drought tolerance and an 85- to 100-day maturation period. What distinguishes it from other beans native to the region is a pine nut flavor and a creamy texture that have inspired the admiration of Sante Fe chefs.

The Four Corners Gold bean has mottling reminiscent of the coats of some breeds of cattle. The base color of the bean is white, with orange-yellow splotching overlaid, and the coloring survives boiling or baking. The dried beans may be reconstituted with water and cooked, and they are commonly incorporated into chili or stew. Those who grow the bean praise its quality both as a green bean (the pods picked at 50 days) and as a fresh shelly bean (picked at 65 days). It is commonly planted in rows spaced 3 feet apart, with seeds planted at 6-inch intervals. Its bush habit requires no support, and the plants grow into one another in the rows. There is a tendency of this variety to twine, or send up runners to climb whatever is near and may be climbed, but it is for the most part a bush bean. The plant sets many white blossoms that generate a plenitude of pods, each pod from 4 to 5 inches in length and housing 4 to 6 beans. The bean averages ¼ inch wide and ⅜ inch long.

What distinguishes it from other beans native to the region is a pine nut flavor and a creamy texture that have inspired the admiration of Sante Fe chefs.

The Four Corners Gold bean was likely a natural cross between the kidney-shaped mottled Jacob's Cattle bean and the Paint bean. The A. P. Whaley Seed Company performed and stabilized the same cross in recent years, selling it under the name Jacob's Cattle Gold shelling bean. Though the Whaley cultivar has not undergone the generations of adaptive breeding and seed saving of the Zuni-nurtured Four Corners Gold, both its flavor and its texture are not far off from the original landrace variety. The preservation and promotion of the bean was an early project of Native Seeds/SEARCH, a nonprofit preservation hub of the Southwest, and it has become one of the better known native landraces employed in traditional Southwestern cooking in the past 20 years.

GUAJILLO
Honey

US ORIGIN OR
MOST PREVALENT IN
Texas

CHARACTERISTICS
*Clear sweetness,
classic honey flavor*

USDA PLANT
HARDINESS ZONES
5b–7a

CLOSE RELATIVE
Catclaw honey

NOTABLE PRODUCERS
*Uvalde Honey
Distributors, Capital
Bee Company Guajillo,
Gretchen Bee Ranch,
Grampa's Honey,
Tejas Honey*

The finest American single-host honey varieties encompass a broad range of flavors, from the acidity of Appalachian Sourwood honey, to the creamy minerality of Hawaiian White Kiawe honey, to the rich citrus, rose, and clove of Tupelo honey. Texas Guajillo honey constitutes something of the golden mean of American honey—simple, elegant, clean, and direct in its sweetness. Some taste a note of lavender or a whisper of chocolate, but most experience its simple and sunny sweetness.

Guajillo is a wild shrub that flourishes on the sandy soils and low ridges in southwestern Texas and northern Mexico, with a related plant called catclaw. Catclaw is a rougher and rarer form of acacia and, with some rainfall in fortunate years, supplies a honey even rarer than Guajillo—Catclaw honey. Guajillo and catclaw blossom at the same time, so in the early years of beekeeping in Texas's Uvalde Valley, the nectar from both plants contributed greatly to early productions of honey in that

Texas Guajillo honey constitutes something of the golden mean of American honey—simple, elegant, clean, and direct in its sweetness. Some taste a note of lavender or a whisper of chocolate, but most experience its simple and sunny sweetness.

first center of beekeeping in the state. Mature Guajillo ranges from 3 to 15 feet in height, depending on soil fertility. It has pin-like leaves that are paired on the stem, like its other mimosa relatives. The globular white flowers bloom from March 15 to May 15 and are much sought-after by bees. Guajillo has adapted well to a dry landscape and requires little rain. It has become a favorite plant of landscapers constructing drought-tolerant gardens.

When Uvalde County was organized in the 1870s, its settlers discovered that honeybees had made the region their home. The oral history of Uvalde features fantastic tales of bee caves gilded with honeycombs and wolf trees housing mammoth bee colonies. Initially, the impulse of farmers was to tame the bees to pollinate their cantaloupe and cucumber fields. But when they tasted the Guajillo honey in the caves and trees, they realized that they had a product that could generate a market much more profitable than any melon field. Several large ranchers organized a network of apiaries with the cooperation of the Southern Pacific Railroad. D. M. Edwards began shipping bulk comb honey from Uvalde in the summer of 1883. In 1903, Uvalde beekeeper J. K. Hill reported to Texas governor S. W. T. Lanham that there were approximately 14,000 colonies of bees in the county, each worth about $500. He estimated that these colonies produced 1,164,000 pounds of honey.

A honey savant described Guajillo honey in the September 1922 issue of the *American Bee Journal*: "The honey is of the finest quality, being very light amber to water white. In fact, some specimens are a milky white and somewhat resemble fireweed honey, making guajillcomb honey ideal for bulk comb packing. It is much sought after by people liking mild honey. As might be expected, this honey granulates very quickly." Bulk comb packing refers to the practice of quickly chopping the honey combs from hives and setting them into shipping containers—

a much simpler and cheaper way of processing honey than extracting and clarifying it for sale in clear containers. Guajillo honey won awards at the World's Columbian Exposition in Chicago in 1893 and the Paris Exposition of 1900. Two key factors influenced these judgments: its simplicity and clarity of flavor was deemed unobjectionable while many more exotic and complexly flavored honeys raised objections from assessors, and Guajillo's origin in a desert country recalled images of ancient Palestine, "the land of milk and honey," giving the Texas sweet a decided mystique.

The heyday of Guajillo honey production in Texas occurred during the first decades of the 20th century. Curiously, the honey was not referred to as Guajillo honey at the time, but instead called Uvalde or Texas honey. While American markets for mono-floral honeys had been established in the 1880s with Orange Blossom honey and Tupelo honey, Guajillo perhaps tasted too much like people's default sense of what honey should taste like to warrant a source identifier. What probably prompted the floral identification was the growing claim that Mesquite honey was "Texas honey" in the mid-20th century. The beekeepers of Uvalde had too great a pride in the history of the Guajillo honey enterprise to let that pass. So in the 1950s and onward, Guajillo or Haujillo honey appeared labeled as such.

Guajillo honey is still produced in Southwest Texas. Most producers use cold centrifuge extraction of the honey from the comb. The descriptors *wild* and/or *native* appear on many labels to indicate that the bees obtained the nectar from uncultivated Guajillo plants and not from apiaries next to acacia plantations. Such wild honey may include Catclaw with the Guajillo. It appears in the market in a range of forms, from clear light yellow to milky white, but it is never dark in color. Guajillo honey is rarely sold in the comb. It is still a beloved and quintessential culinary treasure of the region.

MOON AND STARS
Watermelon

The Moon and Stars watermelon carries with it exciting and contradicting origin stories that tell of Russian, Amish, and Cherokee provenance. The yellow-mottled, green-skinned melon stands out among its fellow watermelons, and its fanciful appearance has inspired the imaginations of growers. But the Moon and Stars watermelon emerged from the breeding endeavors of one of the most prolific centers of melon development in the United States in the early 20th century: Colorado. It's likely a cross between a large, green-skinned picnic melon and a round, yellowish, thin-skinned melon. That said, the patterning from which it gets its name remains a mysterious happenstance.

In the early 20th century, there were more watermelon varieties grown in the Arkansas Valley of Colorado than in any other place in the United States. Rocky Ford, Colorado, has been a hotbed of melon breeding and growing in the United States

since the 1880s. Delavan V. Burrell of Rocky Ford, a breeder of cucurbits—cantaloupes, watermelons, and cucumbers—listed 28 different varieties of watermelon
seed in his 1915 *D. V. Burrell Seed Catalog.* The small town came to national fame
for the Rocky Ford cantaloupe—the model melon of the commercial market in the
first half of the 20th century. Though Rocky Ford is still known for its cantaloupes,
the Moon and Stars watermelon was also a product of the area. Initially it
enjoyed a strong market as a novelty melon, but it declined in public favor
during the middle of the 20th century. After its rediscovery in the late 1970s, it
would become the most recognized and popular heirloom watermelon of the
late 20th and early 21st centuries.

A farmer in Rocky Ford found the yellow-mottled green melon in his field. Rather than hand it over to one of the five biggest melon seed producers in Rocky Ford, he submitted the seed to the Peter Henderson Seed Company in New York to secure its cash bounty paid for new and unusual vegetables. The truly new and unusual variety appeared in Henderson's 1924 *Everything for the Garden* catalog under the name "Sun, Moon and Stars Watermelon." Henderson described it as "something new under the sun. The circles and stars imprinted on its rind are certainly an extraordinary variation from the usual type, and they have persisted for so long a period as to really make Sun, Moon and Stars a new variety. . . . The rind is very thin, medium green in color with an obscure dark stripe, and conspicuously marked with cream-colored circles and star-shaped spots, both large and small." The original Sun, Moon and Stars watermelon had red flesh and brown seeds, and it ripened in 88 days. The foliage shared the mottling of the watermelon's rind (a trait found in some other cucurbits, such as the Dutch Fork pumpkin).

The yellow-mottled, green-skinned melon stands out among its fellow watermelons, and its fanciful appearance has inspired the imaginations of growers.

The visual novelty had been sufficient to keep the unique melon on farms
and in gardens for a few decades but did not suffice to sustain the watermelon's
marketability over time. The Rocky Mountain Seed Company's *Perfegro Catalog*
of 1942 was the last American catalog to offer the melon, labeling it a novelty
melon and including the uninspiring description that "the edible qualities are
about average." By midcentury, the major watermelon seed growers and farmers
of Colorado's Arkansas Valley (A. W. Creager of Ebert Seeds, R. H. James, and

Delavan V. Burrell) grew Kleckley Sweet watermelons as their primary crop and were intensely concerned with its improvement. That dark green picnic melon had become the industry standard for size, sweetness, and seediness.

The Sun, Moon and Stars watermelon variety survived solely by the seed-saving habits of individual farmers. When the Seed Savers Exchange organized in 1975, it drew up a list of lost vegetable varieties they wished to find. One of the original founders, Kent Whaley, took up the melon's cause. A 1977 television interview triggered a letter from gardener Merle Van Doren, who indicated he grew the "Moon and Stars." His seed provided the foundation for the revival of the variety, and other strains soon surfaced. Thanks to these efforts, yellow-fleshed and red-fleshed versions of the revived Moon and Stars watermelon are once again available as seed.

The melons range from 20 to 50 pounds, depending on the growing conditions. Like the Kleckley and Alabama Sweet watermelons, they have a thick rind ideal for pickling. While somewhat vulnerable to viral diseases, the Moon and Stars has enough genetic variety to adapt to local conditions, and if one is careful in selecting seed, 3 to 4 years of planting should provide a productive and healthy field of watermelons.

ROCKY FORD MELONS

How did a small town in southeastern Colorado become world famous for melon growing? Farmers there credit the weather, which during the growing season has sunny, hot days and cool, crisp nights. This range in temperatures helps the melons develop natural sugars. The Arkansas River Valley clay soil also has the nutrients to make the plants thrive.

MOON AND STARS
Watermelon
AND PICKLED RED ANAHEIM
PEPPER
SALAD

ELIZABETH BINDER, *chef and owner*
HAND-CRAFTED CATERING, CALIFORNIA

*Moon and Stars watermelon's sweetness and brilliant red flesh
pair wonderfully with the cool cucumber, spicy peppers,
peppery watercress, and acidic sour notes from the pickle dressing.
If you leave Anaheim peppers on the vine, they will turn red,
resulting in a mildly spicy pepper with smoky, sweet, and tangy notes.
Lemon cucumbers work well with this dish thanks to their mellow flavor.*

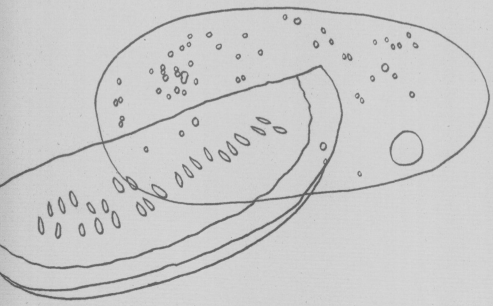

**FOR THE PICKLED
RED ANAHEIM PEPPERS**

**8 Red Anaheim peppers, seeds
removed and sliced into rings**

½ red onion, julienned

**1 red jalapeño pepper, seeds removed
and julienned**

2 cups (470 ml) red wine vinegar

2 cups (470 ml) champagne vinegar

½ cup (100 g) sugar

1 tablespoon black peppercorns

1 tablespoon coriander seeds

FOR THE DISH

**¼ cup (60 ml) of the pickling juice
from the pickled Red Anaheim peppers**

¼ cup (60 ml) extra-virgin olive oil

Kosher salt

**2 cups (180 g) pickled Red Anaheim
peppers, drained and halved or
quartered**

**1 small Moon and Stars watermelon,
peeled and cut into ½-inch (1-cm)
pieces, about 4 cups (610 g)**

**1 medium Garden cucumber or
3 medium Lemon cucumbers, peeled,
seeded, and cut into ½-inch (1-cm)
pieces**

**2 bunches watercress, washed and
stems trimmed**

**MAKE THE PICKLED
RED ANAHEIM PEPPERS**

Place sliced Red Anaheim peppers, red
onion, and jalapeño in a large mixing
bowl. Bring the vinegars, sugar, and
spices to a boil over high heat in a
heavy-bottomed saucepan and simmer
for 2 minutes. Strain the hot pickling
liquid over the sliced vegetables. Allow
to pickle for 30 minutes before using.

ASSEMBLE THE DISH

In a small bowl, whisk together the
reserved pickling juice and olive oil.
Season with salt. Place the remaining
ingredients in a large bowl and lightly
coat them with the olive oil dressing.
Adjust the seasoning, if desired,
and serve.

*Elizabeth Binder is chef and owner of
Hand-Crafted Catering in Napa, California.*

NAVAJO CHURRO

US ORIGIN OR MOST PREVALENT IN
New Mexico

CHARACTERISTICS
Hardiness, used for Navajo weaving and textiles

CLOSE RELATIVE
Churra sheep

NOTABLE PRODUCERS
Herders can be found at Slow Food Navajo Churro Presidium

In 1598, Spanish colonists occupied the lands of the Pueblo People north of Mexico, bringing with them a herd of European sheep called Churra. Records of the expedition claim they had 2,900 sheep in tow. The breed that would come to be known as the Navajo Churro sheep was a creature of such utility that the Navajo regarded it a divine benefaction from the Holy Beings. Ray Kady, who raises the sheep, describes their role in the creation process: "The Diyin Dine'é (Holy Beings) had animals from the beginning of time. When they arranged the world and planned the pattern of the stars in the sky, they first laid the glittering objects out on a sheepskin. The Sun Deity, father of the war gods, possessed a flock of sheep in six colors; his favorite was the Táá Dibéi sheep with thin-bladed four horns, faces made from white dawn/fog, bodies made from clouds, with straight willow sticks gathered for their legs, rainbows used to form their hooves/horns, sheep tobacco placed in their head for ears, and rock crystals also placed in their head to see. A beautiful sheep song was then recited, thus the domesticated sheep came to life, and were given to the Diné people at a later time to care for and in turn care for them."

The sheep adapted to the environment of the American Southwest as the Diné people shaped the breed to become livestock for mutton and fiber for weaving, both of which became major economic assets. As a pillar of the Diné diet, and the heart and soul of their weaving, the Churro sheep became a fixture of Diné life as central as corn.

The Navajo Churro sheep did not set fat, instead becoming narrow bodied and long legged, the better to handle the variable and rough terrain of the region. They bore thick coats of coarse, uncrimped wool with an inner and outer coat that loosely draped the animal's flanks. Rams sometimes developed four or six horns. The fiber is quite strong and not too waxy—ideal for rugs, blankets, and clothes, particularly outer garments. In 1934, agricultural reporter John Howell observed, "[The Navajo] sheep are many-colored, black, grey, bluish, tan, brown, and white. Thus the Navajo has a source for different colored wools from which the famous Navajo blankets are made. These rugs are made of undyed materials." In the 1920s, in order to add reds and yellows to the already broad range, an experiment was made interbreeding Karakul sheep with the Churros. It was the one effort at hybridization that the Diné supported among the multitude of attempts made during the mid-19th century, most intended to improve the breed by introducing breeding rams of larger varieties like the Merino, Rambouillet, and Suffolk.

However, some Churros remained in the remote Hispanic villages, among the isolated Navajos and on the West Coast. These isolated flocks eventually formed the landrace sheep, the Navajo Churro, named to recognize Spanish and Navajo influence. Because the Navajos resisted the settlers who were encroaching on Diné homelands, the US government ordered military actions led by Kit Carson and James Carlton with instructions to destroy Navajo orchards and flocks. There was much bloodshed, and in 1865 approximately 9,000 Navajos were forced on the Long Walk of 300 miles to an internment camp at Bosque Redondo, New Mexico. Terrible conditions there caused the death of many people and their livestock. Some Navajos escaped capture and hid with their sheep in remote canyons of New Mexico and Arizona. After three years, the Navajo were returned to their homeland and were issued two "native" sheep per person from Hispanic flocks.

They became skilled as shepherds and as sheep breeders, yet their aptitude for supporting and increasing the population of this important source of food and fiber eventually became the target of conflicting policies and actions by the USDA and the Bureau of Land Management. In 1930, when the Navajo herd swelled to around 575,000 sheep, the government enforced a cull. There is great disagreement around the number of sheep on the land at the time—the number just quoted comes from the Navajo-Churro Sheep Association website, while contemporary newspapers claimed 1.5 million sheep ranged the region. The droughts of the Dust Bowl era were stressing vegetation, and it was said that the grazing of the sheep exacerbated the problem.

US agents forcibly culled 30 percent of each household's sheep. The Diné greatly resented the significant contraction of their sheep herd, and their distrust of government initiatives grew over the coming decades when agronomists' efforts to improve the herd by crossing them with other varieties led to hybrids that could not thrive in and around New Mexico. "By 1977, the 'old type' Navajo sheep had dwindled to less than 500 head," according to the Navajo-Churro Sheep Association. "A number of motivated individuals along with the Navajo Sheep Project began work to revitalize and save the breed from further depletion. The breed association and registry was formed in 1986."

These "old type" Navajo Churro sheep were found in isolated settlements on the Navajo Reservation of northern New Mexico. Breeders sought to restrict the line to the traits of the old Churro strain and worked with the Southwestern Range and Sheep Breeding Laboratory at Fort Wingate, New Mexico, which supplied the genetic expertise to evaluate the phenotypes. It was the weaving community, not the culinary community, that drove the demand for the return of the classic Navajo Churro sheep. Interest in the restoration project has grown in the past two decades, and the Heritage Livestock Conservancy now regards the Churro sheep to be threatened, replacing its critically endangered status, set in 1980. Many ranchers who are not of the Diné people have secured Churro sheep for their livestock operations. The Slow Food Presidium was organized to benefit the Navajo herders and weavers who depend upon the Navajo Churro sheep for their livelihood. It promotes awareness among restaurateurs about Navajo Churro mutton and celebrates the artistry of traditional Navajo weaving using the natural fibers spun from Churro wool. Eleven Indigenous herders are listed in the Presidium and are a point of hope for the continuation of a breed so important to the Navajo and Diné people.

ROY KADY:
IN THE FOUR CORNERS, SHEEP IS LIFE

Arizona

Navajo Churro sheep are a continuum in Roy Kady's 57 years on Earth, a sacred lifeway he learned from his mother, perhaps his greatest teacher. Roy raises 100 head of Navajo Churro sheep in the Four Corners area of Arizona—the heartland of the Navajo Nation and the place he was raised. He is the president of the Slow Food Navajo Churro Presidium, a collective that works to support the preservation of the breed and the Navajo people who wish to raise them. Roy is the last person in his own community who is raising Churros, as many of his community members have begun raising meatier and more sought-after breeds, like Merinos, "but they eat more than Churros!"

Roy explains that this breed carries a unique spiritual and cultural significance for the Navajo, or Diné, people, saying, "Sheep is life, they're where everything comes into play. . . . Everything about sheep teaches you, because it is a life-giver and a life-taker. It teaches you fatherhood or motherhood, teaches you life in general, from birth to adulthood." The sheep's role in sacred life is closely aligned to its role on the land. "They also care and maintain the land for us so it doesn't just blow or wash away. Being the shepherd and rotating the grazing area, you're a part of that process—[it] definitely helps

you to reconnect and reground yourself." Having been raised with a perspective that centered on land and sheep, Roy embodies those teachings in his own life now and continues to pass on those central values that he learned from his mother, his uncles, and his grandparents.

The Navajo Churro sheep is a story of survival, not just for the sheep but also for its people. The unique species was adopted by the Native people of the Southwest and was once thought to be extinct. But thanks to the resilience and stewardship of the Navajo people who survived the Long Walk with their sheep, along with support and dedication of research and scientific communities, the breed has been revived and is now classified as rare. Though the numbers may never be what they once were, there are many Navajo people like Roy who have made great effort to return the Navajo Churro sheep to their land so that it may remain a centerpiece of Navajo community, spirituality, and cultural life today.

The Slow Food Navajo Churro Presidium, founded in the early 2000s by Roy alongside Gary Nabhan and Gay Chanler, is committed to restoring not just the species but also the traditional methods with which their ancestors stewarded the animals. This loose collective of Navajo sheepherders doesn't register their animals, but the group has been vital to enabling growers to identify their sheep and get products to the local market.

The protocols of the Presidium are in keeping with traditional methods for raising the animals. The sheep graze on open pasture about 80 percent of the time, which makes the meat uniquely tender and flavorful. When it comes to the meat, the Presidium concentrates more on quality than quantity, so the meat stays close to home where the growers can connect with and educate chefs and eaters. While there isn't enough inventory for the meat to be distributed on any large scale, it is readily shared with the Hispanic community in the area, who also play a central role in the sheep's history.

For this reason and more, Roy is proud to raise Navajo Churro sheep in the way his mother and culture taught him, and he is prouder still to enable members of his Navajo community to do the same. The Navajo Churro is as much a foodway as a lifeway for the Navajo people, a testament to the widespread sentiment of Indigenous people in the Southwest: "Sheep is life."

RIO ZAPE
Bean

This black-streaked purple pinto bean may be the most complex and sumptuous of the landrace legumes stewarded by Indigenous growers and taken up by Anglo-American farmers. It became known as the Hopi Purple string bean by settlers in the Southwest before the turn of the 20th century, and the original form of the bean has been stable for centuries. In the late 1950s, archaeologists found three varieties of beans among the excavated ancient plant materials of the Indigenous cave dwellings along the Rio Zape River in Mexico, called La Cueva de Los Muertos Chiquitos—a lima bean, the reddish kidney bean, and a pinto bean. Horticulturists recognized the last of these as a traditional bean of the Zuni collected in 1935.

By the 1970s, many believed that this landrace bean shared by the Zuni and the Hopi, and adopted by a network of Anglo-American farmers, had been revived from the desiccated beans found in the cave—beans dormant since 650 CE that had sprung phoenix-like back into glory upon watering. Those who embraced the story started calling the variety the Rio Zape bean instead of the Hopi Purple string bean. The legend of the resuscitation of the buried bean is one of the most deeply held fantasies among amateur bean enthusiasts; thus the story reinvents itself periodically around different bean varieties.

The Rio Zape bean should be celebrated for being of such great antiquity and developed to such culinary and agronomic excellence that it survived virtually unchanged for well over a millennium and entered into the growing systems of three different cultures resident in the Southwest. Anyone who has tasted the bean can attest to both its distinctiveness and its excellence. Steve Sando, founder of Rancho Gordo beans, a widely respected source for heirloom beans for cooking, says that it was the quality of the Rio Zape bean that inspired him to build a business around preserving and popularizing the greatest heirloom beans of the Americas. Sando writes, "This is the bean that started the whole thing! I was eating a bowl of simply cooked Rio Zapes and I was just bowled over. The flavor was reminiscent of pintos but there was so much more going on. I could detect traces of coffee and chocolate and the velvety texture was like nothing else. I was sold on heirloom varieties after just one bite."

The Rio Zape bean has a creamy texture when boiled or baked and a deep umami, as well as rich flavors possessed by no other bean in the kidney/pinto bean family. On account of its dynamic flavor, Sando recommends it as a "pot bean," one that you cook as simply as possible to serve as a side dish with nothing more than salt, pepper, lemon juice, and maybe chopped onion. Gabe Bullard staged a tasting of heirloom beans for *National Geographic* in 2016. He noted that the Rio Zapes were meatier than the commodity beans he normally used, and lent themselves well to being used as a substitute for meat in chili. The flavor imparts itself to liquid readily, so the broth in which Rio Zape beans are cooked has a range of uses in cooking, and mashed bean gravy is an astonishingly rich condiment. If you aspire to serving a next-level bean dip at a party, look no further than the Rio Zape with its intrinsically robust flavor.

The Rio Zape bean's expanding scale of cultivation has prompted plant breeders to cross the heirloom with the mosaic-resistant Matterhorn Great Northern bean to create a cultivar that will better withstand mass planting. Rancho Gordo will continue to grow the heirloom version. The efforts of Steve Sando, the Rio Zape's inclusion in the Ark of Taste, and a number of chefs and food bloggers have popularized the Rio Zape bean since 2013. It is one of the recent and great success stories of the Ark of Taste.

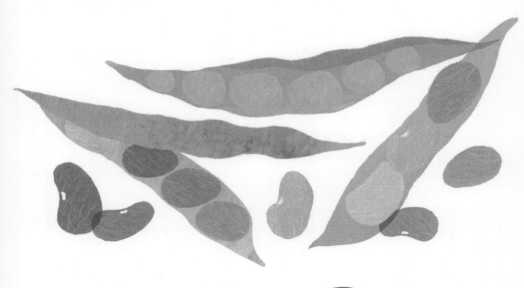

TEPARY Bean

Tepary beans are essential ingredients in the culinary and ecological landscape of the Sonoran Desert. Archaeological records have revealed that Tepary beans were cultivated as human food 5,000 years ago in Tehuacán, Mexico. They have long been grown by Indigenous people in parts of northern Mexico and Arizona. For the Pima and other Indigenous people of the region, the diverse family of Southwestern beans were and are a reliable source of protein that survive heat and drought with unparalleled resilience among legumes. Native Seeds/SEARCH maintains seed for 10 distinct strains of Tepary beans, including four wild landraces collected at Rock Corral Canyon, San Pedro, Santa Catalina, and Sycamore Canyon.

The Tepary bean thrives in the desert because it does not require irrigation in order to survive. Varieties such as Cabora-Ajo and Moctezuma will generate anywhere from 450 to 700 pounds of beans per acre on minimal rainfall. With irrigation, depending on the quality of the soil, an acre can produce anywhere from 800 to 1,500 pounds of beans. Tepary bean plants are also grown and dried for fodder for animals, with an acre producing anywhere from 5,000 to 9,500 pounds of bean hay.

Because Tepary beans are so suited to prosper in rather difficult growing conditions, they were among the first foods the Tohono O'odham successfully reintroduced into cultivation 20 years ago in an effort to move away from the obesity- and diabetes-inducing Western diet. The Tohono O'odham Community Action group sponsored the replanting of the beans as a public health initiative but also, and importantly, as a means of rebuilding Tohono identity. The beans became a vehicle for reeducating Tohono youth in their ancestral stories, including how the white Moctezuma Tepary became mythologized in the story of a hasty coyote running with a bag of beans, tripping, and scattering the contents into the sky to form the Milky Way.

These native legumes possess a level of protein equal to that of most commodity beans in cultivation in the world, yet possess heat resistance and drought tolerance superior to nearly every other landrace bean. This observation, made prior to the general awareness of the speed and virulence of global warming, has taken on even greater trenchancy. Tepary bean seed has been shipped to Senegal and Mali for trials and cultivation, yet it must be said that native African field peas already supply a drought-tolerant, tasty pulse for local consumption. South Asia might be the more appropriate region for experimental plantings. In the American Southwest, Tepary beans have traditionally been grown as a solitary crop, but some Indigenous cultures did intercrop the beans with maize and capsicum peppers.

One challenge of Tepary beans as a garden vegetable is that the pods ripen at different times on the same plant, and ripe pods will shatter and disperse their seed if left unpicked. Traditionally, the beans are harvested by hand as soon as they change color—about 11 to 12 weeks after planting. Harvesting practices differ; some growers uproot the entire plant when the first pod ripens, dry it out, and whack it with sticks to loosen the beans, while others do daily checks of the plants and pick pods when they ripen. The former method is preferred among those growing large quantities of plants in order to sell the dried beans, which store well. Farmers in Arizona claim that the plant is practically disease-free when grown in its dry home environment. Growing Tepary beans in a hot, humid region can lead to the plants falling victim to mosaic virus, white mold, or halo blight.

While Tepary beans can be picked young as a green bean, or picked fresh and steamed as a shelly bean, the most popular mode of preparing the beans is to let them dry and reconstitute them later by soaking them in water and either boiling or baking the beans with a fat and seasoning. The flavor is wholesome, substantial, and touched by a bright minerality.

White SONORA Wheat

US ORIGIN OR MOST PREVALENT IN
New Mexico, Arizona

CHARACTERISTICS
*Soft wheat,
pale golden flour*

USDA PLANT HARDINESS ZONES
7a–9a

OTHER NAMES
Kno Wheat, Trigo Flor
(SPANISH)
*Flor de America,
Trigo Mota,
Sonora Blanca, and
Olas Pilcan*
(PIMA)

CLOSE RELATIVE
Spanish White Lammas

NOTABLE PRODUCER
Ramona Farms

White Sonora wheat was among the first strains of wheat to be planted in North America and the key ingredient in the now ubiquitous and beloved flour tortilla. The variety originates from a landrace European soft wheat brought to Mexico by the Spanish and carried north into the Sonoran Desert by missionary Lorenzo de Cardenas between 1640 and 1650. Cardenas offered the seed to the Eudeve people, who began to propagate the wheat near the rural village of Tuape, Sonora, not far from the present-day US-Mexico border. The wheat was carried throughout the Southwest by the Catholic missionary fathers for use in communion breads. There it began its adaptation to the arid climate of the high desert, which would make it a primary crop wheat of the Southwest for three centuries.

Wheat belongs to a category of tall grasses not native to the Americas, so all wheat in the Western

The traditional foods central to Southwest cookery that are wrapped in or based on the flour tortilla owe their origin to White Sonora wheat.

Hemisphere derives from settler importations. Wheat varieties cultivated in North America in the 1600s were soft, low-gluten varieties that included Red Lammas, White Lammas, and the Mission wheat that was the ancestor of White Sonora wheat. White Sonora wheat was used in the creation of communion bread when it was first introduced to the region, but soon became a staple food for the region's inhabitants. It may have persisted largely as a niche crop if Indigenous people had not made use of the wheat for flour. In seeking a viable crop alternative to maize (sometimes corn crops failed), they leveraged the thriving White Sonora wheat to create the flour tortilla. The traditional foods central to Southwest cookery that are wrapped in or based on the flour tortilla owe their origin to White Sonora wheat.

White Sonora wheat's use as flour to make masa (dough) for tortillas reflects the presence and significance of Mexican culture in the American Southwest. The wheatberry (the entire unprocessed wheat kernel) was also used in traditional dishes such as pinole and posole. Now, the wheatberry is sometimes used to make wheat beer. White Sonora wheat provided an important food source when no other native crops were maturing because it grew over winter for a spring harvest. This off-season harvest led to a doubling of the grain resources of the Sonoran people, which eventually meant the development of a food surplus. In the 19th century, the Pima and the O'odham took the wheat to market and became substantial exporters of the grain, successfully entering the United States commodity markets.

Sonoran wheat is white because it mills to white flour. Mature grains on the stalk are husked in dark reddish glumes, while the berries are chubby and round and can have a pink tinge to the starch. The grains lack awns—the long spikes or beards that some old varieties retain to inhibit insect and bird depredation. The lack of awns makes the chaff (seed husks) easier to separate from the wheat grains. White Sonora wheat grain is resistant to fusarium wilt and the foliage to wheat rust. Because the other landrace soft wheats have vulnerabilities to these pathogens, the White Sonora possesses a distinct agronomic advantage.

By the 1840s, the old European wheat varieties were replaced with spring wheats in Northern states and supplanted by short-season winter wheats like White May, Red May, and Purple Straw in the Southern states. White Sonora wheat persisted through these shifts and has consistently remained in the fields of the Southwestern US since the 1650s—it is the oldest largely unmodified landrace wheat grown in the United States. Purple Straw wheat also remained in the field in substantial quantities throughout the 19th and most of the 20th centuries, alongside White Sonora. However, both of these landraces would be threatened on American grain fields by the development of more productive hybrid varieties. These hybrids, which included Norman Borlaug's Sonora 64 made of White Sonora genetics, were designed for field performance and millability; there was little to no sensory tasting for flavor during the breeding trials. While commodity wheat farmers embraced the new varieties, many people noticed the comparative lack of flavor in the hybrid cultivars. When California and Southwestern chefs and bakers began asking for the old wheat, an effort was made to consolidate the surviving seed stocks to revive White Sonora wheat.

Several circumstances impelled the revival of White Sonora wheat in the 21st century. The rise of American cookery that centered on local ingredients led to the realization that White Sonora wheat was a signature ingredient that anchored an important regional cuisine. The fact that Indigenous, Latin American, and Anglo settler cultures had historically used the product in distinctive ways gave it a unique dimension. At the same time, Southern California began mirroring the efforts of other regions to establish grain hubs—networks of seed suppliers, growers, and millers engaged in concerted efforts to offer alternatives to mass-produced commodity grains—that sought to revive heirloom grains like White Sonora wheat. Native Seeds/SEARCH has been a major catalyst in the effort to make White Sonora wheat a staple grain once again, and other suppliers have joined the effort. Finally, on account of its adaptation to the climate of the Southwest and California, White Sonora wheat has held a peculiar resilience in the face of increasing drought, climate change, and water use restrictions.

WHITE SONORA WHEAT *Tortillas*

NAN KOHLER, *owner and miller*
GRIST & TOLL, CALIFORNIA

White Sonora wheat is considered the original tortilla wheat for communities throughout the Sonoran Desert. This soft white wheat gives tortillas a creamy mouthfeel, a pearly color, and a buttery flavor profile. The tortilla can be eaten on its own with a bit of butter; when used as a vessel for other ingredients, it enhances all other flavors. A food processor is recommended for this recipe due to the very hot water, but you can certainly mix it by hand, whisking the flour and salt together, using your fingers to rub in the olive oil, then drizzling the hot water evenly over the dough and mixing by hand to bring the dough together.

CONTINUED >>

MAKES 12 6- TO 8-INCH (15- TO 20-CM) TORTILLAS

2 cups (240 g) White Sonora wheat flour or other whole wheat flour

½ teaspoon kosher salt

¼ cup (60 ml) extra-virgin olive oil, plus more for brushing the pan, if needed

SPECIAL EQUIPMENT

Pastry brush

Food processor

Tortilla warmer

MAKE THE DOUGH

Bring 1 to 1½ cups (240 to 355 ml) of water (see note) to a boil in a small saucepan. Pour the boiling water into a heatproof liquid measuring cup and set aside.

In a food processor, pulse the flour and salt together until combined. Drizzle in the olive oil while pulsing several times to coat the flour.

With the food processor running, pulse in a scant ¾ cup (177 ml) of the hot water through the feed tube and process until a dough ball forms. The dough should feel very soft.

Turn the dough out onto a work surface and, without adding more flour, knead for about 1 minute. Transfer the dough to a small bowl or leave it on the work surface and cover it well with plastic wrap to prevent it from drying out. Let rest for 1 to 2 hours.

MAKE THE TORTILLAS

Divide the dough into 12 equal pieces and roll each piece into a ball. Keep the finished balls and rolled-out tortillas covered with plastic wrap while rolling and cooking the others.

You can roll each tortilla out on a lightly floured work surface, but we prefer rolling the dough between two pieces of plastic wrap to avoid extra flour being worked into them, and the dough can be rolled thinner this way.

While rolling out the tortillas, preheat a griddle, cast iron pan, or skillet over medium-high heat. If using a well-seasoned pan, there is no need to coat it with oil before cooking the tortillas. Otherwise, brush the surface of the pan with oil. Carefully place a tortilla into the pan and cook until it begins to brown and become mottled, about 15 seconds, then flip and cook the other side. Do not over-cook; the tortillas should stay supple and not be dry and brittle, 15 to 30 seconds per side only. Repeat with the remaining tortillas. Place the cooked tortillas into a tea towel–lined tortilla warmer as you cook the remaining tortillas.

NOTE: Some wheat varieties require more water, depending on location and growing conditions each year, so you may need to add several more tablespoons of water, depending on the specific crop you are using. The important thing is to add enough water that the dough comes together and feels soft and supple—just slightly tacky is okay. If your dough is too wet, add 2 tablespoons of flour at a time until it is soft and pliable but not wet and sticky.

Nan Kohler is the owner and miller of Grist & Toll, an urban flour mill in Pasadena, California.

RIO GRANDE GRAIN: GROWING A LOCAL GRAIN ECONOMY IN NEW MEXICO

New Mexico

White Sonora was first planted in New Mexico in 1599 by the Spanish in Ohkay Owingeh, a Tewa village, just 10 miles away from where Ron Boyd farms today. Ron's voice floats a little when he talks about standing in his fields, mesmerized by the way the wheat moves in a light breeze, the sound it makes brushing up against itself, the way the early light illuminates the golden seed heads. While working a wheat field is undoubtedly less romantic than standing in one, Ron loves growing grain, something he's been doing for a long time.

Ron grew up in a community of farmers east of Pueblo, Colorado, and began his own when he planted some fruit trees on 5 unused acres of his mother-in-law's land in New Mexico in 2000. Without a lot loan to contend with, his farming was not commercial by design. Ron and his wife grew what they wanted—including apples, peaches, and countless varieties of tomatoes—and brought their colorful bounty to market. They took on more of the family land and would eventually come to manage 70 acres of pasture, hay, and seed crops. They began growing grain primarily out of their own interest and because seed production was becoming a bigger part of farming. So when a small band of heritage grain enthusiasts pitched Ron on growing several ancient grain varieties on his land, he enthusiastically complied.

Ron, Alessandra Haines, and Christine Salem, along with several others from the Santa Fe area, met at Grain School, then a project of the Rocky Mountain Seed Alliance and the University of Colorado at Colorado Springs. They have since organized more formally as Rio Grande Grain, which works to "connect growers, millers, commercial and home bakers, and brewers." Christine says they're taking a page out of the Colorado Grain Chain's book in their effort to bring together existing and potential stakeholders of the region's heritage grain. Christine came in as a gardener and seed saver, Alessandra as a bread baker, and Ron as a farmer. The group is motivated to restore the region's grain-growing tradition by bringing heritage grains back to northern New Mexico.

Though it's never been recognized as a particularly commercial agriculture area, New Mexico has an old history of feeding itself and a once-robust grain growing tradition. The state made land available to residents for subsistence farming in the past, and many of those products can still be found at the farmers markets—fruits, vegetables, beans, corn. But Alessandra noticed that "wheat was kind of conspicuously missing." As a baker, the grains that once grew in the landscape she calls home captured her attention, and "it really seemed appropriate to get the grains back up growing here." White Sonora never fully disappeared from the landscape, but the group was particularly interested in bringing it back to northern New Mexico and drumming up enthusiasm for heritage grains with millers, bakers, cooks, consumers, and more farmers.

Whether they're in it for the whispers of their fields of grain, the perfect flour tortilla, or to create a more diverse and flavorful future, they agree that these grains are good for people and good for the environment. "Our genetic diversity has been wrenched away from us as a society . . . by agribusiness conglomerates," says Christine. "We really need to preserve what we can of that diversity and in some ways we can even help increase it through restoring the grains." With the support of farmers and landowners like Ron, the Rio Grande team have worked the fields to trial over 60 varieties of heritage grain before landing on a few favorites that grow well and deliver on flavor and diversity. The varieties they chose were already well adapted to the drought-ridden land and lend themselves to superior baked goods.

Ron's farm has now dedicated more land to a few of the chosen varieties, including White Sonora wheat and Red Turkey wheat. Christine remarks that the White Sonora wheat "feels very rooted to us in terms of being able to connect with the history of that particular grain." The Rio Grande runs along Ron's land, about which he says, "In New Mexico, that's blue gold at its finest." Ron also planted 100 pounds of White Sonora wheat seed at Los Luceros, a state-owned historic farm and ranch, and it has grown exceedingly well there with just two irrigations from the property's acequia (the traditional flood irrigation system that diverts nearby rivers into ditches to water crops). "Sonoran has a history [here], and we're discovering that it succeeds."

The greatest challenge in growing heritage grains in the area is equipment and infrastructure. Farming implements that work for commercial crops on large swaths of land don't work for smaller plots, and grain must go through several steps in processing before it becomes flour for tortillas. The region also has a history of milling—for both flour and corn—and some of the old molinos still stand. But Ron and his fellow grain farmers have slowly begun acquiring the necessary equipment for growing heritage grains, including a relatively tiny combine from China that Christine describes as a three-wheeled motorcycle compared to large, commercial combines. But farmers are getting creative, even sharing equipment where they can. Christine and Alessandra hope that soon they can confidently hand the task off to farmers and get out of the fields, because, as Ron puts it, production is reaching an overwhelming scale for "on-your-knees" farmers.

White Sonora wheat in New Mexico does not stand alone in the current heritage grain revival. Christine notes that they are way behind efforts being made in other parts of the country, but everything they're doing is working—more heritage grain is being planted on farms, local bakers are integrating the grains into their daily offerings, and home gardeners and bakers are seeking out seed and flour. They've found a place among the other national success stories, including Artisan Grain Collaborative in the Northeast, GrowNYC in the five boroughs, Maine Grain Alliance, and the Bread Lab in the Northwest. Growers and millers are enthusiastic about making heritage grains once again thrive on their land. As Ron says, "Grain is the staff of life. It's the beginning of us."

A DATE AKALA (HAWAIIAN RASPBERRY) A
ROUND CHERRY **BLACK REPUBLICAN CHE**
DO **GRAVENSTEIN APPLE** HALALI'I SUGAR
CHELIUM RED GARLIC **JIMMY NARDELLO F**
ONA COFFEE LAUKONA SUGAR CANE LI
LORZ ITALIAN GARLIC MAIKOIKO SUGAR
ARO **MARSHALL STRAWBERRY MISSION O**
IA OYSTER PUA'OLE SUGAR CANE ROCKW
HUBBARD SQUASH SALMONBERRY UA
KALA (HAWAIIAN RASPBERRY) **ALASKAN**
Y **BLACK REPUBLICAN CHERRY DANCY TA**
NSTEIN APPLE HALALI'I SUGAR CANE HU
ED GARLIC **JIMMY NARDELLO FRYING PEP**
E LAUKONA SUGAR CANE LIMU HULUHU
N GARLIC MAIKOIKO SUGAR CANE MAKA
STRAWBERRY **MISSION OLIVE** OHI'A LEHUA
E SUGAR CANE ROCKWELL BEAN SCIO
H SALMONBERRY UAHIAPELE SUGAR CA
RASPBERRY) **ALASKAN BIRCH SYRUP** ALA
LICAN CHERRY **DANCY TANGERINE 'ELE'E**
LALI'I SUGAR CANE HUDSON'S GOLDEN
NARDELLO FRYING PEPPER **KIAWE HONEY**
CANE LIMU HULUHULUWAENA SEAWEE
KO SUGAR CANE MAKAH OZETTE POTAT
MISSION OLIVE OHI'A LEHUA HONEY **OJA**
CANE ROCKWELL BEAN SCIO KOLACE S
NBERRY UAHIAPELE SUGAR CANE ULU
RRY) **ALASKAN BIRCH SYRUP** ALAEA SAL
CHERRY DANCY TANGERINE **'ELE'ELE BAN**
GAR CANE HUDSON'S GOLDEN GEM APPL
FRYING PEPPER **KIAWE HONEY** KIRK-HOW
ULUHULUWAENA SEAWEED LIMU KOHU
MAKAH OZETTE POTATO MANALALILO

ASKAN BIRCH SYRUP ALAEA SALT
RY DANCY TANGERINE 'ELE'ELE BANANA
CANE HUDSON'S GOLDEN GEM A
YING PEPPER KIAWE HONEY KIRK
U HULUHULUWAENA SEAWEED
ANE MAKAH OZETTE POTA
IVE OHI'A LEHUA HONEY OJ
ELL BEAN SCIO KOLACE SPA
APELE SUGAR CANE ULU BREA
RCH SYRUP ALAEA SALT AUNT M
GERINE 'ELE'ELE BANANA FUERT
SON'S GOLDEN GEM APPLE INAM
ER KIAWE HONEY KIRK-HOWE WA
UWAENA SEAWEED LIMU KOHU
OZETTE POTATO MANALAULOA
HONEY OJAI PIXIE TANGERINE OL
OLACE SPANISH ROJA GARLIC SU
NE ULU BREADFRUIT ABBADA DATE
EA SALT AUNT MOLLY'S GROUND
E BANANA FUERTE AVOCADO GRA
EM APPLE INAMONA INCHELIU
KIRK-HOWE WALNUT KONA CO
LIMU KOHU SEAWEED LORZ ITA
MANALAULOA KALO TARO MAR
PIXIE TANGERINE OLYMPIA OYSTER
PANISH ROJA GARLIC SUGAR HUE
READFRUIT ABBADA DATE AKALA
AUNT MOLLY'S GROUND CHERRY BLACK
NA FUERTE AVOCADO GRAVENSTEIN APP
INAMONA INCHELIUM RED GAR JIMI
WALNUT KONA COFFEE LAUKON
EAWEED LORZ ITALIAN GARLIC
O TARO MARSHALL STRAWBERRY

ABBADA
Date

In 1936, rancher Dana Sniff discovered a wild date growing in a dry riverbed near Brawley, California. The plant resembled a Deglet Noor Palm date—the common commercial date popularly enjoyed during the winter holiday season in the US in dishes such as stuffed dates—but its fruit was longer, darker, creamier, and more flavorful. It was less chewy, more creamy, and less malty tasting than the other popular date, the Medjool. Sniff took cuttings of the unusual plant and eventually named the date after his wife and himself, combining Abbey and Dana to get Abbada.

Dates like this one originate in North Africa and the Middle East. So how did Dana Sniff come to find this volunteer sprout in the isolated and dry Imperial Valley of Southern California? Shortly after the turn of the 20th century, the US Department of Agriculture sent plant hunters around the globe in search of fruits, grains, and vegetables that might have commercial potential in the United States. In the early days of that endeavor, a few plant hunters collected dates from the Middle East and shipped them to professional fruit breeders and growers in California and Arizona.

Francis Heiny of Brawley, California, was one such grower, and an ardent lover of figs and dates. In 1911, Heiny planted over 10,000 seeds of Medjool, Deglet Noor, Thoory, and other date varieties in and around Brawley. The plantings were not precisely tracked. Heiny also made intentional crosses of his varieties, while the open pollination of the trees gave rise to natural crosses. It is most likely that a desert storm carried the seed of one such hybrid into the local stream, and that Sniff found a tree sprouted from that drifted seed growing on the dry riverbed on that fateful day.

The Sniffs cultivated plant material in Indio, California, which they mostly sold to a local commercial date grower called Sunnipalms. But by 1960, there were still only two dozen productive Abbada date trees in the United States. It remained a niche variety until the late 1990s, when its beautiful shape, distinctive color, and rich flavor inspired a new enthusiasm among date lovers. More California date groves adopted and planted the Abbada tree, which they continue to grow for the commercial market today.

The increase in popularity of the Abbada date reflects a shift in taste preferences in recent decades toward more brashly sweet, moist, and meaty dates. Before this shift, date consumers preferred the muted, honey-tinged sweetness of the Deglet, Halawi, and Barhi varieties. Today, the Medjool date is dominant in California plantings, culinary contexts, and the commercial market. The Abbada has benefited from that pivot in preference, with its resonant, creamy caramel flavor and a hint of molasses in the finish. The Abbada is more of a confectionary date than a cooking date. Like the Medjool, the Abbada's unembarrassed but smooth sweetness makes it perfect for stuffing or as a simple finale for a great meal.

Dates go through three stages of ripening when harvested—called khalal, rutab, and tamar—before they are deemed cured and shippable. Some varieties, like the Barhi, are occasionally consumed fresh-picked, in what is called the khalal stage. Most dates, including the Abbada, are stored to permit dehydration and concentration of the fruits' sugars. It is dark red when fresh, but cures through the rutab and tamar stages to a lustrous black, often burnished with a silver bloom. When fully cured, the fruit is an average 2 inches in length by ¾ inch wide. The fruit of the Abbada variety can look blistered and wrinkled after curing, but the skin is not too thick to deter someone from eating the fruit out of hand.

In 2016, a patent was issued to Krishna Tawari and Anthony Fortier for the micropropagation of the Abbada date from single cells, a method that would speed up an increase in the number of productive Abbada date trees and potentially push the number of productive Abbada Palms to over 70 in the world. The boarding of the date on the Slow Food Ark of Taste alerted people to the quality of this American-born date variety and helped it win instant converts.

ALASKAN BIRCH Syrup

US ORIGIN OR MOST PREVALENT IN
Alaska

CHARACTERISTICS
Amber color, hint of molasses and soy sauce

CLOSE RELATIVE
Aromatic Black birch syrup

NOTABLE PRODUCER
Kahiltna

Every April, harvesters range the woods of central or southeastern Alaska to tap mature birch trees. Birch syrups have been manufactured not just in Alaska, but also in Russia, the Canadian North, and Northern Europe from antiquity. Traditional uses of birch syrup in the precolonial United States and European cultures was as much medicinal as culinary. Like maple syrup, Alaskan birch syrup is made by evaporating the sap of living Alaskan, Kenai, and Western Paper birch trees until the sugar content rises to over 66 percent of the product. It can have a range of flavors and qualities.

Because much of the natural sugar in birch sap is fructose, which is prone to scorching, rather than the more robust and heat-tolerant sucrose found in maple syrup, the process of reduction is

Most people approaching birch syrup
for the first time expect some version
of the lavish malty sweetness of maple
syrup. Birch inhabits quite another
flavor spectrum—a more austere taste
with hints of molasses and soy.

slow and carried out at temperatures just at or below the boiling point. The ratio of reduction is high, at 100 to 150 gallons of sap to 1 gallon of syrup, depending on the concentration. This rate is twice that of easier-to-process maple syrup. Many varieties of birch grow well in eastern Canada and the United States, so in places where birch trees abounded and maples did not exist, there was little hesitancy in setting up sugar works.

In the early 1900s, timber interests promoted Alaskan birch as a finishing wood in high-end furniture. With public attention focused on birch as an economic engine, Frank Lange of the Anchorage Public Market began demonstrating the manufacture of birch syrup and distributing samples to consumers to generate demand. Lange propelled the development of a birch syrup industry in Alaska by hype. Here is a sample of his promotional writing—notice his referring to himself in third person; hype masters always take care to hype themselves as well as their product: "We are living in a district where nature is more lavish in a food product which is superior to real honest-to-God maple syrup. Mr. Lange informs us that any given amount of birch sap, which runs about the same to the same sized tree as the maple, will yield nearly twice as much syrup of the same consistency." Alas, Lange was incorrect—maple rendered twice as much syrup as birch from the same amount of sap. Because of this fact, the birch syrup industry did not take off around Anchorage over the 20th century, and birch syrup does not hold the same space on American grocery shelves as maple.

Most people approaching birch syrup for the first time expect some version of the lavish malty sweetness of maple syrup. Birch inhabits quite another flavor spectrum—a more austere taste with hints of molasses and soy. There is a sweet center, like caramel, but the overall flavor is much less sweet than that of its counterpart. The color is light amber early in the harvesting season and darker later in the season. Tree variety also plays a part in coloration—the Kenai birch tends to produce darker syrup. The lighter syrup is used primarily to sweeten pancakes and pastries. The darker syrups have a greater range of culinary employments as marinades and glazes, beer sugar, and a component of designer chocolates. Whatever the color, the mouthfeel is smooth and almost plush while the aromatics are woodsy.

The commercial production of Alaskan birch syrup has been local and limited for much of the past century. It has always remained available from individual harvesters. Small-scale local production still exists in towns such as Talkeetna in south-central Alaska. There are excellent artisanal producers such as Daniel Humphrey of Birch Boy Gourmet Birch Syrups. But the scale of production envisioned by Lange a century ago only materialized in the past 20 years, when the local food movement and the benefits of regional signature foods became paramount. The Kahiltna Birchworks has become the center of Alaskan birch syrup production and an emblem of "wild Alaska." Before Kahiltna, the annual production of syrup stood at about 1,500 gallons. Now, production exceeds 3,500 gallons, released yearly and shipped throughout North America.

Producers and local industries are keenly interested in keeping the production of syrup sustainable. *The Alaskan Birch Syrup Producer's Manual* directs that forests with a density of 100 trees per acre of over 8 inches diameter (minimum tapping size) constitute an optimum array. A tapper with 10 acres at their disposal has a profitable stand of trees, and 1 gallon per tap per day for 20 days makes for a good season. In this new age of emergence for birch syrup, local producers have begun exploring new uses for the syrup, like birch vodka, birch water, beer with birch, and birch-infused chocolate.

BLACK REPUBLICAN
Cherry

The Black Republican cherry distinguished the Pacific Northwest as the cradle of sweet cherry production in the United States in the mid-1800s. It bears a name that was then a political slur—to be called a black republican in the 1850s was much like being called a snowflake in the 2010s.

Seth Luelling was a political activist, abolitionist, Quaker, plant breeder, and proud creator of the Black Republican cherry. A native of South Carolina, he had traversed the Oregon Trail in search of prosperity while carrying on his plant breeding work. Luelling was also the founder of the Republican Party in Oregon, when the newly formed party championed the emancipation of slaves and the civil rights of African Americans. Oregon was Democratic and Luelling was condemned by his neighbors for his views, spoken of as a "black republican." Leulling embraced the epithet and then attempted to make those neighbors value the label by giving it to his newest and sweetest agricultural creation.

The cherry upon which he bestowed the name was praised as a masterwork of nature and agricultural innovation, possessing the dark luster and firmness of its Black Tartarian parent along with the smooth sweetness and acidic tang of the Royal Anne. It was the first great fruit bred on the American West Coast in the pioneering nursery started by Seth Luelling's brother, Henderson Luelling, in Milwaukie, Oregon. In 1847, Henderson hauled 700 grafted fruit trees from Iowa to Oregon in wagons converted into soil beds. He transported peaches, pears, prunes, and several types of cherries, including Maheleb, Morello, Royal Anne, Black Tartarian, and May Duke.

Seth took over the nursery in 1854 when Henderson journeyed to California to cultivate fruit trees there. A novice in pomology, the art of fruit growing, Seth learned grafting from his brother, as well as pruning and planting. He read English treatises on fruit breeding and practiced pollinating blossoms in paper bags to control the crossing of varieties in the hopes of getting the best mixture of traits. The Black Republican cherry was the result of one of these crosses, and was created shortly before the outbreak of the Civil War.

No sweet cherry even approached its excellence in flavor in the mid-19th century, and the Black Republican was hailed as "the best of the Bigarreaus (sweet cherries)!" by orchardists. Cherry connoisseurs also praised the cherry

The BING CHERRY

Luelling did not intentionally cross the Black Republican with another of his cherries to form the Bing. It was a chance discovery by Luelling's Manchu Chinese foreman, Ah Bing. Luelling named the variety after Bing to acknowledge his acuity in recognizing the idiosyncrasies of the tree when newly sprouted.

Many of Luelling's cherries were permitted to cross-fertilize so that the cherry seeds could be saved and planted to form rootstock on which to graft Black Republican cherries.

Bing noticed the unique vitality and beautiful configuration of one of these stocks, and transplanted and nurtured it. When Luelling agreed that they had come across something special and began promoting it, the Bing cherry won an instant following. Eventually, it would become the most widely cultivated and beloved American sweet cherry of the 20th century, replacing its forebear, the equally sweet but less meaty Black Republican.

for its meatiness. The Black Republican was prized by home cooks for jams and preserves; it was firm enough to be incorporated into baked goods and sumptuous eaten fresh from the tree.

The cherry's aesthetic appeal—its pleasing shape and beautiful, glossy, deep red color—matched its superior flavor. The cherry is late maturing and grows to a sphere 1 inch in diameter, with a stout stem fixed into a deep, flaring cavity. The thin, purplish-black skin is spangled with barely visible russet spots. The purple-red flesh exudes a rich dark juice, and the small stone is semi-free.

The Black Republican cherry grew large on well-drained and fertile soil with trees about 40 feet apart. Oregon's Willamette Valley, now widely known for grape and wine production, proved to be the choicest of cherry environments, and the Black Republican was planted extensively there. But fruit growers soon found that fruit size would shrink and some trees were simply not productive when Black Republican cherry trees were not grown on optimal land.

Since dependability of production was the primary requisite for cherries for market growers, the variety inspired anxiety outside its ideal environment. Alas, over the course of the 20th century, the acreage devoted to the Black Republican cherry has shrunk to a little under 200 acres, though several nurseries still offer Black Republican saplings for home orchardists, and cherries are available at farm stands and as you-pick fruit in the Willamette Valley and Columbia River Gorge.

Its well-earned rank as the premier sweet cherry variety of the Pacific Northwest and the heart of the sweet cherry market was cut short by its productive and less fickle offspring, the Bing cherry, also bred by Seth Luelling. Unfortunately, history remembers the Bing cherry above Luelling's other groundbreaking plant creations—the Golden prune, the Sweet Alice apple, the Lincoln cherry, and the Royal Anne and Black Republican cherries that established the Pacific Northwest as America's sweet cherry paradise.

DYLAN AND BETH AYRES-McMANUS: LITTLE BEAR HILL'S CHERRY REVIVAL

Oregon

The Columbia River Gorge is a tapestry of mountains, homes, forest, and orchards, all visible from the scenic I-84 highway that runs along the Columbia. The gorge is also the birthplace of the Black Republican cherry, which is being reintroduced to the public by the curious and creative orchardists at Little Bear Hill, a 16-acre cherry orchard in The Dalles. A few years ago, Dylan and Beth Ayres-McManus took over the land to become the third generation of Beth's family to steward the property. And while they respect and honor the efforts of the past generations, they've taken a different approach to caring for the orchard.

Dylan's father-in-law planted Black Republican cherry trees in the 1990s as pollinators to the more marketable Bing and Royal Anne varieties on the orchard. While the cherry experienced a window of popularity in the 1960s and 1970s, the variety doesn't quite fit today's market demand for large, firm fruit that can survive long journeys. The trees yield a great number of fruit and thus a great number of flowers, so it's chiefly kept as a pollinator in the region.

As a visual artist as well as a farmer, Dylan was curious to try the beautiful fruits one sunny day. What he discovered was a taste he describes as entirely unique from other cherries, a complex flavor with earthy sweetness, so Dylan and Beth set out to bring this cherry to market customers in the Gorge. They began with offering them as a snack to exploratory eaters at farmers markets. Many people unfamiliar with the variety shared their affinity for its unique flavor. Dylan also found that an older generation, who grew up with the variety from its heyday in the 1970s, delighted in rediscovering it.

Dylan and Beth began exploring value-added products for the Black Republican cherry to retain its sweetness and complexity in processing. Applying their artists' creativity to the fruit, they turned it into dried cherries, salted cherries, and tart cherry juice. Little Bear Hill now offers their Black Republican cherry products to enthusiastic eaters, which has led to partnerships with cider makers, brewers, and chefs in the area. A curious sample on a sunny afternoon in The Dalles, and a little fresh initiative, have given this deeply flavorful cherry a new life.

DANCY
Tangerine

US ORIGIN OR MOST PREVALENT IN
Florida

CHARACTERISTICS
Easily peeled "zipper" skin, exceptional flavor, ripening period in the holiday season

USDA PLANT HARDINESS ZONES
9b–10a

CLOSE RELATIVE
Pixie tangerine

NOTABLE PRODUCERS
Trees can be purchased at Four Winds Growers and Alder & Oak

The first tangerine came to be by accident in Palatka, Florida, shortly after the Civil War. Planter N. H. Moragne collected an odd seedling tree that had sprouted near a mandarin orange tree originating from Tangier, Morocco. He had no idea what pollinated the flowers that bore the fruit that dropped that first seed. In the 1860s, multitudes of sweet and sour orange varieties filled the air with their pollen alongside the established mandarins, so variations were common.

Veteran citrus grower Francis Dancy was particularly taken by the fruit of what would eventually become the Dancy tangerine. Its thin, leathery skin peeled off readily (in the 20th century it was sometimes sold as the "Zipper tangerine"), its compact size was handy (under 3 inches in diameter), and it had bright juice and a uniquely floral aroma. It retained many of the virtues of its mandarin parent in the slight spiciness on the tongue and deep orange coloration of its peel. Dancy purchased the tree and set about grafting cuttings on hardy orange stocks to create an orchard of identical plants. Dancy knew that uniformity was the future of marketing and would be a primary driver of sales. He suspected that asexual propagation of citrus, either by rooting cuttings or grafting cuttings onto old orange rootstocks, was the only method to ensure uniformity. In 1872 he distributed cuttings to a network of fellow growers. Thus, the Dancy tangerine became the first citrus variety in Florida around which a modern breeding discipline emerged.

HOW FRANCIS DANCY
SAVED THE FLORIDA CITRUS INDUSTRY

In February 1835, a devastating freeze in Florida took out ancient Spanish Seville orange trees, and many planted as far back as the 1600s died to the roots. Cultivators considered abandoning fruit growing altogether and converting their orchards to sugarcane fields. Francis Dancy, then an engineer and later mayor of St. Augustine, managed to dissuade many of them and tip the balance back in favor of citrus. He instructed growers to cut the freeze-blasted trees back to the stumps and wait. Their patience was rewarded with the regrowth of what are now Florida's antique Seville orange groves. Though these sour oranges regenerated, sweet orange plantings proved less vigorous. Only one planting survived the catastrophe, that of Douglas Dummett of Indian River. It was Dummett's plant material that enabled the eventual revitalization of sweet citrus culture. Francis Dancy realized that if citrus would have a commercial future in Florida, something more than simply replanting sweet and bitter orange groves needed to be done. He recognized the potential value of diversified citrus production. Dancy planted lemon trees. He would eventually have 3,000 lemon trees alongside orange trees in his orchards on the east bank of the St. Johns River, but not before he figured out a way to neutralize the depredations of the scale insect.

Naming the fruit after the parent tree's North African origin in Tangiers and also himself, Dancy followed a basic rule of branding: in agriculture, novelty is best paired with familiarity. By 1872, Dancy was a byword in Florida citrus circles.

The namesake Dancy tangerine became a truly national brand in 1890 when the Rolleston Nursery in San Mateo, California, began large-scale commercial propagation of it. From that point until the 1970s, most of the tangerines grown and consumed in the United States were Dancy tangerines. It ripened in early December, and so was shipped and sold as the "Christmas tangerine." Its historical importance as a product was matched by its crucial role as breeding stock. It was crossed with either the pomelo or grapefruit to create most of the significant tangelo varieties—Minneola, Orlando, Sampson, and Seminole. The Dancy is the parent of the Frua and Fortune mandarin oranges, the Dweet and Mency Tangors, and the Pixie tangerine of the Ojai Valley (a fellow Ark of Taste product).

Several factors mark the eclipse of the Dancy tangerine in the 1970s. The Dancy's penchant for bearing only every other year resulted in inconsistent production. Although pruning could compensate for this to a certain extent, this natural cycle of bearing could not be entirely overcome. The Dancy tangerine is also vulnerable to *Alternaria* brown spot, a fungus introduced into the United States from Australia in the final decades of the 20th century. The fungal toxins produced by *Alternaria* can defoliate groves if unchecked. In the early 2000s, the greening disease spread across Florida orchards, putting every heirloom citrus variety in dire peril. Fruit breeders began developing mandarin varieties during the 20th century—Robinson, Sunburst, and Honey (Murcott)—with greater disease resistance, yield, and fruit uniformity than the Dancy. Large-scale growers abandoned Dancy groves for these newer varieties and their more commercial-market-friendly characteristics. They also chose sweeter-tasting tangerines like the Honey variety, betting on the public's increasing preference for high sugar content.

In 2011, David Karp of the *Los*

THE PERIL OF GREENING DISEASE

From the USDA Animal and Plant Health Inspection Service: "Huanglongbing (HLB), also known as citrus greening, is the most serious disease of citrus. The disease is spread by the Asian citrus psyllid (*Diaphorina citri*) (ACP), which has been present in Florida since 1998. ACP transmits the bacteria to the tree when feeding on new shoots. There is no cure for this disease and all commercial varieties of citrus are susceptible to HLB.

Its thin, leathery skin peeled off readily (in the 20th century it was sometimes sold as the "Zipper tangerine"), its compact size was handy (under 3 inches in diameter), and it had bright juice and a uniquely floral aroma.

Angeles Times wrote, "While mandarin cultivation in California has quadrupled over the last decade to about 40,000 acres, the classic Dancy variety has fallen by the wayside, becoming rare to find even at farmers markets. That's a shame, because it's a charismatic, flavor-packed fruit, typical of what mandarins used to be like before they were hybridized with oranges and grapefruit for the sake of larger size and better handling." In 2011, one could still buy the Dancy as a specialty Christmas fruit through Harry & David's seasonal catalog, but the variety is no longer on offer. Producers harvesting old groves of Dancy tangerines decided that the effort required for even small-scale production did not warrant undertaking. Today, while the fruit is not in general supply, many nurseries still sell young trees. And so it comes to pass that arguably the most historically significant and culturally resonant tangerine has nearly vanished from the commercial produce market. But there is hope yet for the variety to live on, as the Dancy tangerine often finds a home in the backyard orchards of citrus lovers.

ʻELEʻELE Banana

Sometime before the eighth century, the ʻEleʻele banana traveled among the dried rhizomes of perhaps as many as three dozen varieties of bananas carried east across the Pacific by Polynesians in the hulls of their oceangoing canoes. Esteemed as a "royal banana," it is the only Polynesian variety with black trunk sheaths and midribs. ʻEleʻele means "black."

The Hawaiian Islands became home to several distinct varieties of banana—namely the Maoli, Iholena, and *Pōpōʻulu*—all of which we can trace to families of bananas found in Polynesia. Most of these bananas, including the ʻEleʻele, are suitable for eating raw when ripe and being cooked when green. The dark fibers of the trunk sheaths were also used in weaving patterned mats and for braided hat bands.

Agronomist W. T. Pope, in his Hawaiian Experimental Station Bulletin *Banana Culture in Hawaii* (1926), described the banana: "The young fruit has the appearance of being badly smoked, and remains rather dark for several weeks following the flower, then gradually changes to dark green, and finally to clear bright yellow at full maturity. The bunches average 60 to 80 pounds in weight, 7 to 9 hands, the fingers varying from 3 to 5 angled, 7 inches long, 1½ inches in diameter, plump, and well-filled to the end . . . skin [is] thick and tough as with other Maoli bananas, clear yellow at full maturity; pulp [is] firm, orange colored; core [is] distinct with numerous underdeveloped ovaries. A good cooking banana."

The ʻEleʻele banana was a mountain banana, grown in the volcanic soil of high, wind-protected valleys, and persisted in Hawaii for centuries. It is one of the few cultivated varieties with a historical origin that maintained a presence in local markets after the Hawaiian Agricultural Experimental Station introduced West Indian, Central American, and Chinese bananas into cultivation shortly after the turn of the 20th century. ʻEleʻele became a crop variety in the 19th century in fields alongside these newly introduced varieties, and confronted the pests and pathogens—nematodes, corm weevils, and bunchy top virus carried by banana aphids—they brought with them, against which it had no natural defense. These maladies decimated the population of ʻEleʻele on the Big Island, and in 1992, the cultivated stands of ʻEleʻele collapsed.

This die-off led to a concerted search for wild and isolated plantings of the ʻEleʻele banana. In 2004, cultivation was rebooted from the plant material of one such discovered stand. Additional trees have been discovered on Molokai. Several growers took up the ʻEleʻele around the year 2010, but its vulnerabilities ensure that it will likely never be more than a rare, specialty banana. Aside from its lack of disease resistance, it requires transplantation in 5-year intervals to hinder nematode degradation. That said, it may be worth the trouble. As the Ark of Taste nomination observes, "when slightly overripe the center of the ʻEleʻele will sometimes gel, creating an extremely sweet treat. Its

THANKING the GODS

FOR THE ʻELEʻELE

A chant offered to the god Kanaloa in the 1600s celebrates the impressive attributes and productivity of the ʻEleʻele banana:

> *Ka maia nui e*
> *ka maia nui e*
> *He umi eka ke hua*
> *Aole hiki ke amo*
> *Elua kanaka hiki ke amo*
> *hiki inoino*

> *The Great Banana*
> *The Great Banana*
> *It will yield 10 hands*
> *The bunch cannot be carried*
> *It will take two men to carry it*
> *With difficulty.*

ability to stay sweet and maintain its firm yet not starchy texture is a fairly unusual and coveted aspect." It tends to be sweet and creamy, with a citrus acidity. The green banana when cooked is like a particularly refined plantain—wholesome, with a plush mouthfeel.

In traditional Hawaiian cookery, the 'Ele'ele is placed in an imu, or pit, dug deep and lined with hono grass. Special heated stones that have never been immersed in water—or else they will explode—are placed in the pit. The bananas are heaped on top of the stones along with taro, breadfruit, and sweet potato, then covered with Ti leaves and mats. The earthen oven bakes the fruits, roots, and vegetables for 4 hours, after which the pit is uncovered and diners enjoy the smoky, flavorful medley.

The future of the 'Ele'ele is uncertain and may depend upon whether a private foundation, the USDA, the University of Hawai'i, or some other institution funds a program of micro-tissue propagation of the variety. That method of propagation is the only currently available technique of ensuring that a population of plants is brought into existence sufficiently substantial to avoid a future wipeout like that of 1992. Angela Kay Kepler has been saving ancient bananas of Hawaii for the past 30 years and enabled the restoration of the 'Ele'ele after its 1992 demise. The revival of the variety may rest in her hands.

GABE SACHTER-SMITH:
THE MORE BANANAS, THE BETTER
Hawaii

While US supermarkets may be dominated by the Cavendish banana, which originated in South America and can be picked green, ripened by ethylene gas, and shipped long distances, there are hundreds of other varieties of bananas in existence. One man in Hawaii is working on making even more. Gabe Sachter-Smith tends the banana groves at Hawaii Banana Source in Hawaii, where he grows 150–200 traditional cultivars and wild species. The varieties Gabe has created himself add even more to the roster. Gabe enthusiastically says his motivation is "to know the story of each different type of banana. With breeding, now I'm helping to write the story."

One of the varieties that Gabe grows is the 'Ele'ele, what can be called a "canoe" plant, as most of the banana types recognized as Hawaiian varieties did not originate there. Instead, Hawaii was the end of the line for Polynesian migration, and "traditional" Hawaiian banana varieties are those that arrived with migratory people via canoe and came to thrive on the islands. Less than half of those varieties—about 20–30 varieties—are still growing there today and some are extremely rare.

The 'Ele'ele is hard to grow and not financially viable as a crop in Hawaii. It is susceptible to a host of pests and viruses, grows large but not quickly, and

is vulnerable to high wind on account of its impressive height. While the 'Ele'ele does not differ terribly from other varieties in its genetic group of Hawaiian bananas, it does have one distinguishing factor: its black color. The fruit grows on blackened stems that make the tree an ornamental garden favorite and a mainstay for hobbyists lucky enough to live in climates like those of Florida and California, where the tree is more populous than it is in Hawaii. It's also grown commercially in South America, where it also does not face Hawaii's environmental challenges and is well integrated into the local markets and food culture.

Noa Lincoln, a professor in the Department of Tropical Plant and Soil Sciences at the University of Hawai'i at Mānoa, grows bananas, breadfruit, and several traditional starchy vegetables on his private farm and at the Amy B. H. Greenwell Ethnobotanical Garden. But, he says, "nobody is growing the 'Ele'ele commercially. . . . None of our heirloom Hawaiian bananas are common at all." Although bananas are not Noa's primary crop, they remain an integral part of his work. "It is preservation in order to ensure we don't lose crop varieties," he says. "Heirloom crop varieties have tremendous value for a lot of reasons." This includes revitalization of Indigenous culture and identity by way of reconnecting to traditional food and foodways.

Although approaching the task from quite different angles, the two banana growers have one specific aim in common: diversity. Noa points out that since the rise of industrial agriculture, "for the vast majority of global food production, we've bred crops very singularly, primarily for yield." In doing so, countless varieties were lost before anyone understood or came to value what they had to offer: flavor, nutritional value, secondary compounds, and so much more. Noa and Gabe are working to preserve plant diversity and the place-specific (not agricultural-system-specific) varieties that remain.

The 'Ele'ele is just one in a long line of bananas worth preserving. Neither Noa or Gabe was overly enthusiastic about its flavor, but the 'Ele'ele variety feels like as much of a gateway to the brilliance of bananas as anything else. Gabe does bring the more unusual varieties to the farmers market on occasion but, like most market farmers, finds that people tend to stick to what they know. That lack of interest among his market customers doesn't bother him much, though; he says, "Why do I do it? It's really for my own shameless amusement. I don't even care if people want them. It brings me joy to go out and walk and see them and learn about them." At the end of the day, Gabe and Noa are both fulfilling their goal of keeping the bananas growing instead of disappearing. Seems all the better if it's that much fun.

FUERTE
Avocado

US ORIGIN OR MOST PREVALENT IN
California

CHARACTERISTICS
Pear-shaped, yellow-fleshed, creamy in texture

USDA PLANT HARDINESS ZONES
8a–10b

CLOSE RELATIVE
A natural hybrid between the Guatemalan and Mexican landraces of avocado

NOTABLE PRODUCERS
Frog Hollow Farm, Griffith Family Farms

Shortly after the turn of the 20th century, Southern California farmers determined that they would develop nonindigenous fruits into American commodities. Farmers associations and big nurseries sponsored plant hunters to explore Central America for good candidates for cultivation. Every introduction was a risk, for plants that had evolved in places with different day length, altitude, and soil conditions frequently did not prosper when planted in different soils and climes.

In 1911, young plant hunter Carl Schmidt traversed the uplands of southern Mexico, searching for avocados. California growers already had some firm opinions about what constituted a good avocado—they favored the hardiness and fattiness of the Mexican varieties and the thick skin, large size, and pest resistance of the Guatemalan varieties. Schmidt found a variety combining these qualities in the markets of Puebla, 80 miles from Mexico City, and tracked down the planting

*The Fuerte was the first crop
avocado in the US and the one
that endeared the taste and texture
of this Central American fruit
to North Americans.*

in the garden of Alejandro Le Blanc. Schmidt secured budwood and shipped it north to his sponsor, West Indian Nursery of Altadena, California. One of his samples (number 15) sprouted and immediately distinguished itself by the vigor of its growth. Newly sprouted avocado varieties would often languish, but number 15 grew vigorously and proved to be cold tolerant, earning its name, Fuerte, which simply means strong in Spanish.

The Fuerte was the first crop avocado in the US and the one that endeared the taste and texture of this Central American fruit to North Americans. Its introduction in the second decade of the 20th century was a textbook instance of a market novelty becoming so attractive to first-time buyers that a durable demand arose. From 1915 until 1950, the Fuerte avocado was the only variety one might find in most markets, despite the efforts of cultivators to introduce new varieties into the United States.

The Fuerte avocado immediately won favor among growers, thanks to its myriad virtues. The Fuerte bore fruit at a younger age than other varieties, allowing growers to harvest the avocados just three years after planting, with a tree bearing about 300 fruits by its fourth year. It ripened in January to early March, a season when other varieties were not yet available, so it enjoyed a midwinter monopoly. The skin, while not thick, was substantial enough to protect the fruit in shipping better than most thin-skinned Mexican varieties. With an average weight of 1 pound per fruit and relatively uniform size, the Fuerte avocado was ideal for the hotel and restaurant trade. A split Fuerte avocado with a miniature salad nestled in the seed cavity became a cliché of restaurant dining in the Jazz Age.

The 1920s saw the extensive planting of Fuerte avocado trees in Central Florida as well as California. In Florida, the variety ripened from November to January. The USDA's foremost avocado expert, Wilson Popenoe, advocated for the variety tirelessly, realizing it would drive the demand for the other avocado varieties he was introducing from Guatemala to the United States. Yet none of

Popenoe's imports—no matter how huge, piquant, or robust—competed with the Fuerte, which constituted 80 percent of California avocado crops by the mid-20th century.

A seedling avocado scavenged from a restaurant dumpster in California and grown by amateur grower Rudolph Hass would eventually overtake the Fuerte in popularity. The Hass avocado did not prevail because of superior flavor, or size, or productivity. In fact, it shared Fuerte's liability of bearing major crops only in alternate years. Rather, the Hass triumphed because it could ripen year round and its rougher, tougher skins kept it from bruising during transport. At a time when grocery stores were trying to overcome the seasonality of food by offering best-selling items year round, the Hass was firmly positioned as the best variety for the job. In 2022, 95 percent of the avocados grown in California were Hass.

The fruit of the Fuerte is pear shaped and has creamy yellow flesh. The delicacy of the flesh is a weakness, for it does not keep well. The fruit has just one day of optimum ripeness before swift spoilage. But for that one day, you can experience a flavor and texture as winning as any avocado can offer. Breeders sought to improve the Fuerte line over the course of the 20th century, and the Newman strain of Fuerte gained favor for productivity and for some additional keeping time.

While Hass remains the leading avocado variety of the commercial market, the Fuerte holds a place in the hearts of avocado lovers as a yard tree on account of its culinary quality. Many heirloom nurseries offer the Fuerte. Modest quantities can also be found on produce stands in the avocado growing regions of California and Florida. If you are lucky enough to bring a Fuerte avocado home, don't let its single day of perfect ripeness pass you by.

GRAVENSTEIN
Apple

US ORIGIN OR MOST PREVALENT IN
California

CHARACTERISTICS
Pale green with red stripes with crisp, flavorful yellow flesh

USDA PLANT HARDINESS ZONES
5–8

CLOSE RELATIVE
Red Gravenstein apple

NOTABLE PRODUCER
Dutton Ranch

While it is now well known that apples are native to Central Asia (Kazakhstan, to be precise), we are less sure of the origins of the Gravenstein apple and how it came to the United States. Author William Kenrick suggests that it came into being during the 18th century in Italy and Germany. The first English-language notice of the Gravenstein apple occurred in an 1822 listing of new apples in London. When John Wilmot forwarded fruit secured in Holland from a Gravenstein tree, he noted that it was "esteemed the best apple in Germany and the Lowcountries." As the variety was new to England in 1822, it could hardly have been in California before then. The legend that Russian trappers planted Gravenstein trees at Fort Ross in the 1820s is dubious. While the Gravenstein's history and arrival to the US are shrouded in mystery, it is certain that the variety was enthusiastically adopted by orchardists later in the 19th century and that it has remained popular to the present day.

*"The flesh [is] pale yellow, crisp, with
a juice vinous and well-flavoured,
fragrant and delicious. Not only
a first rate dessert fruit, but its
abundant juice affords excellent cider;
and it is excellent for drying."*

Here is that first description from *Transactions of the Horticultural Society of London* in 1822: "The skin is a pale green, with dotted stripes of red on the exposed side. Flesh of a greenish yellow, crisp, with a rich and high flavoured juice. It ripens in the autumn, but will keep well till April, and may fairly be considered a rival to our Ribston Pippin." Kenrick provides the first extensive description for an American publication 20 years later: "The fruit is large, round, but varying in form, angular at the crown; the eye is in a broad, deep, knobby cavity; the stalk is very short, deep sunk; color clear straw or yellow, with broken stripes of red next the sun; the flesh pale yellow, crisp, with a juice vinous and well-flavoured, fragrant and delicious. Not only a first rate dessert fruit, but its abundant juice affords excellent cider; and it is excellent for drying."

William Prince's famous Linnaean Garden on Long Island was the first American nursery to offer Gravenstein apple trees for sale in 1831. The variety was first advertised for sale in California by orchardist J. B. Starr in Sacramento in the spring of 1854. The intensive planting of the Gravenstein on the West Coast began in the 1870s, in orchards in Washington, Oregon, and Northern California. By the 1890s, various reputable apple varieties—Baldwin, Esopus Spitzenburg, Ben Davies, Northern Spy, Waxen, Newton Pippin, and Gravenstein—had been cultivated in the region for two decades and demonstrated which kinds thrived in the terroir of the Pacific Northwest. Washington's State Board of Horticulture said of the Gravenstein in 1893, "In the Pacific Northwest it seems to attain a quality of superior merit to any other part of the union. The tree is very vigorous, spreading, forming a large, broad head, a productive and early bear." While many apple trees do not respond well to the drier climates found in the West Coast states, faring better in the cooler, wetter climates of the Pacific Northwest, Gravensteins do quite well without the heavy rainfall of Washington and Oregon.

Sebastopol, California, became associated with the Gravenstein apple sometime after the 1870s, while it was still a relatively new settlement. Nathaniel Griffith planted the first Gravenstein grove in Sonoma County in 1883, orchards sprang up along the Gold Ridge soon after, and by 1910 the fruit had become the signature of the place. The Sebastopol Apple Growers Union organized its first annual Gravenstein Apple Fair in 1910, when apple-covered buildings and floats became the signature of the fair and the foundation for its fame in California. When Prohibition shuttered American cideries in 1919, the Gravenstein's abundantly sweet juice made it the primary sweet cider apple on the West Coast during the interwar years.

Over the course of the 20th century, the Gravenstein apple did not lose its appealing quality as a juice apple or its peculiar suitability to the soil and climate of the Sonoma Valley. Yet cultural forces displaced it gradually from its ideal terroir when the explosive expansion of viticulture in California in the last half century made the land around Sebastopol increasingly valuable for the growing of wine grapes. The profitability of wineries led to many orchards being converted to vineyards. Furthermore, the legalization of marijuana and the stark competition for land within easy transportation distance from the major urban center of San Francisco has made many an orchard owner ponder the sustainability and comparative profitability of growing Gravensteins. Today, there are fewer than 900 acres of Gravensteins planted in Sonoma County.

Because this ideal ecosystem for producing Gravenstein apples stands at risk, Slow Food went a few steps further than simply boarding the apple to the Ark of Taste. The Slow Food Foundation for Biodiversity organized another mode of protection and promotion in the Gravenstein Presidium, in which the environment of an Ark of Taste product is also recognized as being in need of protection. The Gravenstein Apple Presidium connects local producers and institutions like the University of California Cooperative Extension, the AG Innovations Network, the Community Alliance with Family Farmers, the City of Sebastopol, and Santa Rosa Junior College to work together in discovering new markets for the Gravenstein in order to ensure income levels that enable orchardists to resist selling land to alternative and competing crops. The Gravenstein can be found and enjoyed in many places beyond the Sonoma Valley, but it stands as a profound example of the connection between land and culture, ecology and history, and how the concept of terroir extends well beyond wine.

THIN GRAVENSTEIN APPLE AND Rosemary GALETTE

REGINA ESCALANTE BUSH, *chef*
MERCI, YUCATÁN, MEXICO

This tender herbal galette is the French version of apple pie: a thin crust topped with thinly sliced apples, baked to perfection. In France, it's traditionally made with puff pastry, but chef Regina Escalante Bush prefers it with her mother's pie dough recipe.

SERVES 4

FOR THE DOUGH

3 tablespoons whole milk, cold

1 teaspoon white vinegar

1¼ cups (155 g) all-purpose flour

Pinch of table salt

1 tablespoon sugar

2 teaspoons chopped rosemary

8 tablespoons (1 stick/115 g) unsalted butter, cold and cubed

FOR THE FILLING

3 Gravenstein apples

3 teaspoons melted butter

1 teaspoon sugar

1 teaspoon ground ginger

1 teaspoon orange juice

1 teaspoon cornstarch

FOR THE EGG WASH

1 large (19 g) egg yolk

Sugar, for sprinkling

Ice cream (optional)

Honey (optional)

Rosemary (optional)

CONTINUED >>

MAKE THE DOUGH

In a large bowl, combine the milk and vinegar and set aside for 5 minutes in the refrigerator. In a food processor, add the flour, salt, sugar, and rosemary; pulse to combine. Add the butter and pulse until the butter breaks down into pea-sized pieces. Add the milk mixture and pulse again until the dough begins to form. Turn the dough out onto a work surface and wrap it in plastic wrap. Gently press it into a 1-inch (2.5-cm) thick disc and place it in the refrigerator for at least 1 hour or until fully chilled.

MAKE THE FILLING

Cut the apples, leaving the skin on, in very thin slices, approximately ⅙ inch (0.4 cm) thick. Place the slices and the remaining filling ingredients in a bowl and toss to combine.

ASSEMBLE AND BAKE THE GALETTE

Preheat the oven to 350°F (180°C). Place the chilled dough on a lightly floured work surface and use a rolling pin to roll it out into a circle measuring 12 inches (30 cm) in diameter. Place the dough circle on a rimmed sheet pan. Arrange the filling on top of the dough, leaving a 2-inch (5-cm) border of dough. Fold the edges of the dough over the filling and brush the edges with the egg yolk. Sprinkle with sugar. Bake for 20 minutes, or until the crust is golden.

Serve warm with a scoop of vanilla ice cream, a drizzle of honey, and a sprinkle of freshly chopped rosemary, if desired.

Regina Escalante Bush is the chef of Merci in Yucatán, Mexico, and an active member of the Slow Food Cooks' Alliance.

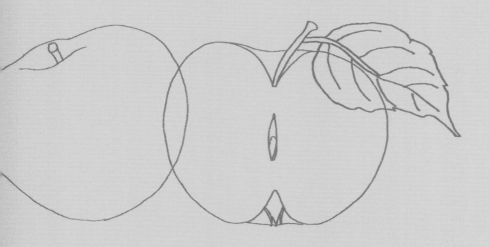

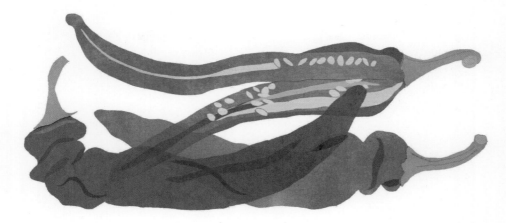

JIMMY NARDELLO
Frying Pepper

US ORIGIN OR MOST PREVALENT IN
Connecticut

CHARACTERISTICS
Thin walled, red, long with a sweet flavor

USDA PLANT HARDINESS ZONES
7b–9a

CLOSE RELATIVE
Peperone di Senise

NOTABLE PRODUCERS
Seed can be obtained from the Seed Savers Exchange, Territorial Seed, Baker Creek Heirloom Seeds, Burpee, Sow True Seed, Hudson Valley Seed, Fedco, Monticello Shop, Truelove Seeds, Sustainable Seed, Kitizawa Seed, Turtle Tree Seed Initiative, Sandia Seed, and San Diego Seed Company.

In 1887, Giuseppe (Joseph) Nardiello and his wife, Angela, transported seeds from Basilicata, Italy, to their garden at Naugatuck, Connecticut. What they brought with them was the famous Peperone di Senise, a thin-walled, long-fruited frying pepper and the signature pepper of that southern Italian region. Just as the Nardiellos adapted to Connecticut, becoming the Nardellos, so the Peperone di Senise adapted to its new environment to be more productive and cold hardy, with long-extending stems that must be staked. The variety possesses a winning sweetness that sets itself starkly apart from the meaty bell pepper, while the fire-engine-red color and 10-inch length of the ripe fruit remain intact from its Italian progenitor. The pepper came to be named after the couple's fourth son, Jimmy Nardello.

All old landrace vegetables, such as this red frying pepper, possess a genetic diversity as great as their adaptability. When planted in new soils and new climates, they effectively become new plants. Peperone di Senise is an ancient landrace that came to Italy via the Antilles—all peppers ultimately hail from the Americas—in the 1500s, eventually spreading to Calabria, Sicily, and Basilicata. Its connection with Senise, however, is so strong that the pepper-growing area there has been awarded IGF protection. Myriad famous and traditional preparations feature the pepper, perhaps none more well loved and used than the sun-dried Peperoni Cruschi.

Though the Jimmy Nardello pepper is designated as a frying pepper, the Nardellos maintained the foodways of their old home, stringing up the harvested red peppers at the end of summer and hanging them in the rafters to dry into the coming fall, so they might always be on hand. Before Jimmy's death in 1983, he conveyed the seeds of his namesake pepper to the Seed Savers Exchange to ensure its preservation and dissemination. We like to think he'd be surprised and delighted at the regard his frying pepper now enjoys. The Jimmy Nardello is a favorite to stem and seed when ripe, lay in a skillet with hot olive oil and perhaps some garlic, and cook until the flesh turns creamy.

If Connecticut was the home of this pepper for the first century of its return sojourn to America, Northern California became its home during the second century. The peppers are greatly popular in the produce stalls at the San Francisco Market, where they are affectionately called Jimmies, and proudly named on many a West Coast restaurant menu. There is great appreciation of the pepper as a raw vegetable, both in its green unripe and red mature states. It is also perfect for frying, prompting Jack Aldridge to write an article explaining the virtues of the Jimmy Nardello for *SFGate.com*: "To roast a good pepper, you need thick, fleshy walls, so you have something left after you char, steam and peel the skins. For frying, however, thin flesh is preferred because it cooks quickly, flattening in the pan more easily than the rigid, thick-walled bell types."

The Jimmy Nardello frying pepper was boarded onto the Slow Food USA Ark of Taste when it was still a novelty among heirloom gardeners. The Seed Savers Exchange was the principal outlet for the seed at the time. Once scarce, it now ranks as one of the more popular heirloom vegetables on the Ark of Taste—a success story in which a family landrace became a West Coast restaurant staple and a star in the produce markets. Today a dozen companies offer seed to the public, in packet sizes ranging from 20 seeds for home gardeners to 1 pound of seed for market farmers.

KIAWE *Honey*

US ORIGIN OR MOST PREVALENT IN
Hawaii

CHARACTERISTICS
Pearly white texture, lightly perfumed flavor

NOTABLE PRODUCERS
Rare Hawaiian Honey Company, Manoa Honey & Mead, Good Job, Bees!

Native to Peru and Ecuador, the Desert Mesquite tree was transported to the Big Island from Mexico in 1837 by Alexis Bachelot, a Catholic missionary. The trees did well in dry seasons and could be grown in the parts of the islands that lacked ample annual rainfall. Thus, they spread throughout the islands over the course of the 19th century. Native Hawaiians, who called it Kiawe, found that the seeds in the pods, once milled, proved a good source of food for livestock, and that the wood made excellent charcoal. The trees prospered on the leeward side of the islands and produced long, narrow, lemon-colored flowers at intervals during the year with no fixed season of blooming.

Honeybees came to Hawaii in 1857, about 20 years after the arrival of the Kiawe trees, when several hives of German black bees arrived from California. Beekeeping and honey production took place on a small scale until the 1890s when ranchers realized that the Desert Mesquite, because of its protracted periods of blooming, would be an ideal host for honey production. A critical mass of bees and trees was reached in the last decade of the century, when 60,000 acres of Kiawe flourished, bringing the first of Hawaii's honey farms into existence. The success of these pioneer efforts convinced some that the mass production of honey might occur in Hawaii. Molokai Ranch, a huge honey production planting, broke ground in 1907 and found that their Kiawe honey won many enthusiastic and ready buyers, particularly in Germany.

WHEN THE AMERICAN PUBLIC DISCOVERED
HAWAIIAN FOOD

When the Broadway musical *The Bird of Paradise* ignited a Hawaiian culture craze in the United States in 1912, chefs on the Islands and on the West Coast began formulating characteristic Hawaiian menus for mainland American consumption. In January 1922 the Hawaiian agency for tourism and trade hosted the following dinner for 350 newspapermen in Seattle. It shows the place Kiawe honey had assumed in the popular perception of edible Hawaii:

MENU
Hawaiian Minted Sliced Pineapple (Hala Kahiki)
Cream of Hawaiian Rice (Laiki)
Canned Hawaiian Tuna (Aku)
Poha Jam Fritters
Hawaiian Beef (Pipi Oma)
Baked Maui Beans (Papapa)
Poi in Koa Calabashes
Hawaiian Fruit Chutney
Guava Jelly
Papaya Marmalade
Kiawe Honey
Hawaiian Crushed Pineapple Ice Cream
Kona Coffee

—from *Seattle Daily Times* (January 29, 1922)

The refined, delicate, and lightly perfumed flavor has notes of vanilla and almond with a slight menthol finish.

Kiawe honey quickly crystalizes, giving the honey's body a pearly white texture when extracted from the comb. The refined, delicate, and lightly perfumed flavor has notes of vanilla and almond with a slight menthol finish. The creamy mouthfeel has long been greatly prized. Kiawe honey is drizzled over fruits or spread over baked goods.

The fate of Kiawe honey in the 20th century has been tied to the decline of the Desert Mesquite populations on the island. Seed mash ceased to be a major source of livestock feed in the latter half of the century, and some of the islands' populations dwindled. Its place on the landscape was also challenged by the invasive Java plum. For decades, honey production in Hawaii has been geographically concentrated in the Puako Forest on the Big Island. The 1,000-acre expanse of trees hosts a number of Kiawe trees 50 to 60 feet tall. The Rare Hawaiian Honey Company and other producers ring the Puako Forest with hives. Yet even in this preserve, other threats to the well-being of the trees and the health of the honey industry have emerged. Fire destroyed half the trees in Puako in 2007, and the island's bee population has declined because of mite infestation. Regardless, a revived interest in Kiawe honey has catalyzed the replanting of Desert Mesquites that will restore the unique tree to Hawaiian forests.

MISSION
Olive

The Spanish Catholic missions were almost as much about agriculture as they were about proselytizing the Indigenous populations of California. Missionaries planted vegetable gardens, grape arbors, wheat patches, and stone fruit groves on the land they settled. Of all the agricultural endeavors and successes staged on these controversial settlements, no crop was more beloved or consequential than the olive. Of all the crops introduced by the missionaries, only three survived the colonial era—White Sonora wheat, the Mission grape, and the Mission olive. The last became a culinary and cultural emblem of California.

The first olives in California were planted from seed brought from Mexico on the grounds of the newly founded Mission of San Diego in 1769. Cuttings from these original trees were used to propagate olive trees on every mission of California and, later, the ranches of Spanish settlers. The original mission trees proved so hardy and disease resistant that many still stood intact when the first history of the Mission olive was published in the *1890 Report of the California State Board of Horticulture*. Until 1881, no other variety of olive was grown in California, and the Spanish families that had plantings were not inclined to undertake large-scale commercial production. In the 1880s, a group of agricultural entrepreneurs, including Elwood Cooper, Frank Kimball, Edward Fries, and C. F. Boop, planted orchards of Mission olives and compared them against at least 70 different European varieties. The Mission olive's strong local adaptation proved enough to counter the larger size, earlier maturity, and greater productivity of the European trees. The Mission olive remained the most widely cultivated variety in the state well into the 20th century.

The oil produced by the Mission olive is markedly shelf-stable, sharp, and peppery.

The fruit of the Mission olive is smaller and more irregular than that of the Spanish Arbequina olive, the variety that would become California's standard crop olive in the late 20th century. Originally cured and brined as a green olive, the Mission olive was initially not pressed for oil. Stone mills for pressing oil were erected at missions and ranches only at the end of the 18th century. The oil produced by the Mission olive is markedly shelf-stable, sharp, and peppery. The cold tolerance of the mission olive enabled it to be grown as far north as San Francisco. For a half century, the variety was also dyed, heavily processed, and sold as a ripe black table olive. But when the olive market globalized in 1998, cheaper Spanish and Moroccan olives outcompeted West Coast varieties in the commercial market. California producers had to reduce prices by finding ways to become more efficient. Unfortunately, the irregular shape of the Mission olive

THE *Mission* GRAPE

Thought to be the earliest vinifera variety to be cultivated in the Americas, the Mission grape was brought to the Pacific coast by explorers. The hearty, long-living vine produces dark, marble-sized fruit, ideal for making sacramental wine. The oldest vine, known as "the Trinity Vine," was planted in the 1770s at the Mission San Gabriel near Los Angeles, California.

made them ill-suited for pitting machines, and growers began eliminating Mission olive groves. However, the simultaneous rise of an artisan oil market that could feature the distinctive and piquant flavor of the Mission olive prevented the wholesale eradication of the crop. Eventually, long-standing olive companies such as Lodestar California rebranded and became Mission olive oil producers.

Biologists attempted to ascertain the lineage of the Mission olive using genetic fingerprinting in the 20th century. Geneticists at the University of Cordoba found no equivalent or close relative in world olive germplasm collections. But California geneticists later discovered a relation to the Picholine Marocaine, a historic Moroccan olive, rendering it possible that the original ancestor of the Mission olive had been a Moorish transplant of a North African olive in Spain that was later brought to Mexico by colonists in the early settlement period.

In 1998, the Mission Olive Preservation, Restoration, and Education Project (MOPREP) was organized to document the history of the iconic variety and compile horticultural expertise about the olive trees of California's 21 historic missions. Soon after, a large-scale project to recover the agricultural legacies of the missions was launched. MOPREP volunteers identified historic trees and collected the surviving material culture of olive processing to replant, prune, and harvest Mission olives. By 2011, the restoration had largely been accomplished, and all of the missions had true Mission olives growing on site once again.

Historically, the production of brined olives overshadowed olive oil production in California. The missionary Fermín Lasuen first pressed oil from Mission olives in San Diego in 1803. The sale of olive oil on the commercial market is first documented in 1822. Sensing in the year 2000 that an artisanal olive oil movement was forthcoming, MOPREP worked to associate the Mission olive with top-shelf olive oil in the public mind, warranting small-scale production throughout the state.

The historic variety is threatened more by real estate development than by a disinterest in its flavor and culinary versatility. Ethnobotanist Gary Nabhan warns that production of the Mission olive has fallen below 30,000 acres early in this century. Nevertheless, in 2020, more than a dozen nurseries offered Mission olive trees for sale. Of all the crops associated with California's colonial and horticultural past, the Mission olive has a promising future with its high esteem among olive oil enthusiasts and deep symbolism for California.

OJAI PIXIE
Tangerine

US ORIGIN OR MOST PREVALENT IN	*Ojai, California*
CHARACTERISTICS	*Seedless, small, sweet*
USDA PLANT HARDINESS ZONES	*8a–10a*
CLOSE RELATIVE	*Kincy tangerine*
NOTABLE PRODUCER	*Ojai Pixie Growers Association*

Grown only in California's Ojai Valley, this seedless hand-sized mandarin has become a cherished emblem of the fertile valley nestled between the Cascade Range and the Klamath Mountains in Ventura County northwest of Los Angeles. The Ojai Pixie tangerine boasts a mystique and distinctiveness that came to monopolize the hearts of the people of Ojai. California won its seat at the citrus table by way of much more common varieties and is known for the navel oranges, red grapefruit, tasty tangelos, and sour lemons that it shipped throughout North America. The groves bearing these varieties still blanket the citrus growing areas of the state, but the Ojai Pixie tangerine holds its place in its namesake valley.

Howard Frost, a breeder at the Riverside Citrus Experiment Station, brought the parent seed of the variety into the station collection in 1927. Frost reported that one parent was the Kincy, a cross between the Dancy and the source of the easily peeled skin, and the King, a tangerine highly favored by the Experimental

Station for breeding. But the parentage was shrouded in mystery and uncertainty, which caused the seed to be sidelined for years. But when citrus breeding trials tested multiple hybrids simultaneously for sample breadth, Frost's seed started being grown out.

James W. Cameron, a maize geneticist, and Robert Soost, a tomato geneticist, were hired by the Riverside Citrus Experiment Station in 1949 to continue Frost's breeding work with citrus. Using classic mandarin pedigrees, they crossed known varieties with mandarin cultivars such as Wilking, Kincy, Dancy, Kinnow, and Kara. Thus, Cameron and Soost undertook the decade-long process of developing and trialing new citrus varieties. Fruit from Frost's seed were improved over a dozen plant generations, making it seedless and increasing the variety's flavor, color, and local adaptability. The Pixie emerged in the late 1950s as a candidate variety. When Cameron and Soost released the variety to the public in 1965, they presented it as a backyard tree for home citrus lovers.

The Pixie came to the Ojai Valley as part of Cameron and Soost's trials. Its adaptability to California's many microclimates was appealing to breeders and growers. Several tangerine varieties were grown in the valley during the mid-20th century. Soost sent the candidate variety to Frank Noyes, who ran a small-scale produce operation. Noyes found the flavor of the new variety remarkable and shared it with Elmer Friend. Friend was impressed with the tangerine and began planting it on his ranch to offer it at his packing house. Sometime in the late 1970s, Jim Churchill sampled Friend's Pixies while on a visit to the ranch to examine avocados. Churchill formed the conviction that he would like to plant Pixie tangerines on a commercial scale. Churchill ordered 330 trees in the 1980s, some of which he sold to Tony Thacher, Friend's son-in-law, who had decided to expand the plantings at Friend's ranches. It took approximately eight years to get the Pixie tangerine trees fully producing. In 1988 the Ojai Pixie first went on the market. As a late-season spring tangerine, it filled a niche in the market. Bay Area consumers bought the variety with great enthusiasm and kept the novelty fruit afloat.

Despite its handy size, fine flavor, seedlessness, and ease of peeling, the Pixie had a few traits that made it less than ideal as a market citrus. It bore fruit only in alternating years and ripened in April, long after the winter holiday season (prime time for tangerine sales). It bruised easily, disqualifying it as a "shipping mandarin." Nonetheless, the variety gained a fervent following in California on account of its great flavor and unique appeal. Capturing an urban market was assuring to Churchill and Thacher, the primary growers of the variety, but their success with the Pixie was cemented by the delight that visitors to the Ojai Valley experienced in encountering a unique mandarin variety that came ripe during

. . . success with the Pixie was cemented by the delight that visitors to the Ojai Valley experienced in encountering a unique mandarin variety that came ripe during the most splendid weeks to visit the valley, from late March to early May.

the most splendid weeks to visit the valley, from late March to early May. By the mid-1990s, visitors began to actively seek out the Pixie tangerine, influencing other citrus growers to plant trees. It quickly became part of the Ojai Valley's identity, and there are now an estimated 25,000 Ojai Pixie tangerine trees in cultivation in the area.

The Pixie's status as a specialty tangerine has not been without tribulation. Growers in the Central Valley saw the public response to the tiny mandarin with the endearing name and countered with Cuties. Size and kid-friendliness were the chief selling points of the Cutie, and the Central Valley growers rolled it out with a national ad campaign heavily slotted on the Nickelodeon channel. The Cutie sold at a lower price point than the Pixie, and the Pixie's growers in Ojai rightly felt they were being undercut. Furthermore, the growers did not wish to be absorbed by big citrus brands like Sunkist. They formed an association to strategize on marketing campaigns and respond to pest and pathogen invasions. Alliances with local government led to the creation of Ojai Pixie Month in April, when hotel packages and restaurant discounts in the region inspired visitation by tourists. Local eateries eagerly feature the fruit in menu items that highlight local and seasonal goods, and mixologists have gotten creative with Ojai Pixie tangerine juice and peel in craft cocktails.

Though the appeal and charm of the Ojai Pixie tangerine remain strong enough to keep the variety in cultivation in the area, growers have also taken the precaution of developing other lines of valuable citrus like the Kishu and the Page Tangor tangerines so that revenue streams are diversified on citrus farms. The Ojai Pixie Growers Association has periodically introduced new themes and angles in marketing the variety, like touting the Pixie as a lower-acid tangerine in 2019. The association has the good fortune of promoting a product whose quality is immediately apparent when enjoyed by consumers. If you've never had the pleasure of a slice of Pixie or a sip of its juice, plan your next California adventure in pursuit of that unique delight.

OLYMPIA Oyster

This single native oyster of the American Northwest once grew as far south as the Baja Peninsula with beds skirting the entire coast of California. Farther north, the oyster beds in the Puget Sound of Washington were particularly extensive. Though the oysters were slow growing and only attained the size of a half-dollar, their clear, briny, and bold umami flavor kept the demand steady.

San Francisco during its post–gold rush boom became the first consumption hub for these small native oysters. Demand grew for the nutty, flavorful bivalve in the city's taverns and eating houses. The oyster population of that area was irrevocably overfished by get-rich-quick watermen in the mid-1800s to service the demand. By 1868, shipments of the highly coveted Olympia oyster and others began arriving from Olympia, Washington, to replace the vanished oysters. Consumers in California and Washington State vendors began calling it the Olympia oyster from its port of origin. Indigenous

Though the oysters were slow growing and only attained the size of a half-dollar, their clear, briny, and bold umami flavor kept the demand steady.

fishermen in the Pacific Northwest engaged in a brisk trade of the shellfish to supply consumers in San Francisco.

Rampant overfishing took place in the Washington waters as well, and several bays and sounds became nearly devoid of oysters in the 1890s. The local population of native oysters declined so greatly that watermen began importing the heavy-shelled Pacific oyster from Japan to seed their beds. Quite unfortunately, the Asian oyster drill tagged along with that shipment.

Despite the predation of invasive pests and the competition of two species of imported oyster, the Olympia held its own until 1928, when an additional peril to its well-being emerged. Another of Washington's resources—lumber—would prove toxic to the Olympia. When a pulp mill in Shelton dumped its sulfite waste into Oakland Bay, a major spawning ground of the Olympia, the pollution killed off half the population of the bay within five years. The pulp mill remained open for the duration of the Great Depression, and the factory spewed on. By the mid-1950s, the Olympia was nearing failure. In 1957, E. N. Steele published *The Rise and Decline of the Olympia Oyster*, a prophecy of the total extinction of the oyster industry unless water quality improved. The Shelton Plant closed in 1958. By then, it was believed that 91 percent of the Olympia oysters had been destroyed by its effluent in the 30 years of its operation.

The Olympia staged a comeback in the 1960s, though the flatworm and the predatory oyster drill sea snail prevented a more robust restoration of the nursery. Oyster growers organized to build clutches and seed more beds. Their actions were timely, because additional environmental pressures began to fall on the Olympic Peninsula. The coastal waters struggled with chemical runoffs and bacterial blooms fueled by failed septic tanks and medical waste, all of which threatened the sensitive oyster populations of the Olympia waters. Civic authorities imposed strict chemical usage and discharge regulations to wrest the situation under control. Tenacious efforts in environmental regulation and proactive work by oyster farmers stabilized the Olympia oyster in the 1980s.

With the aid of the Puget Sound Restoration Fund, a succession of inlets were reseeded soon thereafter—Budd, Henderson, and Hood Canal. The same farmers had introduced two additional oysters into Washington's waters—the Belon from France and the Kumamoto from Japan. While it would appear on the surface a counterintuitive way of preserving a native oyster, producers were building public recognition of varietal distinctiveness. When the consumer began thinking about the taste and characteristics of particular types of oysters, the conditions would be favorable for reviving the Olympia as a consumer category. This happened in the 1990s, and the Olympia was often sold as the "Pioneer oyster" or, more simply, "nuggets of gold."

Because the Olympia oyster is a native resource, Indigenous tribal resource officers have been greatly involved in the past and current effort to rebuild the population. It seemed apparent at the end of the 20th century that commercial fisheries would deter the effort to reestablish the population, and the Olympia oyster was not commercially exploited. But two Washington entities—Olympia Oyster Company and Taylor Shellfish—joined in efforts for the replenishment of the waters and, effectively, retailing of the oysters. Today, they are both still your best chance at getting a taste of this unique gem.

Because Washington State prohibits recreational harvest of oysters of less than 2½ inches in diameter, the Olympia is protected against private harvesting. Indigenous communities in the region are permitted to harvest the oyster, but not for commercial sale or use.

The restoration of the Olympia in recent decades has not been restricted to Washington waters. Various environmental groups have been attempting to build populations in California bays and estuaries, Oregon inlets, and British Columbia. Going forward, climate change and sedimentation will be major challenges, but work and hope for the sustainability and full restoration of the Olympia oyster as a food resource persists.

JOHN ADAMS:
FOR THE LOVE OF OLYS

Washington

John Adams lives in the house that his grandfather built almost 100 years ago overlooking the Little Skookum Inlet. When he learned about the Native people who had inhabited that land for the last 6,500 years and the native Olympia oyster that had been an integral part of their foodways, John made it his mission to keep the once-bountiful oyster thriving there. He has been harvesting and farming Olympia oysters there since 1995 as Sound Fresh Clams & Oysters. John shucks them at the farmers market for friends old and new, alongside Pacific oysters and Manila clams. Today, John's primary goal is preserving a healthy population of the only oyster native to the West Coast while fostering meaningful connections with the community.

After joining the Slow Fish community at Terra Madre in 2014, John changed his business model to even out the quantity of each of his shellfish offerings, despite the fact that the "Olys" are less productive and can be more challenging to grow. Since retiring from the army to the peaceful bay, John has closely observed the species throughout the seasons, noting ongoing changes in its environment. His efforts at preservation have been supported by the many organizations that recognize the value and importance of preserving native and heritage food species.

With the help of the USDA, John built a reef structure consistent with the environment in which the Olys have developed well in the past. Through this project, John learned a lot about the species. Olympias are brooders, which means the mothers hold on to their eggs for a couple of weeks before releasing them into the water, where they flutter down to the substrate to find an object to attach to in a good shady spot, where they'll spend their life. They created what they believed to be the most robust environment possible for the Olys to live and set, and assumed that the oysters would accumulate there. However, he learned that Olys don't necessarily come back to set in the same place they were released by their brooding mothers, as was the common assumption. Despite not seeing the return of the oysters set there, the reef has a 100 percent rate of survivability for all the Olys that do take up residence.

Thanks to his vigilant observations of the oysters in the dynamic habitats on John's land, he has a uniquely accurate view of the seasonal spawning patterns of the Olympia oysters, a day-by-day percentage, and an idea of when they're setting. They're usually done spawning by July, but the Olympias are extremely susceptible to changes in environmental factors and not always so predictable. In September 2021, the bay got an unexpected wild Olympia oyster set for the first time in seven years. A local biologist thought the heat dome had reset the population to go into another spawning phase, but the abnormal heat caused a change in the tide and current system that brought the Olympias in and caused a larger portion of them to spawn at one time. Since the ever-more-unpredictable currents dictate their timing, and timing is everything when it comes to the Olys, John will keep watching.

John's story of Olympia oysters is one of love and commitment, flexibility and adaptation, and navigating a coastal treasure by quite literally going with the flow. On that beach where John watches and cares for the Olympia oysters, he hosts shellfish foraging dinners where curious eaters can learn about the precious oyster and create a connection with the variety that will keep them in demand and alive. John's commitment to the preservation and promotion of the Olympia oyster has given him a unique sense of purpose and stewardship on that beautiful bay, and connecting the community with their native oyster has proved to be a worthy mission.

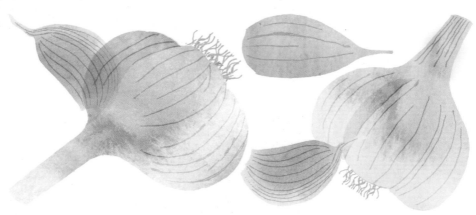

SPANISH ROJA *Garlic*

US ORIGIN OR MOST PREVALENT IN
Pacific Northwest

CHARACTERISTICS
Hardnecked, red tinge appearing blue or purple, refined taste, low sulfur, nice spice

USDA PLANT HARDINESS ZONE
7

CLOSE RELATIVE
Silver-Skinned garlic

NOTABLE PRODUCERS
Seeds from Burpee, Urban Farmer

The name of this aromatic allium is something of a misnomer. The Spanish Roja is a member of the Rocambole garlic family, a group of hardnecked and multicloved varieties that thrive in northern latitudes with colder winters. In other words, the variety most likely comes from a climate almost unknown in Spain. Farmers in Oregon have had the longest known acquaintance with this flavorful allium, and call it Greek Blue as much as they call it Spanish Roja. The red tinge appears to some as blue and to others as purple. But the foreign origins suggested in these names were marketing ploys of relatively recent vintage. When the variety came to the Pacific Northwest around the turn of the 20th century, promoters adopted a name that suggested Hispanic antiquity, hoping it would capture the attention of growers and catch on as a local signature.

Garlic has been beloved for centuries not only as a culinary product but also as medicine. The specific origin of cultivated garlic isn't terribly clear, but most varieties seem linked to Central Asia and the eastern Mediterranean. As numerous garlic varieties made their way to world markets, spinning stories with imagination-inducing names became a common practice in vegetable selling. The Rocambole garlic family collected a number of commonly used monikers, some with a modicum of history to them: Bavarian garlic, Top-Setting garlic, Sandleek garlic, Serpent garlic, and Spanish garlic. The Spanish Roja adapted exceedingly well to the climate and growing conditions of the Pacific Northwest and is most prolifically grown for seed and sale in and around Oregon.

The signal feature of the Rocambole garlic varieties is an array of bulbils in the shape of a globe at the apex of the seed stalk. These pea-sized seeds could be planted to propagate the plant, as well as the cloves (most garlic is propagated by planting its most robust cloves). The scapes form a loop as they extend beyond the leaves and toward the sky. Horticulturists Gayle M. Volk and David Stern describe the external appearance of the bulbs as "generally white with some faint violet or brown stripes, or splotches across the locations." The cloves tend to be large in plants grown in Oregon and Washington State, with five to eight cloves per bulb. Because mechanical harvesting bruises Rocambole garlic, the majority of the Spanish Roja crop is hand harvested, which is labor intensive. But given the premium paid because of its taste quality, many small-scale allium cultivators find growing it worth the trouble.

Spanish Roja is planted in western Oregon in October, for it is a winter variety requiring quite a number of chill hours (hours below 40°F) to thrive. It is harvested the following August. It became part of farming schemes in Oregon because it afforded winter work for farms in the season opposite to the common spring-planted Silver-Skinned garlic. The early Oregon seed companies—Burt's, Portland Seeds, Posson's, Fletcher & Byrd's Seeds, Routledge Seed & Floral—tended not to distinguish varieties in their listings. The Gill Brothers of Portland offered two varieties: "common" and "French"—the former being the Silver-Skinned Creole garlic grown throughout North America since the early 19th century. Silver-Skinned garlic was famed for its sulfurous bite; in fact, it was the variety responsible for garlic breath and garlic's bad reputation in polite company. French garlic, according to the Gill Brothers, was nearly double the size of what they were calling common garlic, and notably prolific. There is a strong probability that Gill Brothers' French garlic is what we now know as Spanish Roja.

Garlic farming began on some scale in the Pacific Northwest in the 1880s. The Tualatin Valley west of Portland was the first great place for garlic growing in Oregon. Beaverton, the most populated town in the valley, reported major harvests as early as 1911. The *Oregon Journal* purported that "[t]he garlic crop of

Early in the 20th century, the Rocambole of Oregon—French garlic or Spanish Roja—became "the other garlic" among West Coast culinarians. It had won their favor with its looser skin, easier peel, and sweeter, richer flavor.

the section is not only very liberal, but of very fancy quality." The writer reported that 10 tons had been derived from a single farm and that portions of the harvest would be shipped to San Diego. Since vast quantities of Silver-Skinned garlic were grown in California's Central Valley, this observation suggests that the San Diego demand stemmed from a desire for a "fancier"—that is, hardneck Rocambole—variety.

Rocambole garlic developed a reputation for superior taste, particularly the Spanish Roja, a quality that was attested to in a marathon set of tastings conducted by Chester Aaron across the United States in 2002. In 50 blind comparative samplings, Spanish Roja consistently ranked in the top three of all varieties. Rocambole garlic was altogether a more refined family of garlics, with a rich, sweet taste, spice taking the place of sulfur, and an inviting aroma when cooked. Early in the 20th century, the Rocambole of Oregon—French garlic or Spanish Roja—became "the other garlic" among West Coast culinarians. It had won their favor with its looser skin, easier peel, and sweeter, richer flavor. The loose skins meant a shorter storage life, but the superior flavor meant that they were used more frequently, skirting the all-too-common fate of some garlic lingering in the kitchen long enough to become garlic dust in a slipper.

Indeed, in the small-farm garlic boom of the late 20th and early 21st centuries, many people have pointed to the Spanish Roja as the variety that established the specialty market for fine garlic. In 2021, it was grown on at least two dozen heirloom organic farms in the United States, and its cultivation has stretched well beyond the Pacific Northwest. If you let your imagination take the lead and send you eastward from the garlic fields of Oregon, the variety might just make a perfect match for tapas, paella, and seafood dishes.

MICHELLE WEEK:
UNDER THE WHITE OAKS

Oregon

Michelle Week grows close to 100 different food varieties on about two acres of rain-soaked farmland she leases just outside of Portland, Oregon. But her heart lives in the soil she also tends under the White Oaks of her ancestral Sinixt land. Drawing on her affinity for the outdoors, a childhood of gardening, and a strong desire to dig deeper into the Sinixt heritage she gets from her grandmother, Michelle started farming in 2017 with a business partner and a goal of giving away as much food as they sold. The following year, Michelle started Xast Sqit Farm, which translates from the Sinixt language to Good Rain Farm, and focused her attention on traditional foods. "The farm is focused on native food sovereignty and bringing back our traditional, culturally relevant foods to the dinner table more widely than they are currently available," says Michelle. "That's why part of my choices for what we grow on the farm come from the Ark of Taste."

Before Michelle became a full-time farmer, she worked in food co-ops and grocery stores, motivated by an interest in cooperative business models as alternative economic models designed to better support communities. That's where she learned about the Ark of Taste, which she used as a guide for seed selection from the start. Xast Sqit Farm's CSA program is what enables Michelle to grow so many heirloom, heritage, and rare varieties each season, many of which have relatively low yields. The team puts a lot of energy into storytelling so that their CSA members and followers understand the value of the varieties they're growing and why they're doing it, aside from their great taste.

Michelle's Indigenous ancestry is rooted in the Arrow Lakes community, from the headwaters of the Columbia River that spans what is now the US-Canada border, and later part of the Confederated Tribes of the Colville Reservation. That border and the subsequent forced relocation split up the

Arrow Lakes tribal members and Michelle's family landed in and around what would become the Portland Metro area. Today, Portland hosts one of the largest populations of Indigenous people on the West Coast, but that population is now made up of diverse tribal members from across the United States. So while Michelle spends much of her time learning about first foods of the Pacific Northwest and the Colville Tribes, she has also taken to growing many first foods from other regions and peoples.

"Farming became this place where I could do meaningful, foundational support for community, which is feed them, so that they can be creative, innovative, and helpful in other ways," says Michelle. "I can steward the land, which I have a deep passion for." The roster of produce at Xast Sqit is never the same year over year, as Michelle incorporates new foods that might excite her CSA members and varieties that are well suited to sometimes extreme changes in weather patterns. Michelle seeks to decolonize "rare" foods and retell their stories, but contributing to biodiversity by growing a broad selection of foods is equally important to her selections. In the 2022 season, Michelle grew the Cherokee Purple tomato, Spanish Roja garlic, Cherokee Trail of Tears bean, Hidatsa Red bean, and Amish Paste tomato, all of which are found in this book. The most cherished feedback Michelle gets is from someone having a first taste of something since they moved off the reservation or an elder in their family passed away. Michelle revels in increasing access to first foods to the tribal members in her community.

Normalizing foods only recently considered rare is a big part of the mission at Xast Sqit Farm, in addition to making these products accessible and economical. In order to do that, Michelle communicates with members about the dynamics and usages of much of her produce, like the Hidatsa Red bean, which can be eaten either as a green bean or dried. Similarly, Spanish Roja garlic offers not only robust heads of garlic, but also scapes and spring garlic. The Cherokee Trail of Tears bean gives eaters a glimpse into the taste preferences of the land from which it comes. The Amish Paste tomato, true to its name, is an excellent tomato for sauces and pastes, while the large, juicy Cherokee Purple tomato is divine eaten fresh.

Michelle is deeply connected to the native Oregon White Oak, which she tends to on her father's land, but she'd like to make that tree and many other perennial natives a bigger part of her farming practice in the future. Those perennial crops account for many of the native first foods of this zone, like red flowering currant, thimbleberry, salmonberry, blackberry, gooseberries, cattails, camas, nettles, hazelnuts, elderberry, and Oregon grapes. Michelle is able to grow many local indigenous foods, like nettles, miner lettuce, Makah Ozette potatoes, and strawberries. Michelle believes deeply that "It's so important to keep those foods alive, keep that diversity alive, keep that exploration alive."

Michelle is doing deep work as a farmer, but goes beyond simply growing food to act as an environmental steward, storyteller, Native foods educator, activist, community supporter, champion of biodiversity, and seed saver. She was awarded the Slow Food USA Snailblazer award in 2020 for her work in farming and a Slow Food USA microgrant in 2021 for the Good Rain Save Our Seed program. The stories she tells with each CSA box will continue to shift perspectives on food, community, and the Native history of the land. In other words, Michelle is using the Ark of Taste to do exactly what it was created to do—identify, rediscover, and champion important and delicious traditional foods to keep them in production and on our plates. And in doing so, she is honoring the human history of the food that has long grown on the lands we call home.

WELCOME ABOARD THE ARK OF TASTE!

In recounting the history of each food featured in this book and getting to know some of their growers, we are reminded that food is inextricably linked to people, history, and culture. Sometimes saving a corn variety is as much about genetic diversity as it is about honoring the people who planted it long ago and continue to tend it today. We all have a role to play in keeping these flavorful foods alive, and we must do this work together. We have immense gratitude for every person who has done their part to revive or preserve even a single plant or species.

Some of the foods in this book are success stories—plants and animals that have been revived in recent years on account of that hard work and the increased demand for them from gardeners and eaters alike—while others are still endangered. Our great hope is that the stories in this book entice you to find the foods that you don't want to live without, and to join us in making sure you never have to. Here are some ways you can do just that:

- Learn more about local foods and the people who cultivate them.
- Nominate something to the Ark of Taste.
- Plant a seed from vendors and producers mentioned in each entry.
- Support your local farmers, eat at the restaurants putting these products on the table, and ask for the foods you love in markets and at your favorite eateries.
- Advocate for federal, state, and local policies that support culturally diverse farmers and local economies, end exploitation of workers at all stages of the food chain, restrict corporate privatization, increase biodiversity, and address climate change.
- If you're a chef, add regional products to your menu.
- If you're a farmer, tell the stories of what you grow.
- Join a Slow Food chapter, community, or affinity group.

Are you aware of a producer of an Ark of Taste product that we should know? Do you have more details about the foods in this book? Please share with us! Visit our full Ark of Taste catalog at slowfoodusa.org/ark-of-taste, and get in touch with us at arkoftaste@slowfoodusa.org if you have questions, corrections, or updates, or want to get involved with an Ark of Taste committee in your region.

THE ARK OF TASTE

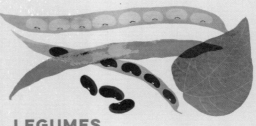

FRUIT

Abbada Date
Arkansas Black Apple
Belle of Georgia Peach
Black Republican Cherry
Bradford Watermelon
Dancy Tangerine
Dyehouse Cherry
'Ele'Ele Banana
Esopus Spitzenburg Apple
Fairfax Strawberry
Fuerte Avocado
Gravenstein Apple
Hewes Crab Apple
Marshall Strawberry
Meech's Prolific Quince
Mission Olive
Moon and Stars Watermelon
Norton Grape
Ojai Pixie Tangerine
Pink Champagne Currant
Wilson Popenoe Avocado

LEGUMES

Apios Americana
Cherokee Trail of Tears Bean
Christmas Lima Bean
Four Corners Gold Bean
Hidatsa Red Bean
Rio Zape Bean
Tepary Bean

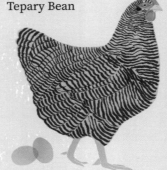

MEAT

American Guinea Hog
Bourbon Red Turkey
Cayuga Duck
Navajo Churro Sheep
Ossabaw Island Hog
Plymouth Rock Chicken

NUTS & GRAINS

American Chestnut
Butternut (Tree)
Carolina African Runner Peanut
Carolina Gold Rice
Cocke's Prolific Corn
Manoomin (Wild Rice)
Purple Ribbon Sugarcane
Purple Straw Wheat
Red Turkey Wheat
Tuscarora White Corn
White Cap Flint Corn
White Sonora Wheat
Yellow Creole Corn

SEAFOOD

American Paddlefish
Great Lakes Whitefish
Olympia Oyster
Wellfleet Oyster

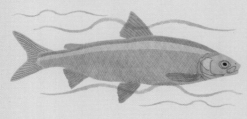

SYRUP & HONEY

Alaskan Birch Syrup
Guajillo Honey
Kiawe Honey
Tupelo Honey

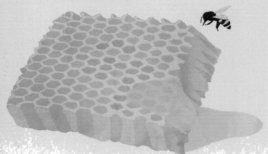

VEGETABLES

Amish Paste Tomato
Boston Marrow Squash
Candy Roaster Squash
Cherokee Purple Tomato
Chiltepin (Bird) Pepper
Early Rose Potato
Fiddleheads
Fish Pepper
Hayman Sweet Potato
Hinkelhatz Pepper
Jimmy Nardello Frying Pepper
Livingston Globe Tomato
Long Island Cheese Pumpkin
Perfection Pimento Pepper
Spanish Roja Garlic
Tennis Ball Lettuce
Whippoorwill Pea

ACKNOWLEDGMENTS

Every entry on the Ark of Taste exists because of the work and deliberation of a community—the six regional committees across North America that first recognize and "board" an endangered or rare food onto the Ark; the nominator whose passion for an ingredient or dish prompts research and documentation; the growers, seed savers, school educators, home cooks, and professional chefs who keep plants, animals, and preparations alive; and the teams at Slow Food International and Slow Food USA who inspire and coordinate the network. We are grateful for the care and commitment of this grassroots movement for deepening our kinship between plants, animals, and humans for the last two decades in the United States.

The narratives in each Ark of Taste entry are rooted in the history and stories provided by nominators, but this book also presents significant new research and information. While we recognize some of the most influential people in each entry, our thanks extend to everyone who has touched these foods. Trailblazing seed companies like Seed Savers Exchange, Native Seeds/SEARCH, Southern Exposure Seed Exchange, and many others have preserved not just the seed but also the stories of countless Ark of Taste items, and so deserve our heartfelt gratitude.

Putting together this volume has been a labor of love. Authors Giselle Kennedy Lord and David S. Shields carefully researched each item and introduced us to many growers who are committed to biodiversity. Illustrator Claudia Pearson shone a light on the unique beauty of each Ark of Taste item with her beautiful line art. Art director Carol Bobolts has worked with Slow Food for years, and brought her in-depth knowledge of the Ark of Taste into full color. Lori Paximadis provided the painstaking work of copyediting, along with recipe reviewer Sarah Strauss and proofreader Susan Schader Lee. Slow Food USA staff Mara Welton, Brian Solem, and Anna Mulè helped coordinate recipes, photography, and provided support with editing and fact checking.

Our heartfelt gratitude goes to Dinah Dunn, editor extraordinaire at Indelible Editions who saw the potential of the online database and worked hand in hand every step of the way to bring it to fruition. And Michael Szczerban and his team at Voracious, Hachette Book Group, expertly guided the process to create a delightful read from cover to cover. Thank you.

INDEX

ABOUT SLOW FOOD

In 1986, a shiny new fast-food restaurant was set to open next to the iconic Spanish Steps in Rome. A group of Italians gathered to resist the homogenization of their vibrant local food culture. Instead of throwing rocks, they set out long tables and served pasta on the street, chanting, "We don't want fast food. We want slow food!"

That spark lit a fire around the world as more and more communities saw their traditional foodways overpowered by multinational corporations seeking global dominance and privatization of shared resources. At its heart, the Slow Food philosophy rejects the modern obsession with speed and productivity and instead celebrates diverse flavors, community, culture, and equity at all levels. It's about creating a world where all people can eat food that is not only good for them, but also good for the people who grow it and the planet we share.

This vision comes to life with small and dynamic groups of volunteers who are aligned with the Slow Food mission and are committed to making change in their own neighborhoods. The Slow Food movement set down roots in the United States in 1999 and has since grown into a national association with more than 80 chapters, more than 10 national community action teams, and a robust leader network. We are dedicated to uniting the joy of food with the pursuit of justice.

SLOW FOOD USA: *slowfoodusa.org*   SLOW FOOD INTERNATIONAL: *slowfood.com*

The Slow Food **ARK OF TASTE** initiative began in 1996 with a vision to preserve the vast biodiversity of foods that were at risk of extinction. Just like the biblical figure Noah built an ark and boarded animals two by two to save them from being eliminated by a widespread flood, Slow Food began to "board" seeds and animals, traditional recipes, and unique processes to the Ark of Taste to safeguard them. Today, more than 150 countries have boarded nearly 6,000 items to the Ark of Taste, including more than 300 in the United States.

What makes the Ark of Taste particularly engaging is that it is an open invitation to the eaters of the world to participate in the preservation of the distinctive foods and biodiversity of their region. Anyone can nominate a food to the Ark of Taste—you don't have to be a farmer, fish harvester, or even a Slow Food member to nominate a product to this living catalog of delicious and distinctive foods facing extinction. All you need to do is to pay attention to the lands and waters around you, respect the people who tend them, listen to their stories, and open your taste buds to new flavors.

The stories in this book are just a sampling of the foods in the Slow Food USA Ark of Taste catalog, and our website serves as a database that continually grows and evolves.

ARK OF TASTE USA CATALOG: *slowfoodusa.org/ark-of-taste*
ARK OF TASTE GLOBAL CATALOG: *fondazioneslowfood.com/en/what-we-do/the-ark-of-taste*

ABOUT THE AUTHORS

GISELLE KENNEDY LORD holds a master's degree in gastronomy from Boston University and was named James Beard National Scholar Northwest in 2018. She spent the first decade of her career as a short-form documentary videographer, learning to navigate farm rows and tight kitchens with a camera in hand. Giselle has worked on farms from the Pacific Northwest to Patagonia; she has cooked for crowds from her backyard to Beirut. Giselle became ever more enamored with the Ark of Taste while working as the director of communications for Slow Food USA, where she championed the preservation of food culture and the importance of biodiversity. She lives in Portland, Oregon, with her husband, son, and pets and spends her free time making magic in the kitchen, weekending in a converted short bus, and growing what some would consider too many tomatoes.

DAVID S. SHIELDS is the Carolina Distinguished Professor in the College of Arts and Sciences, University of South Carolina. His scholarship explores the fields of early American literary culture, American performing arts, photography, and food studies.

Shields is currently the chairman of the Carolina Gold Rice Foundation, the nonprofit group whose mission is to preserve and restore the agriculture and cultivars of the American South. He also chairs Slow Food's Ark of Taste Committee for the South. The rationale and the work of these restorations were explored in his 2015 culinary history, *Southern Provisions: The Creation and Revival of a Cuisine*, which chef Sean Brock calls "the most important book written about Southern food." In 2016 the Southern Foodways Alliance awarded Shields its "Keeper of the Flame" award for his efforts.

Shields's 2017 title, *The Culinarians: Lives and Careers from the First Age of American Fine Dining*, the first-ever collection of biographies of American chefs, caterers, and restaurateurs, was a finalist for the James Beard Book Award in food scholarship. In 2018 Shields was also awarded Slow Food USA's "Snailblazer" award for biodiversity. In 2021 his survey of South Carolina foods, *Taste the State: South Carolina's Signature Foods, Recipes, and Their Stories*, co-written with Kevin Mitchell, was published by the University of South Carolina Press.